BIBLE
TRAINING INSTITUTE
GLASGOW

WORLD
CHRISTIANITY
oceania

Leonora Mosende Douglas, Editor

WITHDRAWN

Published by MARC and MARC EUROPE

WORLD CHRISTIANITY
OCEANIA

U.S.-ISBN 0-912552-48-4
Europe-ISBN 0-947697-49-7
MARC a Division of World Vision International
919 W. Huntington Drive
Monrovia, CA. 91016

WORLD CHRISTIANITY SERIES

Oceania is the fifth volume in the *World Christianity* series published by MARC and, for the first time, MARC Europe.

The Missions Advanced Research and Communication Center (MARC), in an effort to motivate the Church in the world to the task of evangelization, produced thirty-five country profiles in 1971. These profiles attempted to describe the status of Christianity in those nations. They were subsequently used at the International Congress on World Evangelization held in Lausanne in 1974. Since that time, other countries were added, and older profiles revised. In 1978 the profiles were collected by sub-regions, and material on unreached groups was added to the text from the Unreached Peoples Database. This fifth volume with its new format is the work of many and varied people whose viewpoints add balance. To each we express our gratitude.

This work has been carried out in close cooperation with the Strategy Working Group of the Lausanne Committee for World Evangelization. The information contained in this and previous volumes is part of the MARC/LCWE attempt to display the task of world evangelization in a way that will help the Church identify and evangelize the peoples of the world in their historical context and reality, and to recognize the political division of the world into nation-states.

Any report like this must be considered "work in progress." Therefore, we welcome comments, corrections, or additions that Christians throughout the world might supply.

Edward R. Dayton
Samuel Wilson

Series Editors

Previous volumes in the series:

World Christianity: Middle East
World Christianity: Eastern Asia
World Christianity: South Asia
World Christianity: Central America and the Caribbean

Volumes to appear in the near future:

World Christianity: Southern Africa
World Christianity: Western Europe
World Christianity: Eastern Europe

MARC....... Lausanne Committee for World Evangelization
Missions Advanced Research & Communication Center ... LCWE

Table of Contents

FOREWORD

This book is yet another attempt to provide for Church and secular leaders an overview which will help them understand more fully the situation of the Church of the Lord Jesus Christ on the islands that stud our blue, blue Pacific. The information is not perfect, and never can be, because of the continual changes that go on in life. People live and die, denominations are established, or disperse, and so the records continue to furnish changing information. Nevertheless, the hope of this book's editors is that whatever information it has been able to collect will be of some use to the man or woman who wants to be used of God to serve the Church and further the Kingdom here on earth.

We, the Pacific peoples, and our cultures have been the subject of research and studies, of conferences and workshops, of books and magazines; of videotapes and films. Sometimes we are elevated to be the easygoing, loving, gracious occupiers of paradise; sometimes we are the offspring of savage and fierce cannibals and devil worshipers who will quickly revert to them at the least provocation. The Church coming into the Pacific has sometimes been labeled as the destroyer of our culture, while at the same time propagating the western culture and almost equating it with the gospel it preaches. The fact of the matter is that we are exactly the same as missionaries and other people in the world -- children of Adam, therefore, sinners by nature and practice -- needing forgiveness, cleansing and salvation that the Lord Jesus Christ alone can and does give!

The Pacific is a political playground for the big powers. The possession of strategic military bases in the northern Pacific by the U.S.; the U.S.S.R.'s wooing of Pacific nations with lucrative turnover for fishing rights; France's resolution on nuclear tests and her unwillingness to grant independence to her Pacific territories; and the growing number of trade agreements between other nations and our nations bear testimony that we are no longer able to be totally free to live as we please.

We are beset by a growing materialism that comes with economic development, by the diversity and complexity of modern life, the increasing numbers of crimes, high inflation rates, an increasing number of jobless people, and increasing breakdowns in marriages and family relations, frustrated youth, delinquent parents, in the midst of these, the Church of the Lord Jesus Christ is entrusted by God with the only message that will bring meaning and relevance to life on this earth and ensure peace and everlasting life afterwards.

This book does not bring life, but it is an instrument that the Church can use to do its work better in addressing that Message to the princes, the prophets/priests and the people (the leaders -- political and others, the church leaders and the people generally) as Ezekiel of old was commanded to do.

Maika R. Bovoro
Special Associate
for Pacific Relations
World Vision South Pacific
Suva, Fiji
July 25, 1986

ACKNOWLEDGMENTS

We thank the Almighty for guiding, inspiring, and seeing this volume through to fruition. The list of individuals who have contributed to this task is long indeed. We can only name a few.

To the staff of World Vision International/South Pacific, MARC, Word Processing and Decision Support, we express our appreciation for facilitating, researching, writing, and/or processing the manuscripts/text of the book. Maika Bovoro and Barton Magasim contributed materials on Fiji and Papua New Guinea, respectively. Robert von Oeyen wrote the Vanuatu section and contributed to the Chapter One overview of the region. Harley Schreck wrote the Unreached People and People Group sections of the country profiles; Mary Janss Forrest researched and wrote the Micronesia chapter and coordinated the publication of the book; Burt Singleton and John Pentecost contributed research; Word Processing staff members did an excellent job of sorting through the endless drafts; Marian Carney and Dayton Roberts were publication managers; Dana Buckley was proofreader; and Carol Brown was the artist who coordinated the formatting and book cover. To Jack Cooper, Director of Research and Information; and Sam Wilson, Director of MARC, many thanks for the stalwart support and perseverance in seeing through the completion of the project.

World Vision New Zealand and World Vision Australia research units contributed the chapters for those countries, respectively. We thank them and the Zadok Centre for giving us permission to reprint.

A special thank you is extended to Charles Forman for his time and response to our eleventh-hour appeal for consultancy.

We acknowledge input from the following organizations:

Bible Society, P. O. Box 18, Port Moresby, Papua New Guinea.

Evangelical Alliance of Papua New Guinea, Pastor Martin Wain, Tokorara Christian Fellowship, P. O. Box 333, Boroko, Papua New Guinea.

Melanesian Council of Churches, Boroko, Papua New Guinea.

Baptist Union of Papua New Guinea.

Roman Catholic Church in Papua New Guinea.

Salvation Army in Papua New Guinea.

South Sea Evangelical Church of Papua New Guinea.

Foremost, we thank the people and church leaders of this region who have shared with us their experiences and insights into the workings of the Holy Spirit amongst their fellow men and women. Their stories need to be told to others as models as well as for unity in our Christian experience.

PREFACE

MARC's World Christianity series provides general background information on missions, churches, parachurches, ecumenical bodies; issues and concerns facing the Church in different parts of the world.

This volume on Oceania aims to provide a broad sweep of the status of Christianity in this island region in the context of two centuries of Christian experience. Profiling the Christian influences past and present has been a formidable task. As experienced by other investigators, the very geography and state of the oral tradition of the peoples of Oceania proved to be major challenges to the survey process we went through. We employed various research methods. Literature review was foremost--sifting through seemingly endless volumes of published materials on mission history in Oceania. On the other hand, current developments on the Church scene needed face-to-face interviews with resource people and key informants. We barely scratched the surface in this regard owing to the distances and travel costs in the area. Group and individual interviews, expert opinion were utilized. Prepublication reactions were sought from consultants both in the Pacific and in the United States and England.

The terms *Oceania* and *Pacific* are used interchangeably in this volume. Hawaii, which is part of the Polynesian cultural group, is referred to in regard to the coming of European and American missionaries in the 19th century. We did not include a profile of Hawaii in this volume. Australia and New Zealand, both First World countries in terms of their current socioeconomic categorization, have been linked intricately with the spread of Christianity in the island nations through the mission boards that operated from these two bases. They also continue to play a role in regional political-economic power affecting the Pacific islands. Since census data are readily available in these two countries, and since published materials on the church scene are numerous, both Australia and New Zealand status of Christianity profiles differ in the treatment of data from the reporting on the island nations. Trends and patterns of Christian practices are derived from the census and published sources for Australia and New Zealand.

On the other hand, as we gathered scanty information from some island countries, we realized the danger of presenting an unbalanced picture. The issue of proportionality will continue to be problematic in a compendium work like this. The absence of comparative statistics and the level of mass communication in the different island nations are realities we researchers have had to contend and live with. The effort to be all encompassing also presented a dilemma. Introductory materials such as ours remain on the descriptive level. Analyses of data to hypothesize cause and effect relationship of events are best left to other investigators. We did not intend to oversimplify the explanation of certain events in a locality. We can only point out "watersheds."

Oceania has had rich mission history. Historiographical materials chronicling this history have been thoroughly investigated by others. For instance, John Garrett's reconstruction of the onset and subsequent work of conversion and propagation of Christianity in Oceania in the 17th to 20th centuries is well researched, insightful and fascinating. Charles Forman provided historical accounts that led to the emergence and formation of national churches from these mission churches' background. On the other hand, Darrell Whiteman has shown the successful role of the missions in bridging traditional and western cultures. Missionaries have brought about in different parts of Oceania the contact of the local culture with the wider societies--both within the ethnolinguistic groupings and outside them.

Long before the concept of indigenization attracted the present-day theologians, the indigenous missionaries from the Samoas, Tahiti, Tonga, and Fiji had shown what it was like to spread the Word of God meaningfully among their own people. The churches of Oceania have also demonstrated contextualized liturgical forms. The quality of Christian faith, practice, and/or teaching, of course, needs to be analyzed further. Syncretism and nominality occur in many parts of the Christian world.

Oceania remains exciting, challenging, and even exotic to the outsider. The western world has long been enamored of the accounts of conquest and Christianization in the South Seas. Yet today, despite the transition from colonies to independent nations, from mission churches to national churches, Christianity in the Pacific is flourishing and deepening. As the countries undergo social changes, so too the churches face challenges of the times. The role of the Christian Church, which for centuries was intricately interwoven in the domestic affairs of the people, has been transformed anew; this time, in helping steer the newly independent nations on courses that involve Christian values and traditions.

Oceania is unique in this sense. The ability of the people of God and their leaders to help influence the paths their respective countries take, is manifested in many ways. Christian leaders occupy many political positions in the Pacific. Political consciousness is apparent in the Church's involvement in the quest for independence. Issues of nuclear-free Pacific are addressed alongside issues of social justice. These agenda are brought to the world forum with determination. The world, indeed, is more enriched as people know of the great strides and efforts Christian workers are making in Oceania today.

As we paint this multi-faceted portrait of Christian influence and current work in these islands, we hope we are able to share with the peoples of the world the tasks that have been accomplished in the past and the challenges and opportunities that remain for Christian laborers.

Nora Mosende Douglas
Hong Kong
August 30, 1986

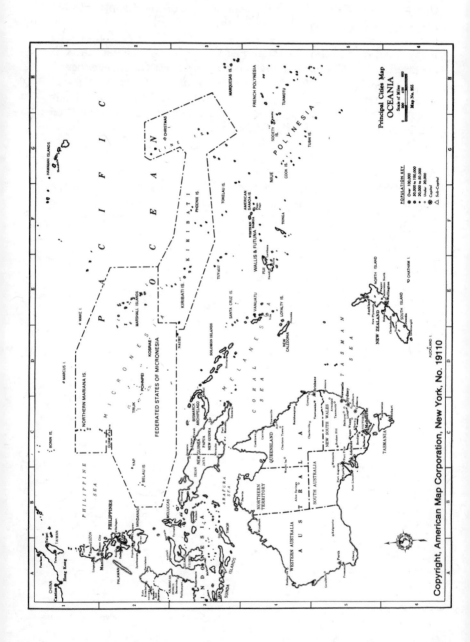

Principal Cities Map
OCEANIA
Scale of Miles
Map No. 965

POPULATION KEY
- Over 100,000
- 50,000 to 100,000
- 20,000 to 50,000
- Under 20,000
- Capital
- Sub-Capital

Chapter One: *Oceania Overview*

Geography
People and Culture
Historical Notes
Mission History
National Churches
Ecumenical Agencies
Parachurch and Mission Groups
Major Concerns
Other Religions

OCEANIA: Overview

To the reader unfamiliar with the area, it may come as a surprise to know that Oceania is one of the most Christianized regions of the world. For over two centuries, Christianity has spread across the Pacific, permeating and intertwining itself in the lives of the people. It has become the traditional religion of most of the Pacific island countries.

In this volume we examine the current status of Christianity in Oceania against a backdrop of history of missions, people groups, current geographical, cultural, socio-political and economic conditions. We also describe the present structure, composition and activities of Christian churches, agencies, and groups. Statistical data are analyzed for Australia and New Zealand which continue to have links with the island nations for missionary initiative and cooperation.

GEOGRAPHY

Location:

Oceania, as a region, covers the area bordered by and including the islands of New Guinea and the Pacific Island Trust Territory in the west; Hawaii and Easter Island on the north and east; and Australia and New Zealand in the south. There are about 25,000 islands within the region. Taken together, these islands comprise only about 1.6 million square kilometers, whereas the sea area is more than 88 million square kilometers.

Island Types:

Oceania has four major kinds of islands: continental, volcanic, atoll, and coral reef. Continental islands have rugged interior mountain ranges, plateaus, interior valleys, narrow coastal shelves and swamps. This topography tends to create small linguistic and political communities among the inhabitants. Examples of these are the Melanesian islands of Papua New Guinea, the Solomon Islands, and Vanuatu.

Volcanic islands have steep cliffs and mountain ranges divided by deep valleys. These islands are often surrounded by fringing reefs.

Hawaii, Tahiti, Cook Islands, Pohnpei, and Kosrae are examples of these.

Atolls are made up of a series of islets which typically, but not always, enclose a central lagoon. These islets are composed of coral reefs which have formed from corals and algae. Most of the islands of eastern Micronesia are atolls.

Coral reefs, a type of low island, are similar in composition with atolls. However, in terms of structure, the central lagoon has partially or totally disappeared. The reef's border has been elevated above the surrounding sea. Examples of this are Nauru, Banaba (Ocean Island), and Niue.

PEOPLE AND CULTURE

Cultural Areas:

Oceania has been divided into three general cultural areas: Melanesia, Micronesia, and Polynesia.

Melanesia, meaning "black islands," comes from the Greek word "melanin" - the chemical in the skin that accounts for dark pigmentation, a physical characteristic of the Melanesians. Countries included in Melanesia are Papua New Guinea, the Solomon Islands, New Caledonia, Vanuatu, and Fiji. The eastern part of New Guinea island, Irian Jaya, is inhabited mainly by Melanesians, although politically, this area now belongs to Indonesia. There are about five million Melanesians in these islands. The New Guinea highlands contain a quarter of them. The Fijian people are mostly Melanesian, but culturally are related to both Polynesia and Melanesia.

Polynesia, meaning "many islands," is made up of the islands of French Polynesia, Pitcairn Islands, Cook Islands, Tuvalu, Tokelau, the American and Western Samoa, Niue, Tonga, and Wallis and Futuna. It has a larger geographic area than Melanesia and has greater distances between the island groups. Hawaii is a major part of Polynesia.

Micronesia, meaning "little islands," includes about 2,000 islands of the atoll type. Five island groups with culturally distinct peoples comprise Micronesia: Palau and Yap in the west; the Carolinian atolls of Truk, Pohnpei and Kosrae in the south; Mariana Islands to the north; Marshall Islands in the east; and Kiribati and Nauru to the southeast.

People In Oceania

Oceania is inhabited by people whose ancestors populated the region in a number of migrations. The earliest to arrive in the South Pacific were the ancestors of the Australian Aborigines. The exact date of arrival of these people in Australia is unknown. Geographic isolation and cultural evolution have acted in concert to result in a distinct group of people with strikingly different cultural patterns from those found in the rest of the Pacific.

Settlers and migrants from Europe, and more recently from other parts of the world, comprise major people groups in Australia and New Zealand. Migrations to Australia, especially during the arrival of European refugees from Communist nations and Roman Catholic nations, in southern Europe, shifted the religious profile of that country. These groups are described more fully in Chapters Two and Five, respectively.

The Melanesians are frequently called "Papuans" which is a Malay word for "frizzy haired." They vary in skin color from the rich black of the Western Solomons and Bougainville to the lighter skin of the Trobriand Islanders. Chowning reported in her study that the Melanesians and Africans, including the "pygmy" populations of the two areas, could not be linked genetically.

Melanesians who live in the interior of the New Guinea Island, both Papua New Guinea and Irian Jaya, are mainly root-crop agricul- turalists. They have developed elaborate systems of cultivation in the highland valleys of New Guinea. Those who are found in the coastal areas of the larger islands and throughout the smaller islands of Melanesia, practice a mixture of agriculture and fishing. They have developed various types of watercraft, including sailing canoes.

Micronesians probably migrated from Melanesia, although the exact path of migration and timing of the migration is still unclear. Palauans, Carolineans, Chamorros, I-Kiribati, and Marshall Islanders make up the Micronesian peoples. Micronesian cultures are based upon a mixture of agriculture and utilization of ocean resources. Micronesians tend to have egalitarian types of social systems. They are noted for having developed the most sophisticated sailing canoes in the southern Pacific.

Polynesians are found over a great area of the Pacific from Hawaii, south to New Zealand, and from Easter Island to Fiji. Polynesians migrated from Melanesia and appear to have split at the Marquesas, with one group going north to Hawaii and the other group going south to New Zealand to become the Maoris. Except for the Maoris, Polynesians again practice a mixture of agriculture and fishing. Polynesians throughout the area developed a stratified political system and an elaborate religious systems.

SOCIAL ORGANIZATION

On the other hand, Melanesian social organization differed from Micronesian and Polynesian societies. It tended to be organized in smaller political units within a large cultural-linguistic group. There were no true tribes with a chief as a leader of the entire group, in contrast with those of Micronesia and Polynesia. Leadership in the political unit was achieved through personal skills and abilities. Individuals owed their allegiance to this small unit where they worked, fought, and/or celebrated together.

The Melanesian type of social organization accounted mainly for the difference in the patterns of conversion to Christianity compared with that of Polynesia. Tippett characterized the Polynesia pattern in terms of People Movements. The paramount chief in a Polynesian society, in consultation with his ruling body of elders, would choose to become a Christian, then the rest of the followers would convert. In Melaneisa, conversion occurred in smaller units. The task of church planting was more difficult and took a longer time than in Polynesia.

The Maoris are the indigenous people of New Zealand. They are Polynesians who modified their culture to adapt to the colder climate of the area. They originally came from the Cook Islands and the Society Islands, northeast of New Zealand.

AUSTRONESIAN LANGUAGES

The Micronesian, Polynesian, and newer languages of Melanesia all belong to the Austronesian family. Their roots go back to proto-Malay. This family of languages is the most widespread in the world. Linguistic diversity in Oceania is directly related to the length of time migrants have been in a particular area. Polynesia, for example, is linguistically the most homogeneous, being the last area settled. It has about 17 languages within a central triangle of islands and 11 in outlying areas. Micronesia is somewhat more diverse linguistically, and Melanesia, which has been settled the longest, is the most complex. The latter has about 1,200 languages (700 to 800 in Papua New Guinea, alone).

The large number of languages in Oceania pose all kinds of difficulties, not only to outsiders, but also to the governments trying to work within these cultural areas. The development of linguas franca (common languages) has eased these difficulties. Pidgin English, known as *Tok Pigin* in Papua New Guinea, and *Bislama* in Vanuatu are used as linguas franca. The Solomon Islands has its own Pidgin language, also.

HISTORICAL NOTES

Major Explorers "Discovered" Oceania

Famous world explorers reported the existence of the Oceanic islands and peoples during the 16th through the 18th century. These voyages and reports eventually paved the way for the coming of Europeans and Americans. Among these were the missionaries who introduced Christianity to the Pacific peoples.

The following illustrates the western presence in the region:

1500-1600

Portugal was in the East Indies; Spain was in Guam, Philippines, Solomon Islands, Marquesas Islands. World explorers: Magellan, Mendana, and de Quiros.

1600-1700

The Dutch replaced the Portuguese in the East Indies. Navigators discovered Northern Australia. In 1642, Captain Abel Tasman sailed around the southern part of Australia and "discovered" Tasmania, New Zealand, Tonga and parts of Fiji.

1700-1780

The Dutch explorer Roggeveen "discovered" Easter Island. Tuamotus, and the Samoan Islands in 1722. From 1764-1769, the English Captains Byron, Wallis, Cartaret, explored the Pacific area. Wallis found Tahiti. The Frenchman Bougainville followed Wallis to Tahiti and proceeded to the Samoan islands, New Hebrides now Vanuatu, New Guinea, and the Solomon Islands.

At three different times between 1768-1779, the British Captain James Cook explored the Society Islands, New Zealand, New Caledonia and Norfolk Islands. He charted the new islands of the Tuamotus, Cook, and Marquesas.

1780 marked the end of the major exploration and new discoveries era.

The major explorations eventually led to the colonization and administration of Oceania by western powers. This will be discussed under the individual country sections.

Economic Developments: Ventures and Adventurers

Between 1780 and the 1860's, more outsiders came to the islands, some even settling there, especially in Polynesia and Micronesia. Among these arrivals were various beachcombers, sailors, whalers, and traders. Some jumped ship from an explorer's ship; others were shipwrecked. Some were malcontents, others adventurers. Many of them were undesirables, bringing alcohol and new diseases to pristine areas. Many formed long-term liaisons or married island women, and a few became advisers or mediators between European traders and the local chiefs, having learned the local languages.

By 1820, British and American whalers operated all over the region, carrying on a thriving industry until the whaling grounds were depleted around 1880. During this period, the whalers traded liquor, guns, hardware, and textiles for food and sexual partners. Rampant venereal disease, violence, indigenous conflicts, and alcoholism caused the depopulation of many island groups. With the end of the whaling era, copra trading became dominant all over the region.

Colonial Period

Between the 1800's and 1900's, Australia and New Zealand became financial centers for the Pacific. Commerical developers from these two countries obtained lands in different parts of Oceania. They grew copra, sugar, cacao, vanilla, fruits, cotton, and rubber, among others. The need for labor in these plantations, especially in sugar fields, brought indentured workers to the Pacific. Indians came to Fiji; Filipinos, Japanese, and Chinese went to Hawaii.

The indentured labor system obliged the island workers to work for a few years in exchange for food, a small wage, and a bonus of cash and goods upon returning home. In reality, the workers were tricked or trapped into the arrangements without being paid. Many islanders were victimized and did not return home. The persons who made the labor arrangements for profit were known as the blackbirders. *Blackbirding* occurred mainly for large plantations, including those in Peru and Australia. It was partly in this slave trading context that the early Christian missions had to operate.

While the Micronesian islands such as the Marianas and Guam were ruled by the Spaniards in the 17th century, for the most part, colonialization of the Pacific occurred in the late 19th century to the mid-20th century. Great Britain, Germany, France, the United States, Japan, and Australia occupied various parts of the Pacific Territories. Colonial administration was tied with the economic, political and military interests of these nations.

The churches in Oceania during this time were strongly identified with the missions which provided them leadership. Hawaii's church life developed somewhat differently from the island nations with the strong presence of Asians and Americans. New Zealand and Australia, with white settlers in the majority, had a different set of directions and problems in their church development.

Meanwhile, the period between 1900 and 1942 was described as being the high point in the life and influence of South Pacific Christianity. The people and the churches had a relative period of stability. The Pacific churches, although still under the leadership of foreign missionaries, developed their own character and distinctive life. Influenced both by missionary teaching and the local culture, the Pacific Islander Christians developed their own understanding of the faith and their own moral code.

The churches in Polynesia were mainly self-supporting. They constructed their own buildings and provided for the pastor's salary and housing. Often, the pastors grew their own food. Younger churches in Melanesia were receiving financial assistance from foreign mission boards.

World War II Period (1942-1945)

The war experience, especially in the areas where military confrontation occurred, is said to have strengthened the sense of identity and independence of the Pacific Islanders. They developed a new sense of importance of the Christian faith apart from the tradition-al island life after the harrowing war experiences. Also, they had exposure to other ways of life through the troops that inhabited the islands during this period. On the other hand, foreign missionaries were cleared from the islands where they were considered enemies by the warring nations. Missionaries in Papua New Guinea were severely treated; many of them died.

Deprived of their founders and leaders, the churches in the Pacific responded by developing strong local leadership. In many villages church life continued; local leaders led worship services. A yearning for independence had started to take root among the people.

Post-World War II Period

The island nations in the Pacific were in a state of rapid transfor-mation. The factors of improved communication, education, economic development, and urbanization affected the church and mission situation. The island churches, especially the long es-tablished ones in Tahiti, Samoa, Tonga and Fiji, started to assert their independence from the founding missions. They started to undertake their responsibilities as moral and spiritual leaders in the Pacific. Thus, in the 1960's and 1970's national churches emerged as self-governing, self-propagating, and self-supporting churches. This development coincided with expressions of nationalism.

In the meantime, the post-war years brought a heavy influx of missionaries to the different parts of Oceania, particularly to the New Guinea island. Missionary groups came from New Zealand, Australia, Europe, and America. Australian Protestant and Catholic missionaries served in various parts of Oceania. The American Board activated its mission in Micronesia, dividing the field with their Leibenzell missionary counterparts. American Jesuits came to the Carolina and Marshall Islands; the American Capuchins, to the Marianas. The Jesuits were assisted by the Maryknoll Sisters and the Mercedarian Sisters. The Lutherans and Catholics strengthened their work in the Papua New Guinea highlands. Pacific Islander church workers joined their Methodist colleagues in their work in Papua New Guinea. Indigenous workers from the Melanesian Brotherhood and their Anglican Papuan churches joined the efforts in the highlands. The Sepik district also opened up for the missionaries.

The foreign missionaries who came to Papua New Guinea highlands at this time represented smaller and newer missions and churches with a strong evangelical bent. Group conversion was not as emphasized as individual conversion.

MISSION HISTORY

Mission History In Oceania: First Contacts

Mission work in Oceania has evolved through the precolonial, colonial, and post-World War II periods. Each period posed different challenges to the missionary work as major cultural, political, social, and economic developments in the region.

Pre-Colonial Period

Among the characteristics of the pre-colonial, first missionary contact of the 17th to 19th century were the presence of traders, whalers, and other adventurers in the islands. Island chiefs were engaged among themselves in warfare in their battle for supremacy. Eastern and central Oceania, which are Polynesian in culture, had hierarchical social organization while the western Oceania islands had more egalitarian yet more individualistic systems.

Australia/New Zealand became a major base for the European missionaries who came from Tahiti in the east, and the others who were stationed in central Oceania. Five major mission groups dominated the scene at this period: the Congregationalist London Missionary Society (LMS), the Anglican Church Missionary Society, the Wesleyan Methodist Missionary Society, societies and religious orders belonging to the Roman Catholic Church, and the Congregationalist American Board of Commissioners for Foreign Missions (ABCFM). Also present at this period was the Presbyterian mission in Vanuatu (formerly New Hebrides). The Lutheran missions came to the northern part of New Guinea in 1886 when Germany annexed the territory. The mission of the Seventh-day Adventists also had its start at the turn of the century, basing itself at Fiji.

By 1900, Christianity was planted in Oceania. Eastern and central Pacific had large churches encompassing whole populations; western Pacific had its young churches in their beginning stages of growth. Missionaries played a major role in the political developments of islands such as Hawaii, Fiji, Tonga, Wallis and the Cook Islands.

ROMAN CATHOLIC MISSIONS

Priests who came with the 17th century Spanish explorers introduced Christianity in parts of Micronesia ruled by Spain. When
Guam became a Spanish port between the Philippines and Mexico,
the Spanish brought the Catholic mission. The priests worked with
the paramount chiefs to gain converts. Catholicism spread to the
Mariana Islands. Subsequently, war broke out between the Spanish
and the Chamorros of Guam, where thousands of the latter were
killed.

Widespread Catholic evangelization in Polynesia and Melanesia
developed much later than the Protestant missionary work. In 1827
the Holy See assigned eastern Oceania to the apostolic care of the
Congregation of the Sacred Heart of Jesus and Mary, known as the
Picpus Fathers. The Picpus Fathers and the Marist Fathers entered
Polynesia through Hawaii and Southeast Tahiti in the 1830's.

Western Oceania was entrusted to the Society of Mary with the
first missionaries directed by Bishop Pompalier in 1937. Missionaries reached New Caledonia in 1843. Other congregations, such
as the Missionaries of the Sacred Heart and the Divine Word
Fathers, spearheaded missionary activities in mainland Papua New
Guinea.

During the 19th and 20th century colonial period, the French
government aided the Catholic missions through promotion of the
French language and culture. Some of these missions were in
French Polynesia, New Caledonia, Wallis and Futuna, and Vanuatu.

THE LONDON MISSIONARY SOCIETY

The missionaries of the London Missionary Society (LMS), mostly
Congregationalists, spread Christianity primarily in Polynesia
through Tahiti, the Marquesas, and Tonga. This British mission
came to Oceania in 1797 at the time when island chiefs were still at
war with one another; and when traders had come and beachcombers had settled in some Polynesian areas. The first mission group
met many difficulties. Contact was made at this time with Sydney,
Australia through Samuel Marsden, an Anglican clergyman and
trader.

The second LMS mission group included John Williams and Lance-
lot Threlkeld; they were stationed in the Leeward Islands which
became the nucleus for the early propagation of Christianity in

Polynesia. Local churches developed in Huahine, Raiatea, and Borabora under the guidance of the LMS missionaries. These churches became the first Polynesian-sending churches utilizing the trained island evangelists. These indigenous missionaries became pioneers, advisers, and informants to the European missionaries, in different parts of Polynesia. They worked effectively, through initial hardships, with the local chiefs and within their cultural patterns. These Pacific Islanders laid the foundation for the evangelization of Oceania. Notable among them were Anaa in the Tuamotus; Tubuai and Raivauae in the Australs; Rapa in the Marquesas and Fiji.

In 1830, the LMS spread westward through the Society Islands to Cook and Samoa Islands, becoming known as the Tahitian web in the spread of Christianity in Oceania.

In 1871 using pastors from the Loyalty Islands LMS pioneered missionary work in the Melanesian island of New Guinea. A more detailed account of the spread of Christianity through LMS work will be given in the individual country and status of Christianity chapters following this.

THE CHURCH MISSIONARY SOCIETY

Organized in Britain, the Church Missionary Society (CMS) came to New Zealand in 1814 to spread the gospel to the Maoris. This spread of Christianity has been known as the Maori strand. This evangelical Anglican mission started out as a chaplaincy for convicts in the New South Wales penal settlement in Australia. The most effective chaplain at that time was Samuel Marsden, who worked with released convicts and who established a self-supporting colony through farming and livestock raising.

Marsden also aided the LMS missionaries in Tahiti with necessities and trade goods. Through a Maori chief named Ruatara, who asked Marsden to expand the mission to New Zealand, the Church Missionary Society established the first mission in New Zealand at Rangitowa, northwest of the Bay of Islands. Later the work with the Maoris expanded southward. The mission churches tried to preserve the language and early culture of New Zealand.

The mission encouraged the development of the missionary arm of the Australian and New Zealand Anglican churches. The Melanesian Mission worked with the people in the Banks, Loyalty, and Solomon Islands. By 1866 they had established a mission school on Norfolk Island.

WESLEYAN METHODIST MISSIONARY SOCIETY

British interest in missions to the Pacific increased in the early 1800's. The Wesleyan Methodist Missionary Society established a station in the Bay of Islands in New Zealand in 1820 under the leadership of the Rev. Samuel Leigh. It was to supplement the work of LMS. It expanded later to Tonga and Fiji. Walter Lawry of the British Wesleyan Conference was appointed to Tonga. He worked in areas where Tahitian LMS missionaries had been shipwrecked at Nuku'alofa. Earlier, LMS Tahitian teachers, Borabora, Taute, and Zorobabela had laid the foundation for evangelization.

John Thomas, a Weslyan Methodist missionary, later succeeded in converting Topou, a supreme ruler of Tonga, and his family to Christianity. Mass conversion, and later, revivals characterized the missionary efforts in Tonga.

Missionaries with the Wesleyan Methodist Society came to Fiji through Tonga. David Cargill and William Cross came in 1835. Tongan teachers assisted them with the task of evangelization. Foremost among them was Joeli Beru who became a leading figure in Fiji Methodism. Fiji at this period was characterized by deep division among the ruling chiefs. Wars and cannibalism occurred.

Among the Wesleyan missionaries who came to Fiji later was John Hunt who became widely respected for his works and who laid the foundation of a Fijian church. He guided the emergence of a church established within the framework of customary laws. Fiji *lotu* had its own liturgical character using sonorous local chanting and action songs and other unique expressions.

Wesleyan mission work spread from Lakeba, Somosomo, Rewa, Bau, to Viwa where the local chief Varani converted to Christianity. The conversion of the warrior-king Ratu Cakoban marked the widespread movement of the people to Christianity.

In 1830, John Williams and Charles Barff of the LMS met with the Wesleyans in Tonga to discuss mission work in the South Pacific. The two groups agreed upon areas in which they would operate, and thus, the first comity was signed. Samoa was to be an LMS area, and Tonga and Fiji would be left to the Wesleyans. The influences of this and similar agreements are still evident in the dominant churches and denominational affiliations of the national churches in the present nation states of the Pacific.

NEW HEBRIDES PRESBYTERIAN MISSIONS

The London Missionary Society supported the work of the Presbyterian mission that came to the New Hebrides (now Vanuatu), in the 1850's. Earlier, LMS Cook Islanders and Samoans worked on the islands of Aniwa, Futuna, Aneityum, Tanna, and Efate.

John Geddie from Nova Scotia, became the pioneering Presbyterian missionary in the New Hebrides. With other missionaries, he emphasized the Calvinism of the late Evangelical Revivals in Scotland. Conversion, then education, was the main approach. Geddie tried to develop self-governing presbyteries early on. By 1855 Geddie ordained deacons, and charged church officers with tasks assigned by elders and ministers within the church session. Elders in the Presbyterian Church of the New Hebrides developed the tradition of church government which lent itself to application in wider social and political situations. This pattern still exsts in Vanuatu today.

Geddie's efforts for self-government of the local church were considered by the Scottish and Nova Scotia churches as premature. For many years to come, white missionaries tended to dominate the proceedings of the developing church (see "Christianity," section for Vanuatu in Chapter Three of this book).

At about this time, sandalwood trading and *blackbirding* for slave labor were underway in the New Hebrides. The missionaries during the course of their voyages to the different parts of the island, encountered problems with them. John Paton, a recruit of the Presbyterian mission, wrote extensively at that time of his indignation over the Melanesian labor trade.

THE AMERICAN BOARD OF COMMISSIONERS FOR FOREIGN MISSIONS (ABCFM)

Congregational missionaries of the Boston-based ABCFM came to Hawaii in 1820. They came to the islands, then called the Sandwich Islands, shortly after King Kamehameha died; a group of chiefs kept conditions stable, but the people were curious and expectant regarding the powers of the God of the white sailors and traders. The missionaries succeeded quickly by working through the highest chiefs of the island. Altogether 12 groups of American Board missionaries arrived from 1820 to 1848. They brought Christian and Protestant values for ingenuity and hard work. An autonomous Hawaiian church emerged between 1848 and 1900.

Children of the missionaries later staffed the Hawaiian-based missions to Micronesia. By 1850, ABCFM missionaries and some of their Hawaiian converts expanded to the Eastern Carolines, the Marshalls, and eventually to the Gilberts, now Kiribati.

SEVENTH-DAY ADVENTISTS

In 1899, the American missionaries John Fulton and Calvin Parker established the Fiji Mission at Suvavou. Fiji remained the center of the mission until 1973 when its headquarters moved to Auckland, New Zealand. Renamed the Central Pacific Mission, the regional headquarters monitors and coordinates the activities of mission in Fiji, Cook Islands, French Polynesia, Pitcairn, Samoa, and Tonga.

Other Contributions Of Missions

In addition to introducing Christianity in the Pacific, the early missions provided education and medical care to the people long before these services were offered by colonial governments. In translating the Scriptures, missionaries developed orthographies for the unwritten languages and taught people to read. From this beginning the area progressed to the point that most people of the Pacific were literate in either the vernacular or a local Pidgin language.

The period between the missionary outreach in the 1700's to the early 1900's bore bountiful harvests in propagating the Christian faith. Consolidation and integration of Christian beliefs and behavior occurred in different levels among the believers. Many traditional mores found their expression in the Christian celebrations and forms of worship. Western influences also left their marks on the people.

The influences of particular missions are best seen in the denominational affiliation of the national churches in Oceania today. Table 1 outlines the major denominations in each of these countries.

The following section discusses the current composition, structure and major activities of the main denominations in Oceania. Not included are the recently arrived Pentecostal groups. The section also deals with the non-Christian influences in the region.

TABLE 1

MAJOR CHURCHES IN OCEANIA

COUNTRIES	DENOMINATIONAL AFFILIATIONS
Australia	See Chapter 2, Table 4
Melanesia	
Fiji	Wesleyan
	Methodist
	Roman Catholic
	(Hinduism)
New Caledonia	Roman Catholic
	Evangelical Church
Papua New Guinea	Roman Catholic
	United Church
	Lutheran
	Anglican
Solomon Islands	Anglican
	United Church
	Roman Catholic
Vanuatu	Presbyterian
	Roman Catholic
Micronesia	
Belau (Palau)	Roman Catholic
Federated States	
of Micronesia	Roman Catholic
	Congregational (Kosrae, Truk and Pohnpei)
	United Church of Christ
Guam	Roman Catholic
Kiribati	Roman Catholic
	Congregational (KPS)
Marshall Islands	United Church of Christ
	Roman Catholic
	Congregational
Nauru	Congregational
Northern Mariana Islands	Roman Catholic

New Zealand	See Chapter 5, Table 7

Polynesia

American Samoa	Congregational
	Methodist
	Roman Catholic
Cook Islands	Congregational
	Roman Catholic
	Seventh-day Adventist
French Polynesia	Evangelical Church
	Roman Catholic
Niue	Congregational
Pitcairn Islands	Seventh-day Adventist
Tokelau	Congregational
	Roman Catholic
Tonga	Methodist
	Roman Catholic
Tuvalu	Congregational
Wallis and Futuna	Roman Catholic
Western Samoa	Congregational
	Methodist
	Roman Catholic

THE ANGLICAN COMMUNION

The Anglican Church in the Pacific has generally been Anglo-Catholic, stressing the sacramental side of the church. Until the 1930's, most of the Anglican missionaries came from England. After World War II, indigenous leadership expanded and today these indigenous leaders lead their churches throughout the Pacific.

Organizationally, the Anglican churches in Melanesia have become a self-governing Church in the Anglican Communion. Until 1975, Melanesia was linked with the New Zealand church through the Provincial Synod. Papua New Guinea was connected with Australia until 1977. In parts of Solomon Islands and Papua New Guinea, the Anglican Church has become an indigenous church. In Polynesia, it tends to be an expatriate's church, playing a significant chaplaincy role.

The Diocese of Polynesia is part of the Church of the Province of New Zealand. Except in certain matters, the bishop, the clerical and the lay representatives elected by the synod of a Missionary Diocese have the same rights as those of the dioceses of New Zealand. The Church of the Province of New Zealand has been working with the

Associated Churches of Christ, the Methodist Church, the Presbyterian Church, and the Congregational Union in regard to the issue of uniting as one church body.

The Church of the Province of Melanesia was formed in January 1975. The Archbishop of the province is based in Honiara, Solomon Islands, with bishops in Malaita, Temotu, Vanuatu, and Ysabel. The Papua New Guinea Province has bishops in Lae, Dogura, Rabaul, Popondeta, and Port Moresby.

The South Pacific Anglican Council acts as a constitutional body to deal with matters referred by the General Synods of the member provinces of Melanesia, New Guinea, and Polynesia. Membership by the Council incudes all bishops of the area, one clergy and one lay person.

ROMAN CATHOLIC CHURCH

Dioceses in the Pacific were originally classified as vicariate apostolic, having a missionary status under the supervision of the congregation for the Propagation of the Faith in Rome. The missionary order nominated the bishops. Growing interest in localization led to the change from vicariate to diocesan structures. In 1966 Pope Paul VI decreed the establishment of the regular hierarchy throughout the Pacific. Apostolic Nuncios and delegates coordinated the Catholic Church in the Pacific; they are also the main link to the Vatican in Rome. One Apostolic Nuncio based in New Zealand oversees two hierarchies: one for New Zealand and Fiji, and the other for all South Pacific islands. The other Apostolic Nuncio presides over Papua New Guinea and the Solomon Islands.

Each hierarchy is coordinated through its own Bishop Conference. CEPAC (Conferentia Episcopalis Pacifici or Catholic Episcopal Conference of the Pacific) covers a wide region. It is comprised of 11 dioceses and archdioceses. Five are French-speaking and six are English-speaking. The three Metropolitan Provinces include the Archdiocese of Suva, the Archdiocese of Papeete, and the Archdiocese of Noumea.

Fiji and Rotuma belong to the Archdiocese of Suva. The suffragans to this archdiocese include Apia in Western Samoa, Tokelau, Tarawa in Kiribati, Tuvalu, Nauru, Rarotonga in Cook Islands, Niue, Caroline and Marshall Islands. The Society, Austral and Tuamotu Islands are part of the Archdiocese of Papeete. Taiohae of the Marquesas is a suffragan. The Archdiocese of Noumea includes

New Caledonia and Loyalty Islands. Port Vila, Vanuatu, and Wallis and Futuna are suffragans.

The Diocese of Tonga belongs to CEPAC, but comes directly under the Holy See of Rome. The vicariate of the Caroline and Marshall Islands, which first remained with the hierarchy in the United States, became a diocese in 1979.

Another system of regional organization for the Catholic Church is the orders of priests, brothers or nuns who undertake specific tasks such as teaching, nursing, etc. Among these orders are the Jesuits, Marist priests, brothers, and sisters.

Protestant Churches

Adherence to and/or affiliation with major Protestant churches in Oceania remains strong among the majority of the people. The major strong traditions are as follows: Evangelical churches in French Polynesia and the Loyalty Islands, New Caledonia; Congregationalists in the Federated States of Micronesia and the Marshall Islands; the Cook Islands, Niue, Kiribati, Nauru, Tuvalu, and the Samoas; Presbyterians in Vanuatu; Wesleyan Methodists in Fiji and Tonga; and Lutherans in Papua New Guinea.

The last decade has seen the union of several of these Protestant churches; thus membership figures in individual churches may have dropped. The individual country status of Christianity sections in this book detail these developments. Briefly, the following table gives membership and some church workers' statistics for denominations most directly affected by unions:

TABLE 2

METHODIST/WESLEYAN CHURCHES

	Member-ship	Community
Australia		
The Uniting Church in Australia	560,174	1,500,000
Australian Aborigines	1,000	2,000
Methodist Church of Australia		
Continuing	48,000	75,000
The Church of the Nazarene	909	1,800
The Wesleyan Church	535	1,100
Fiji		
The Methodist Church	170,270	250,000
Papua New Guinea and Solomon Islands		
The United Church (part formerly		
Methodist)	92,000	300,000
The Wesleyan Church	1,368	3,000
The Church of the Nazarene	1,633	3,000
New Zealand		
The Methodist Church	25,000	100,000
The Church of the Nazarene	463	1,000
Samoa		
The Methodist Church	30,146	60,000
The Church of the Nazarene	138	300
Tonga		
The Free Wesleyan Church	452,000	10,215
The Free Church of Tonga		
The Church of Tonga		
TOTALS	941,790	2,349,200

PRESBYTERIAN/CONGREGATIONAL CHURCHES

Presbyterian Church of
Australia -- 776 congregations; 324 parishes, 389 ministers and home missionaries in 1981.

Uniting Church of
Australia -- 3,200 congregations; 3,200 ministers in 1980.

Congregational Union of
New Zealand -- 73,934 members; 500 congregations; 555 preaching stations; 660 men and 30 women ministers, 5,992 men and women elders.

Congregational Christian
Church in Samoa -- 85,000 members; 22,426 communicant members; 10 districts (sessions); 220 ministers; 32 elders. Women not ordained elders or ministers as of 1980.

Presbyterian Church of
Vanuatu -- 45,000 members; 10,000 communicant members. 49 congregations; 200 preaching stations; 59 ministers; 300 men and women elders; 2 deaconesses; no women ordained ministers as of 1981.

SEVENTH-DAY ADVENTIST (SDA)

The Seventh-day Adventist (SDA) work in the Pacific started with the pioneer work of John Fulton who opened a mission training school in Fiji in 1904. From this school a corps of national workers became SDA missionaries to other Pacific islands. By 1941 the Fulton College had opened its doors to all Pacific denominations. The College became a regional training institution and was renamed the Union Training College for the Central Pacific.

In 1949 the Central Pacific Union Mission was established in Fiji. Today, from its base in New Zealand, it monitors and coordinates the activities of the SDA missions in Fiji, Cook Islands, French Polynesia, Pitcairn, Samoa and Tonga.

Church departments and activities include youth, health, lay activities or evangelistic outreach, Sabbath school, publishing, communication-radio, television, Bible correspondence, education and stewardship. The denomination operates hospitals and health clinics in the region. It also contributes to community welfare through the care of needy families.

Radio broadcasts are made throughout the Central Pacific Mission. Radio Tonga and Samoa carry the denomination's religious broadcasts.

ECUMENICAL AGENCIES

The last 25 years have seen the development of regional and intranational conferences and councils of churches in the Pacific. The Pacific Conference of Churches is in the forefront of ecumenical cooperation among Christian churches. National councils and similar organizations have been formed to address the ongoing ministry needs and interests of member churches. Invariably, these councils and individual churches affiliate with wider world bodies such as the World Council of Churches.

Pacific Conference Of Churches (PCC)

Led by indigenous Pacific church leaders in the early 1960's, the seed for the formation of a regional organization of Pacific churches and mission agencies came into being. Meeting at Malua Theological College in Western Samoa, these leaders shared the work and the needs of the Pacific churches, particularly the need to upgrade the theological training for ministers and church workers. One of the results of this meeting was the creation of the Pacific Theological College in Suva, Fiji.

The Pacific Conference of Churches was formally established at the 1966 assembly at Lifou in the Loyalty Islands of New Caledonia. The Conference has met every five years since then. It has developed and promoted several programs and services throughout the region. These include the Christian Education and Communication Program, Christian Family Life Program, and the Church and Society Program. From the conference grew the publishing house Lotu Pasifika Productions; the Pacific Churches Research Center based in Vila, Vanuatu (now inactive); and the Chaplaincy at the University of the South Pacific.

The 1970's and early 1980's saw PCC's involvement in programs and issues for integral human development, Pacific identity and solidarity; theological education; independence movements, i.e. Vanuatu and New Caledonia; nuclear-free Pacific; participation of women and youth; impact of transnational corporations; effects of tourism, and motivation and priorities of aid and development.

National Councils of Churches and some provincial councils have been formed also in the last decade. Concerned with intra-country ecumenicity, these councils are in different stages of growth and cooperative endeavors. The Melanesian Council of Churches in Papua New Guinea and the Solomon Islands is one of the most active in the region. It has seven member churches and two associate members. It has grown from a missionary-initiated-and-led council of foreign missions to a council of autonomous churches led by Melanesians. Among its recent activities are the establishment of rural development information center (the Liklik Buk Information Center); ecumenical planning and integration of development projects; social programs; and support of the establishment of the Provincial Council of Churches.

Council For World Mission
(Formerly London Missionary Society)

Formed in 1977 by churches linked with the London Missioanry Society, the Commonwealth Missionary Society, and the Presbyterian Church of England, the Council has six member churches in the Pacific region.

It has 15 missionaries with the United Church of Papua New Guinea and the Solomon Islands; four with the Kiribati Protestant Church; two with the Congregational Church in Samoa; one with the Tuvalu Church; and two with ecumenical bodies. In turn, Pacific missionaries serve elsewhere. Four Congregational Christian Church in Samoa (CCCS) missionaries serve in Europe and Africa. One from the Presbyterian Church of New Zealand works in South India; and two from the United Church of Papua New Guinea work in Tuvalu.

The member churches of the Council undertake urban ministry projects and Christian youth training.

**Communaute Evangelique De L'Action
Apostolique (CEVAA)**

Based on the former Paris Evangelical Mission, this group helps French-speaking Protestant Christians in the Pacific. It groups together Third World and former "sending" churches in an equal partnership for mutual assistance. It has assisted the evangelical churches in Tahiti and New Caledonia, the Pacific Theological College, and the Pacific Conference of Churches.

PARACHURCH AND MISSION GROUPS

The following section lists some of the missions operating in Oceania today. The list is far from exhaustive; Papua New Guinea alone has about 80 mission agencies at work.

Mission Agencies

LUTHERAN MISSIONS

The Evangelical Lutheran Missions work with the Evangelical Lutheran Church of Papua New Guinea, where they have 550,000 adherents. About 2,530 indigenous pastors, evangelists and Bible women work in the mission. The Missouri Synod Lutheran Church in the United States, the Lutheran Church in America and the American Lutheran Church have given assistance to the Lutherans of Papua New Guinea.

LIEBENZELL MISSION

The Liebenzell Mission works in Micronesia and parts of Papua New Guinea. It has stations on Truk, Yap, and Palau. Cooperative churches include the Evangelical Church of Truk since 1906; the Evangelical Church of Yap since 1959; and the Evangelical Church of Palau since 1929. Total adherents in these churches in 1985 were 15,000.

In Papua New Guinea, the Liebenzell Mission is stationed in three places: Sepik Province with the South Sea Evangelical Church (SSEC) since 1963; the Evangelical Church in Manus since 1914; and the SSEC in New Britain since 1977. There are about 4,000 adherents in these churches. Three hundred and fifty indigenous pastors, evangelists and Bible women have worked with the missions in the Sepik Province of Papua New Guinea. Another 26 have worked in Manus. Missionaries stationed in three areas in Papua totaled 45.

WESLEYAN MISSION

There has been a large Wesleyan/Methodist mission working in many parts of the Pacific including the highlands of Papua New Guinea. The mission in Papua New Guinea has become a part of the United Church. (See Papua New Guinea section of Chapter Three in this book.)

Australian Wesleyans entered the highlands of Papua New Guinea in 1961. American missionaries joined the Australians later in developing interior stations and establishing a headquarters base in Mt. Hagen. They succeeded in planting and organizing churches within five districts. Leadership was under the national district superintendents. Outreach continues into other needy areas of the highlands and the coastal area of Lae. Japanese missionaries from Immanuel General Mission assist the Wesleyan missionaries in the pioneering urban work.

SOUTHERN BAPTIST MISSION

Southern Baptists missionaries have worked in Guam since 1961. In 1984, eight missionary staff worked with three Southern Baptist churches. Church membership was 450. In Fiji, a missionary couple came to Nadi to work with local Baptist churches. In 1984, a national pastor served 80 members in two churches.

ROMAN CATHOLIC MISSIONS

The Roman Catholic mission groups can be categorized under the religious orders of sisters, brothers and fathers. They operate in various parts of Oceania. The following comprise some of the missionary orders:

> Columban Fathers, the Daughters of Our Lady Compassion, Indian Missionary Society, Missionary Sisters of the Society of Mary (SMSM), the Marist Brothers, Marist Sisters, Monfort Brothers of St. Gabriel, Sisters of Our Lady of Nazareth, Daughters of Charity of St. Vincent de Paul, The Carmelite Nuns (OCD), Sisters of St. Joseph of Cluny, Vincentian Fathers, Picpus Fathers, the Sacred Heart Order, and the Christian Brothers.

CENTRAL PACIFIC UNION MISSION (CPUM):
SEVENTH-DAY ADVENTIST

CPUM was founded in 1949 after the Seventh-day Adventist Church reorganized its administration in Australasia. With headquarters in Auckland, New Zealand, its members are from Cook Islands, Fiji, French Polynesia, Pitcairn Islands, Samoa, and Tonga. The mission promotes, administers, and coordinates the religious, educational and welfare work of the Seventh-day Adventist Church in member countries. It administers development projects in these countries, and the Fulton College in Fiji. The Adventist mission also operates the publishing house for the South Pacific, Trans Pacific Publishers of Fiji. It has numerous lay activities, stewardship and pastoral instructional programs.

Parachurch Agencies

Education, nursing, translation, printing, social welfare, and many other Christian efforts are not new in Oceania. Many positive things have resulted from the work of past missions. Situations and conditions in the region have changed, yet there is continuity in the ministries of past and present Christian workers.

The following section narrates some of the activities of the parachurch groups operating in Oceania today. Groups working n Australia and New Zealand are listed in their respective profiles, Chapters Two and Five.

LITERATURE DISTRIBUTION

The Bible Society Of The South Pacific

The main task of this society is to translate God's word and publish the Scripture. Of the 265 languages in 16 countries of the South Pacific, the full Bible has been translated in 12 languages: in Solomon Islands, in Nauru, Kiribati, Fijian, Tongan, Samoan, Niue, Cook Island, Maori, Tahitian, Vanuatu and Lifou in New Caledonia. The Bible is currently being translated in Bislama Pidgin, the lingua franca in Vanuatu. Revision of the New Testament in Fijian will be in print in 1986. The Bible Society of the South Pacific (BSSP) works with the Summer Institute of Linguistics in some translations.

Distribution in 1984 included the following: Bibles--72,976; Testaments--30,587; Portions--23,809; Selections--1,792,512; New Reader Selections--263,304.

The Scripture Union

The Scripture Union is an interdenominational organization which aims to help people of any denomination to read the Bible with understanding. It started in England in 1867. Pacific Islanders who trained in Australia and New Zealand and who used Scripture Union materials later promoted the use of these materials in their respective countries. National committees were formed in Tonga, Fiji, Papua New Guinea, Vanuatu, Solomon Islands, New Caledonia and Samoa.

The national committees in some countries are linked to the National Council of Churches and work together with the Bible Society to promote Bible reading. The committees provide local churches with study guides based on a five year curriculum of daily readings from the Bible. Notes have been produced in local languages. Notes covering the whole Bible have been produced in local languages of Tonga and Samoa, simple English, and Nguonese (Vanuatu). Notes on the New Testaments are available in Bislama, Pidgin, and Fijian. The committees also distribute standard English and French notes. Scripture Union in New Zealand produces Bible reading calendars for its Pacific Island groups in such languages as Cook Islands, Maori, Niuean, Samoan, and Tongan.

The ministry of the Scripture Union assists Christian churches through Bible reading materials for all ages, Christian Fellowship in schools, youth, children, family outreach, and leadership training.

Lotu Pasifika Productions

Lotu Pasifika Productions, based in Suva, Fiji, was incorporated in 1973 as the production unit of the Pacific Conference of Churches, its Christian Education and Communication Program, and the churches they serve. It began as a producer of Sunday school curriculum and evolved into a producer of books, records, and cassettes. The materials are 90 percent Christian literature while 10 percent are used as supporting programs to schools. It publishes about 20 to 24 books a year. Lotu Pasifika serves the Eastern Pacific Christians with their communication needs.

In the late 1970's Lotu Pasifika encountered problems with high cost of production and distribution. These difficulties included unreliable ship freight, exorbitant airfare, and expensive materials. In the early 1980's, the Pacific churches decided to emphasize publication in the vernacular. Local authors, indigenous ideas, cultural values, specific needs, and legends and stories in the Pacific were incorporated in the curriculum materials and books.

Among the current issues Lotu Pasifika has identified as crucial to the churches are the untold influences of the video industry coming into the country. In addition, it raises the issue of the role of the church as moral guardian of the people. That role needs to be reiterated and strengthened.

Summer Institute Of Linguistics (SIL)

SIL is a private volunteer organization funded by civic groups, churches and individuals. It assists in the development of the South Pacific people through study and research of the many languages and cultures in the area. It produces literature in the previously unwritten languages. Its members are from Australia, New Zealand, Papua New Guinea and the Solomon Islands. Its work in Papua New Guinea started in 1954; among the Australian Aborigines, in 1961; in New Zealand, in 1963; and in the Solomon Islands, in 1977. Its language programs now operate in over 250 language groups in the Pacific area.

THEOLOGICAL SCHOOLS/COLLEGES

Pacific Theological College (PTC)

Established in 1965 following a decision of the Conference of Churches held at Malua, Western Samoa, in 1961, the PTC is involved mainly in education, training, and research with emphasis on Pacific theological education. It engages in research and reflection on issues facing the Pacific churches. The College has members from 14 countries in the South Pacific. It has a special women's program which provides training for women and wives of students.

Pacific Regional Seminary (PRS)

The seminary trains candidates for the Catholic priesthood and to give in-service and refresher courses to Catholic church workers in the Pacific. Established in 1972 as a result of a decision by the CEPAC Bishops, it now serves the Caroline and Marshall Islands, Cook Islands, Fiji, Kiribati, New Caledonia, Samoa, Tonga, and Vanuatu.

Christian Leaders Training Colleges (CLTC)

Founded over 20 years ago the CLTC has a sprawling campus located in Banz, Papua New Guinea. Its students come from many Pacific islands to study theology and Bible or agriculture at this Evangelical Alliance institution. Although most of the approximately 200 students are from that tradition, the college accepts individuals from a variety of theological and educational backgrounds.

Other theological schools in the Pacific Islands are the following:

> Ecole Pastorale Hermin, Tahiti
> Davuilevu Theological College, Fiji
> Tangintebu Theological College, Kiribati
> Sia'atoutai Theological College, Tonga
> Bible College of the Presbyterian Church, Vanuatu
> Lololima Seminary, Vanuatu
> Ecole Pastorale Bethanie, New Caledonia
> Assembly of God College, Papua New Guinea
> Crusade Bible College, Papua New Guinea
> Holy Spirit Seminary, Papua New Guinea
> Martin Luther Seminary, Papua New Guinea
> Newton Theological College, Papua New Guinea
> Rarongo Theological College, Papua New Guinea
> Pacific Adventist College, Papua New Guinea
> Bishop Patterson Theological Center, Solomon Islands
> Piula Theological College, Western Samoa
> Moamoa Theological College, Western Samoa
> Malua Theological College, Western Samoa
> Kanana Fou Theological Seminary, American Samoa
> Takamoa Theological College, Cook Islands

COMMUNICATION/BROADCASTING

Unda Oceania

UNDA is the International Association for Radio and Television in the Roman Catholic Church. Latin for "wave," UNDA symbolizes air waves of radio and television.

UNDA Oceania was formed in 1973. National members include Australia, Federated States of Micronesia, Marshall Islands, Guam and Northern Marianas Islands, New Caledonia and Vanuatu, New Zealand, Solomon Islands, Tahiti and Marquesas Islands, Fiji, Samoa, Tonga (UNDA VITI), Cook Islands, and Wallis and Futuna.

The general objectives of UNDA are to promote a truly human and Christian spirit in all activities of the media; to help achieve effective religious broadcasting and to promote media training and media education programs.

Through UNDA many national organizations received financial grants for basic equipment, training or preparation of religious broadcasting programs.

Some members of UNDA are associated with the World Association of Christian Communication. A representative of the Pacific Council of Churches attends the annual UNDA Oceania Assembly. The French-speaking areas of the Pacific have not been represented in the group. There is a felt need to reach these groups.

The Pacific Regional Association Of The World Association For Christian Communication

The World Association for Christian Communication is primarily concerned with electronic media, radio, television, and Christian literature development. Formed in 1979, the Pacific Regional Association-WACC has 14 corporate members with four personal members. The association is linked with worldwide communication programs and receives information about developments in other parts of the world.

The objectives of the WACC-PAC are basically to promote the development of all communications media in spreading the gospel of Christ in ways appropriate to the needs and realities of the Pacific peoples.

There are two wholesale distribution centers in the region: one in Port Moresby to serve the West Pacific groups of Papua New Guinea and the Solomon Islands, and the other in Suva, Fiji to serve the rest of the Pacific.

RESEARCH/TRAINING

The Micronesian Seminar

A brainchild of Francis Hezel and other Jesuit priests serving in Micronesia, the Micronesian Seminar as a group has evolved to become a pastoral-research institute on the needs of Micronesia, and an evaluation of church activities in the region. The main function of the institute is "to stimulate socio-theological reflection to raise questions relative to the islands today in the light of the gospel and to help pastors bring these problems to the parishioners... and to coordinate and sponsor renewal programs for mission personnel."

The Micronesia Seminar has published pure and applied historical research on the region. It is also linked with Pacific historians at the University of Hawaii, and Australian National University. It has some working relationship with the Melanesian Institute at Goroka, Papua New Guinea.

The seminar also assists priests, brothers and sisters in various seminars, workshops, conferences, theological and spiritual renewals. It has extended assistance to grassroot community development educational programs. It offers assistance to Protestant pastors and Catholic workers and to government agencies in devising tools by which people can educate themselves as to the realities of Micronesia today.

The Melanesian Institute For Pastoral And Socioeconomic Service

This institute aims in helping the churches in Papua New Guinea and the Solomon Islands in understanding and responding to the needs of the Melanesian people through an integrated approach of research, teaching and writing. The fundamental issue undergirding the institute's activities is the relationship between Christianity and Melanesian cultures.

It stresses the need for missionaries working in Melanesia to have deep knowledge and understanding of the people, the culture and traditions of Melanesia. It analyzes the socioeconomic/political movements in the region and relates them to human development programs.

Founded in 1968 by the Association of Clerical Religious Superiors of the Catholic Church in Papua New Guinea and the Solomon Islands, the Institute now has ecumenical membership. Its members are the Anglican Church in Papua New Guinea, the Catholic Church in Papua New Guinea and the Solomon Islands, the Evangelical Lutheran Church of Papua New Guinea, and the United Church of Papua New Guinea and the Solomon Islands.

Pacific Churches Research Center (PCRC)

Although now inactive, the PCRC was a Pacific Conference of Churches regional research center. Established in 1976, it undertook church-related research on various aspects of religion, language, culture, social organization, history, and social problems. Pacific Churches Research Center was staffed by indigenous researchers. It published the journal *Reo Pasifika* in English and French.

STUDENT FELLOWSHIPS

Campus Crusade For Christ

The Campus Crusade for Christ has ministries in Fiji, French Polynesia, Papua New Guinea, Solomon Islands, Tonga, Vanuatu and Western Samoa. It plans to expand to all 16 countries of the South Pacific. Its evangelistic programs include a Here's Life Training Center operating in Port Moresby, Papua New Guinea. This evangelistic program provides training of leaders at four levels. In 1984, 42,244 evangelistic contacts were established.

Campus Crusade for Christ has worked in the Solomon Islands with the Church of Melanesia and the United Church. It conducted its Way of Life Church Development leadership training program, which was introduced with churches in Fiji, particularly with the Nabua Methodist Church. Leadership training classes are also held at the University of the South Pacific in Suva, Fiji.

In Vanuatu, Campus Crusade is developing its ministries with high school students particularly with Matevulu High School in Espiritu Santo. In Tonga, a young Tongan woman has developed a multi-generation discipleship ministry among the local high schools. The Way of Life Plan for local church growth and outreach is being implemented by the Methodist Church.

Pacific Students For Christ

This interdenominational evangelical Christian organization is concerned with the spiritual welfare of tertiary education students, graduates, and workers in the the South Pacific. This organization promotes Christian fellowship in 19 institutions in four countries. Among its activities are evangelism, Bible studies, prayer meetings, fellowship evenings, seminars, workshops, retreats, mission lay training programs.

Student Christian Movement

The only SCM presence in the Pacific is in Fiji, particularly in the University of the South Pacific. At one time, the student members involved themselves in rural development projects. Its main thrust is in creating a Christian witness as students concern themselves with political and economic issues in the communities where they live.

The SCM is a member of the World Student Christian Federation, a regional and international federation of students established in 1895. The Pacific is part of the Asia region based in Hong Kong.

Christian Fellowship Of The University Of The South Pacific

This group is a full member of the International Fellowship of Evangelical Students. Several students in the University of the South Pacific organized in 1971 to focus on Bible study, prayer and fellowship. More recently, represented in the fellowship are Fijians, Indians, Chinese, Rotumans, Tongans, Samoans, Solomonis, Vanuatuans, Kiribatis, Cooks, and Niueans. Their major aim is to witness for Christ and to have fellowship with other Christians.

WOMEN'S GROUPS

Young Women's Christian Association (YWCA)

The YWCA groups in the Pacific are affiliated with the World YWCA. The local groups cooperate with governments, churches, and other agencies in their work affecting women and families. The association is Christian, although its membership is not necessarily so. It does not have an evangelistic role.

The regional YWCA office in the Pacific was set up in 1974. National offices and some local programs exist in Papua New Guinea, Fiji, the Solomon Islands, and Samoa. It works with women and youth in development programs and projects. Training and experimentation on the application of applied technology for women are being undertaken. Other social programs include work with urban squatter women, kindergarten programs, youth clubs for boys and girls, sport and recreation and public affairs programs. Among its constraints are its limited resources, human and financial; the authoritarian structures in many Pacific cultures; and difficulties with western-based volunteerism concepts.

The Girls' Brigade Asia-Pacific

Engaged mainly in non-formal education, the Girls' Brigade originated in New Zealand and spread to several Pacific islands. Today, the member countries of this group include Vanuatu, Solomon Islands, Papua New Guinea Cook Islands, Tokelau, Tuvalu, Brunei, Singapore, Malaysia, Hong Kong, Western Samoa, American Samoa, Australia, New Zealand, and Niue. The Asia-Pacific Committee is based in Auckland, New Zealand.

Formerly known as the Pacific Fellowship of the Girls' Life Brigade, the Girls' Brigade has grown significantly in the most recent decade.

MAJOR CONCERNS

Today, the Church in the Pacific is going through a period of significant change. Since World War II and particularly in the last 15 or 20 years, there have been upheavals in Pacific society and in religious practice unparalleled since the days of initial European-Pacific contact. Some of the important trends strongly affecting the Church in the Pacific today are as follows:

1. Increasing Pluralism

The Pacific Church has been and to a large extent in most countries remains predominantly Protestant. Out of a Christian population of about five million, there are well over 2.5 million evangelical Protestants and Anglicans, as compared to nearly 1.5 million Roman Catholics. Yet there are hundreds of thousands of other Islanders who call themselves Christians but are not Protestant, Anglican, or Roman Catholic. Their number is growing dramatically, especially in Papua New Guinea and some countries in Polynesia.

A case in point is Papua New Guinea, clearly a pluralist Christian nation. It has been pluralist since the 1890 Comity Agreement for evangelization among the London Missionary Society, Anglicans and the Methodists in Papua and the Lutherans in German New Guinea. Other unreached areas of that vast island region were worked by Catholics. Today, there are no real comity agreements, and there are numerous religious options close at hand. The new conservative evangelical or fundamental churches are growing, and the number of Pentecostals is nearly twice that of the Anglicans when all the different Pentecostal groups are added together.

In Tonga the Church of Jesus Christ of Latter-Day Saints (Mormons) is the second largest religious denomination, almost half as large as the predominant Free Wesleyan Church. The Mormon adherents in 1985 numbered 23,500.

Among indigenous Fijians, the Methodist Church claims the allegiance of at least 80 percent of the population. But the Assemblies of God are now one-fifth the size of the Methodist Church.

In French Polynesia, about 87 percent of the total population claim to be Christians yet the number of those practicing their faith is much smaller.

In the larger Polynesian countries, the "predominant" Protestant Church may not long be in a majority position. In an era of national independence and religious freedom, increasingly church leaders accept that they are only a voice among other voices in national affairs.

In most of the smaller Polynesian and Micronesian political units, the old mission churches still represent from 70 to 80 percent of the population. But even here, in political and economic affairs, voices other than those of church leaders usually seem to carry more weight.

The most strongly felt issue, however, in this emerging era of pluralism is that religiously the "predominant" churches find themselves to be just one option among many.

2. **The Pacific Missionary Impulse And The Present Need For Spiritual And Evangelical Revival**

The unique success of the spread of Christianity in the islands of the Pacific in the 19th and 20th centuries was due to the evangelical zeal of Pacific Islander missionaries. In islands all across the southern Pacific, they and European missionaries effectively proclaimed the freedom and peace and renewed purpose in living that is found in Christ alone.

Their spirit still lives on in the area. A survey undertaken to update the "Record of Pacific Islander Missionaries" at the Pacific Theological College showed that the number of new missionaries sent out in the past decade was the same or greater than the average number recorded over each of the previous 15 decades. These missionaries went not only to the Pacific, but to all parts of the world, even to those countries from which the first European missionaries came. This is something for which to praise God with fervent joy.

During the last 20 years a number of church leaders and observers have lamented the rise of secularization and "repaganization" in the Islands because of outside influences, urbanization, and the breakdown of traditional social and religious structures in the towns and among islanders returning from abroad. Even where church practice is strong, gospel conviction may not be nearly as strong. Some observers even fear that church leaders all too often seek to enforce church practice and promote their ecclesiastical authority more for the sake of trying to retain traditional Christian structures than for the sake of promoting the gospel itself.

Spiritual renewal and evangelical revival is needed, but to be truly effective it must develop from within the Pacific and be attached to the deep roots of Pacific evangelical tradition. There must also be a recognition of the new era of religious pluralism and all the challenge and opportunity that this provides. If the presence of new sects and denominations in the Pacific helps stimulate that recognition, they will have done the Church in the Pacific a great favor, whatever other spiritual renewal they may provide for some.

One of the hopes for spiritual and evangelical renewal in the Islands is that the churches will be better able to share their strengths with each other. Perhaps too much emphasis is still being placed on retaining old denominational ties, while more fresh channels of cooperation need to be developed all around the Pacific, channels based on equality and mutuality.

3. **Justice And Freedom Issues In The Pacific**

Numerous grass roots movements and organizations have been formed in the Pacific around the issue of a nuclear-free Pacific including the abilities for self-determination of local political and justice issues. Many of these groups originated with the concern of Christian people that justice be done in the region.

One of the most active of these movements is the Nuclear Free and Independent Pacific Movement which took its mandate from the People's Charter for a Nuclear Free and Independent Pacific drafted at the first Nuclear Free Pacific

Conference held in Fiji in 1975. Since then, three other conferences have been held in the Pacific to discuss issues of justice relating to nuclear use by First World countries in the area and to self-determination efforts by indigenous minorities: in 1978 on Pohnpei, 1980 in Hawaii, and 1983 on Vanuatu. As a result of the Hawaii conference the Pacific Concerns Resource Center (PCRC) was established there to provide resources and networking coordination for protest and solidarity campaigns organized by Pacific peoples to address the above issues.

Organizations currently involved in the resolution of similar justice issues include:

Task Force on Militarization in Asia and the Pacific
475 Riverside Drive
New York, NY 10115

Micronesia Coalition
475 Riverside Drive
Room 616
New York, NY 10115

Pacific Resources Coordinator
United Methodist Office for United Nations
777 United Nations Plaza
New York, NY 10017

South Pacific Peoples' Foundation of Canada
407-620 View Street
Victoria, BC V8W 1J6
CANADA

Religious Task Force for Peace and Justice
85 South Oxford Street
Brooklyn, NY 11217

American Friends Service Committee
1501 Cherry Street
Philadelphia, PA 19102

The nuclear-free issues of the Pacific are especially significant for those islands and their people already affected by nuclear testing or dumping. The U.S., Britain and France have exploded nuclear devices in the Pacific affecting areas mainly in French Polynesia and the Marshall Islands.

Self-determination and freedom are issues of indigenous minority peoples. The Maoris in New Zealand, the Aborigines in Australia, and the Kanaks in New Caledonia are among the most actively involved in the pursuit of these.

Pacific church groups involved in justice issues include the Pacific Conference of Churches, the Roman Catholic Church and Eglise Evangelique de Polynesie Francaise. Local involvement in justice is experienced as a natural part of church life and as it relates to the whole person within his/her community.

OTHER RELIGIONS

Church Of Jesus Christ Of Latter-Day Saints (LDS or Mormons)

The Church of Jesus Christ of Latter-Day Saints (Mormons) started mission work in the region in 1850. Today, the Pacific is one of the 12 ecclesiastical areas. The Hawaii-Pacific Island Area includes Hawaii, Samoa, Tonga, Tahiti, Fiji, Micronesia, and the nearby islands. An Executive Administrator operates the area through the regional structure supervised by representatives. Families make up wards, the basic unit of the church; 10 to 15 wards comprise a stake; three to five stakes comprise a region.

Supporting the ecclesiastical leaders are the professional groups of the church. Brigham Young University in Hawaii has an enrollment of about 1,700. The Church Education System operates 23 schools in the South Pacific with enrollments of about 5,470. About ten percent of these students are not LDS. The Bishoperic Office provides services such as building and maintaining meeting houses, translating and printing materials into local languages, keeping records of finances and membership, giving technical help in welfare functions. A new service group -- Genealogy -- gathers oral and written genealogies of the Polynesians for use by concerned families.

Summary of Church Membership, 1985:

Australia	43,466
American Samoa	3,933
Federated States of Micronesia	838
Fiji Islands	27,222
French Polynesia	6,422
Guam	764
Marshall Islands	1,142
New Caledonia	418
New Zealand	39,572
Tonga	19,733
Western Samoa	25,860
Cook Islands	551
Total	**145,441**

Jehovah's Witnesses

The following figures are based on the 1984 Service Year Report of the Jehovah's Witnesses for the Pacific:

TABLE 3

	NO. OF CONGS.	AVERAGE PUBLISHERS*
American Samoa	1	80
Australia	591	39,052
Belau (Palau)	1	
Cook Islands	4	61
Fiji	24	849
Guam	1	211
Kiribati	1	12
Marshall Islands	2	155
Nauru	2	4
New Caledonia	8	593
Niue	1	14
Papua New Guinea	83	1,601
Pohnpei	1	69
Saipan	1	20
Solomon Islands	32	591
Tahiti	11	561
Truk	2	38
Vanuatu	2	59
Western Samoa	2	141

*NOTE: "Publishers" do visitation and conduct Bible studies.

Hinduism

Hinduism was brought primarily to Fiji by Indian indentured laborers more than a century ago. During this period which lasted until about 1919, Hindu Indians learned Hinduism from the religious book *Ramayan* by the poet Tulsi Das. One of the Hindu teachers was Totaram Sandhya, an indentured laborer himself. The *Ramayan* became familiar to the Hindus through oral recitation, public readings, and the festivals of its hero, the Lord Rama. Rama, an incarnation of Vishnu, is celebrated as God, and a manifestation of the Supreme Being.

In Fiji, the majority of Hindus belong to the orthodox Sanatan. Sanatanis have formed several associations or *Sabhas*, some of which promote educational or political works. Ramayan remains the most popular festival and social religious event among the Fiji Indians. A minority reform movement within Hinduism, the Arya Samaj, claims membership from among the Fiji Indians.

The Baha'i Faith

In 1953 and 1954, a handful of followers of the Baha'i faith were found in Fiji, New Caledonia and New Guinea. Since then, Baha'is from Australia, New Zealand, United States, France, and Panama settled in different parts of the Pacific. Called pioneers, they would then form a local Spiritual Assembly, the basic administrative unit of the community.

In 1963, the Baha'i faith in the Pacific spread to over 200 localities with 43 Spiritual Assemblies. Two regional assemblies, one based in Suva, the other in Honiara, have jurisdiction of the island territories. Among their activities were translation of Baha'i literature, establishment of elementary schools, holding conferences and summer schools, and spreading the message of Baha'u'llah, their prophet.

Islam

There are about 250,000 Muslims in Australia, found mainly in the cities of Darwin, Hobart, Sydney, and Perth. These Muslims are migrants from the Middle East, Asia, and Europe. About 10,000 Muslim students from Malaysia, Singapore, and Indonesia study in Australia.

The various ethnic and national Muslim communities in Australia have formed their own Islamic societies for cultural and spiritual advancement. The Australian Federation of Islamics Council (AFIC) links these various Islamic groups.

Fiji also has a large Muslim community in the Pacific numbering about 50,000. Descendants of indentured laborers between 1879 and 1916, these Muslims have maintained their cultural and religious identity. Sixty percent of Fiji Muslims are farmers and live in rural areas. Fijian Muslims have established schools and social service institutions to meet the needs of their community. Relationships among the major religious groups in the country are cordial.

The Muslims in the Pacific cooperate through national Islamic groups in New Caledonia, New Zealand, Australia, Papua New Guinea, and Fiji.

Chapter Two: *Australia*

AUSTRALIA

Profile

NATURAL FEATURES: **Land area:** 7.7 million sq. km. **Terrain:** low-lying and varied. **Climate:** relatively dry, temperate in the south, semitropical in the north.

POPULATION (1985): 15.8 million. **Annual growth rate:** 0.9 percent. **Ethnic groups:** European (97 percent), aboriginal (1 percent), Asian (.6 percent), others, 1.4 percent.

RELIGION (1981 census): **Christians:** 76 percent. **Non-Christian:** 1.4 percent. **No religion:** 10.8 percent. **Not stated:** 10.9 percent.

LANGUAGE AND LITERACY: English, aboriginal language, native language of immigrants. **Literacy:** 100 percent.

GOVERNMENT: Democratic, federal-state system, recognizing British monarch as sovereign represented by Governor-General. **Executive:** Prime Minister and Cabinet responsible to Parliament. **Legislative:** Bicameral Parliament including a 64-member Senate and 125-member House of Representatives. **Judicial:** High Court and other federal and state courts. **States and Territories:** New South Wales, Victoria, Queensland, South Australia, Western Australia, Tasmania, Northern Territory, Australian Capital Territory. **Principal cities:** Canberra (capital), Sydney, Melbourne, Brisbane, Adelaide, Perth and Hobart.

ECONOMY: Per Capita GDP (1983): US $9,810 **Average inflation rate:** 9.8 percent. **Natural resources:** lead, zinc, copper, iron ore, others. **Agriculture products:** livestock, wheat, wool, sugar. **Industry:** mining, manufacturing, and transportation.

Historical Background

The Aborigines migrated to Australia about 40,000 years ago. Nomadic hunters and gatherers, they scattered across the continent adapting to both the fertile coastal region and the harsh, dry inland.

In 1770, Captain James Cook became the first European to contact the Paleolithic aborigines. He claimed the east coast for Great Britain. In 1788, Captain Arthur Phillip founded the colony of New South Wales with a convict settlement at Port Jackson, now Sydney. Many of the first settlers were convicts, some of them condemned for offenses that would be considered trivial today. A policy of emancipation of convicts began in mid-19th century. Immigration of free people started. The discovery of gold led to increased population, wealth, and trade.

Australia obtained complete autonomy in both internal and external affairs from Great Britain with the Statute of Westminster Adoption Act on October 9, 1942.

Immigration from Europe increased dramatically after the Second World War. The largest number of postwar immigrants were from Britain, followed by Italy, Greece, the Netherlands, the Federal Republic of Germany, Yugoslavia, and Austria. In mid-1971, the government instituted progressive reductions in immigration. However, the country took in about 66,000 Indo-Chinese refugees in 1975-1982.

Much of Australian culture reflects a European influence, particularly the arts -- opera, music, painting, theater, dance, and crafts. However, distinctive trends are evolving from a concern for the environment, interest in the aboriginal culture, and the influence of Australia's neighbors.

PEOPLE GROUPS

Australians are predominantly of British origin. Other principal national groups include Irish, Italian, Greek, Maltese, German, Yugoslav, and Dutch. The aboriginal population, estimated to be

160,000 in 1985, constitutes one percent of the total. The majority of the people live in cities and towns on the east and south coasts.

The aboriginal inhabitants numbered between 250,000 and 300,000 when the first European settlers came in the 18th century. As many as 500 tribes spoke different languages. Aboriginal tribes have complex systems of religion, law, social organization and culture expressed in mythology, bark paintings, engravings and dance. Today, aboriginal population continues to decline. They lead a settled but traditional life in remote areas of northern, central, and western Australia. Mixed descent aborigines have settled in the urban centers of the southern states.

Socio-Political Conditions

Of immediate social concern in Australia is the plight of the Aborigines. Located primarily in the Northern Territory, Queensland, and Western Australia, thousands of them live in poverty and poor health. After almost two centuries of neglect, the government and the public have just begun to respond to their needs and rights. Recently enacted social legislation, dealing with the land rights of Aborigines and their integration into society, will improve their situation.

About ten million Australians live in seven major cities -- four million people in Sydney alone. High urban concentration contributes to rising unemployment (9.5 percent of the labor force in 1984), increasing crime rate, and other problems associated with the urban poor.

Natural disasters such as periodic brush fires, floods, cyclones, insect plagues, and drought also create problems in some parts of the continent.

The great majority of Australians take an active interest in sports and entertainment. Numerous television and radio stations, newspapers, and magazines provide information and entertainment to the public.

The three main political groups are the Liberal Party, representing urban business-related groups; the National Party, nominally representing rural interests; and the Australian Labor Party, nominally representing the trade unions, working classes, and liberal and left-wing groups. All three parties work on domestic welfare policies and favor economic protectionism and conservation of natural resources. Among the issues having strong bipartisan sentiment is the Australian commitment to the ANZUS Alliance.

Economic Condition

Australia has a diversified and affluent economy. It has one of the highest levels of real income per capita in the world. Traditionally, its prosperity has been based on agricultural and mineral exports, but the contribution of finance, business services and community services to the GDP (gross domestic product) has risen from 47 percent in the mid-1950's to 61 percent in the early 1980's. The mining sector has also grown because of important discoveries of iron ore, petroleum, coal, natural gas, and other minerals.

Agriculture still makes an important contribution to total exports, although its share of total overseas earnings fell from 65 percent in the mid-1960's to 32 percent in 1982/83. The world recession in the early 1980's affected Australia's rate of economic growth, and unemployment reached 10.4 percent in 1983. Today, Australia continues to recover from that recession.

Status of Christianity

Table 4 shows the denominational affiliation of both Christians and non-Christians in absolute numbers and proportional distribution nationwide. It must be noted that in 1976, the Uniting Church was formed with the Methodist Church, the Congregational Union, and a substantial majority of the Presbyterian Church of Australia, thus the decrease shown in the individual denominations.

Census data are used to determine in one level of interpretation the status of Christianity in Australia.

An analysis of census and survey figures shows a significant decline in the number of Australians willing to acknowledge any affiliation with the Christian church through the ten-year period, 1971-1981, with total Christian affiliation declining from 86.2 percent to 76.4 percent.

The accompanying growth in non-Christian religions, while significant in relative terms -- 75 percent over the last decade (0.8 percent in 1971; 1.4 percent in 1981), is still small in absolute numbers and is accounted for largely by immigration e.g., from Turkey and the Middle East (Muslim); and refugees from Indo-China (Buddhist).

Clear evidence exists of the differences in religious affiliation between the various Australian states. According to 1976-1981 census figures, New South Wales (NSW) remained the state with the strongest Christian affiliation sharing with Tasmania the lowest proportion of "No Religion" respondents. The Northern Territory had the smallest proportion of Christian affiliation, with the largest proportion of "No Religion," and the largest group of "Not Stated."

TABLE 4

CHRISTIAN DENOMINATIONS AND NON-CHRISTIAN RELIGIONS IN AUSTRALIA

Christians	%	1976	%	1981
Baptist	1.3	174,151	1.3	190,259
Brethren	0.2	20,720	0.1	21,490
Catholic	25.7	3,482,848	26.0	3,786,505
Churches of Christ	0.6	86,850	0.6	89,424
Anglican	27.7	3,752,221	26.1	3,810,469
Congregational	0.4	53,445	0.2	23,016
Jehovah's Witness*	0.3	41,539	0.4	51,817
Latter-Day Saints*	---	---	0.2	32,446
Lutheran	1.4	191,548	1.4	199,760
Methodist (inc. Wesleyan)	7.3	983,240	3.4	490,467
Orthodox	2.7	372,234	2.9	421,281
Pentecostal	0.3	38,393	0.5	712,148
Presbyterian	6.6	899,950	4.4	637,818
Salvation Army	0.5	63,335	0.5	71,570
Seventh-day Adventist	0.3	41,472	0.3	47,474
Uniting Church	---	---	4.9	712,609
Protestant Undefined	1.5	206,159	1.5	220,679
Other Christians	1.7	236,929	1.7	253,769
Total Christian	78.6%	10,644,851	76.4%	11,133,301

Non-Christian

Buddhist	NA	NA	0.2	35,075
Jewish	0.6	53,441	0.4	62,127
Muslim	0.3	45,205	0.5	76,794
Other	0.2	30,422	0.2	23,557
Total Non-Christian	1.0%	129,069	1.4%	197,573

Other

Indefinite	0.4	51,270	0.5	73,551
No Religion	8.3	1,130,300	10.8	1,576,618
Not Stated	11.8	1,592,959	10.9	1,595,195
Total Population	100.0%	13,548,449	100.0%	14,576,338

*NOTE: These two groups were listed as "Christians" in the original source.

Source: Australian Bureau of Statistics, 1976 Census and 1981 Census.

NOTE: The 1981 statistics include a number of groups that are regarded by the Christian churches as being outside the limits of Christian orthodoxy e.g., Jehovah's Witnesses and Latter-Day Saints. There is a case for excluding them from the "Christian" section of the table.

Gallup Poll data between 1966 and 1976 indicated a drop from 88 percent to 76 percent of Australians who said that they believed in God. Age groups varied in their belief in God and in Jesus Christ, with a higher percentage of believers among older people.

Church attendance records from 1950 to 1981 showed considerably less decrease than the drop-off suggested in the census figures. Approximately half of the Australian population rarely if ever goes to church, and this proportion (after allowing for sampling variations) has changed very little during the last 30 years.

Other statistical data is available which is helpful in giving more substance to an understanding of the actual religious practice of Australians.

It was estimated that 97 percent of all funerals in Australia used religious rites. Until the mid 1960's, 90 percent of all marriages were performed by religious celebrants. In 1976 the figure had dropped to 71 percent, and by 1979 it was down to 64 percent. This proportion might be affected by the limitations which restrict the clergy of several major churches/denominations from participating in remarriage of divorced individuals.

During the period 1963-1974 there occurred a noticeable and widespread net decline in Sunday School attendance (59 percent). A 20 percent decline in baptisms conducted and a 41 percent decline in the number of people confirmed were also recorded.

Regarding church membership data, the evidence here is scanty and not strictly comparable, since few denominations use the same criteria in keeping statistical and membership data. Conclusions which can be drawn, keeping in mind the limitations of the data, are that:

1.   Small, theologically conservative or charismatic denominations have recorded large increases during the last decade; e.g., Wesleyan Methodists, Christian and Missionary Alliance, and Assemblies of God have all at least doubled their membership during the last decade. It should be noted, however, that these denominations all started from what was, in absolute terms, a very small base.

2.   There has been a drop in the combined membership of the denominations entering Union when the membership of the Uniting Church is examined. This is after allowance is made for membership of the congregations that did not go into Union.

     These statistical observations, however, do not indicate that many people included in the dropping figures had felt that their needs were not met by the new ecumenism. Many of them had joined smaller, more theologically conservative groups (see 1. above) because they tended to offer more satisfying expression of faith in line with their original congregational life and practices.

3.	In most Anglican dioceses there has been an upturn in the number of Anglicans receiving Communion. The turning point seems to have occurred in 1979.

AUSTRALIAN CHRISTIANITY: INTERPRETATION

Much care is needed in interpreting the decline in both Christian affiliation and stated belief in God. Understanding the historical background of the forms of Christianity brought to Australia and the historical background is vital to a balanced approach to the sociological data, which seems at first to indicate decline and little else.

On the one hand, from the Wesleyan tradition, evidence shows the formation of an Australian religious character. Wesleyanism came from free Cornish miners of England, not from convicts. These miners who came to the goldfields adapted their English roots to the Australian mining world; established their own modified social and family structure; and built their churches from which a distinct religious character emerged.

In addition, Methodist Union at the time of Federation came out of a long wave of revivals.

On the other hand, Australian Christianity, particularly from the Anglican tradition, has never been characterized by the revivals that have been so much a part of the American Protestant experience. The most likely explanation is that the evangelicalism reaching Australia had already been absorbed into the forms and style of the English church life that were taken there. The Protestant Churches in the 19th century by and large represented the religion of a heart that was already "strangely warmed." The Christianity that reached there was already informal; it was a religion of a heart already revived. The process of organized church extension that dominated Australian church activity in the late 19th Century was not, then, at the expense of revival; it was, rather, an expression of it.

Nevertheless, the evidence of the last 20 years suggests that Australia was only superficially Christian. Why were its roots into the Australian environment to prove so shallow?

Again an examination of the historical record is fruitful. Australia was founded as an English jail. It ultimately fell between two major fronts of Christian missionary endeavor taking shape at the end of the 18th Century and beginning of the 19th: The outreach was to the unchurched working class and urban proletariat on the one hand and to the "heathen masses" of Africa and Asia on the other. Until the 1830's and 40's, nearly half a century after the initial settlement, the spiritual needs of the convict and free settler Britons alike were largely overlooked.

The Anglican Chaplaincy in Sydney was supplied with small grants from the Society for Promoting the Gospel (SPG) and the Society for the Promotion of Christian Knowledge (SPCK). The newly-formed Church Missionary Society (CMS) refused appeals for help from the colony. However, they encouraged efforts to form a New South Wales (NSW) auxiliary to raise money for "overseas missions." In a similar vein, the London Missionary Society and the Baptist Missionary Society received more money from the colony than they spent on it.

Because of this weakness, the Australian Anglican churches were placed in a position of continuing dependency vis-a-vis their parent churches in England, Scotland, and Ireland who found the "nominal" Christianity of the colonies much less exciting and challenging than their mission to "heathen" lands. The tendency of Australian churches to "look back home" to the churches in the home country, with their apparent strength and security, was reinforced. These home country churches provided the standards for theology, worship and evangelism.

Australian Wesleyanism presents a different picture. The Methodist Church of Australasia (Australia and New Zealand) separated structurally from Great Britain in the 1850's. It formed its own State and General Conferences, operated as a whole autonomous church, with Tonga and Fiji as mission fields, and systematically took over the whole financial burden. It was entirely independent from Great Britain.

This quick historical summary provides some explanation for the failure of Christianity in Australia to develop a truly indigenous character. Returning to the contemporary scene, it is crucial to note that the recent decline in church affiliation has, for all that, left the core of the church very much intact. It was pointed out earlier that church attendance has declined much less than "affiliation." There is also evidence of an actual upturn in attendance in numbers of denominations. The shrinkage that has taken place has been in the civil or social role of Australian Christianity. Christianity has been discarded as a cultural assumption by a significant minority of Australians; however, among those who still remain committed there is a tendency for the commitment to deepen.

Since 1945, as a result of factors including migration, lower cost of travel, increased educational opportunities and television, a pluralistic society has developed in which there is no longer any broadly-based religious consensus. Given the continuing operation of the factors underlying this development, the church is faced with a major challenge: It must demonstrate the truth and relevance of the gospel within the framework of people's everyday experience.

MAJOR CONCERNS

Frontiers For Mission

UNREACHED PEOPLES GROUPS

Traditional, animistic religious practices are still widely found among **Aboriginal** groups. However, Christianity has made inroads among the Aboriginal population. In general, Christianity is strongest among the Aboriginal groups found in urban situations or near mission stations or small towns.

Traditional religious practices and beliefs are important to the cultural identification of the more "traditional" Aborigines. There is a possibility that as the Aboriginal population becomes more active politically, traditional religious forms will again begin to be more widely followed by those persons in urban areas. A thoroughly contextualized Christian church is needed among the various Aboriginal groups.

The small **Chinese** population is predominantly non-Christian and urban. As is found in many other overseas, resident Chinese communities, language and family responsibilities are important factors in the maintenance of a distinct sense of peoplehood. Religion has become less important; and, in general, the Chinese population is increasingly non-religious or secular in its religious orientation.

Almost 60,000 **Turkish peoples** live in Australia. Over 98 percent of these persons are Muslims. The degree of adherence to orthodoxy varies greatly from the very orthodox to cultural Muslims; however, Islam is an important element in the Turkish identity of all members of this people group. Turkish peoples have only been arriving in Australia for the past 20 years; assimilation into Australian life has been difficult. In addition, ties to relatives and friends in Turkey have been made more difficult by greatly increased restrictions on immigration to Australia with the recent worldwide recession. This has led to barriers blocking effective ministry and interaction between Turkish peoples and Christians in Australia.

Although the percentage of active church participants is low, there has not been a concerted effort to understand the Australian population in terms of unreached people groups. Little is known about the distribution of religious fervor and participation among the various people groups which can be defined in Australian life.

In addition to non-Christian religions in Australia, two potential areas for missions exist -- one geographical, the other attitudinal/ intellectual.

THE URBAN FRONTIER

By whatever measure is used -- church attendance, numbers of ministers, financial resources -- there is across the major urban areas a massively uneven distribution of Christian presence and activity.

Studies of Baptist churches in Sydney and Melbourne and the Uniting and Continuing Presbyterian churches in Sydney show that Protestant churches are notable for their relative absence in lower socio-economic areas. The evidence clearly shows of a historically-rooted cultural alienation of working-class people from Protestant churches -- a pattern now deeply entrenched into the geography of major urban and suburban areas. While efforts have been made by individual churches and small groups of Christians to reverse this trend, there is no evidence of any significant shift in the priorities of any denomination.

The Catholic church is in a somewhat different position in terms of a historically close contact with the labor movement and those in the lower socio-economic levels, although the impact of these factors is currently weakening.

THE SECULARIZED RELATIVIST FRAMEWORK

While the Urban Frontier presents a challenge of cultural alienation and broadly includes that 50 percent of people who rarely attend church, the group that claims "No Religion" presents a special challenge. It is made up of people who consciously deny the reality of anything beyond the world of everyday experience. It is skeptical in mind, relativist in temper, and "religious" in its commitment to limiting religion to the private sphere. Comprising 15-16 percent of the Australian population, those who stated "No Religion" are (1) predominantly male, 130 males per 100 females (1981 Census); (2) semi-skilled workers or tertiary educated rather than white collar workers; (3) Australian or British in origin.

NATIONAL CHURCHES

Roman Catholic Church

BRIEF HISTORY

The Roman Catholic Church could be said to have arrived in Australia -- at least in spirit -- with the Irish convicts in the First Fleet in 1788. However, with the exception of a brief period in 1803-4, there was no public celebration of Mass in the colony until 1820, and the first bishop was not appointed until 1834. The Church took on a strong Irish identity in terms of both membership and clergy. By the 1870's, Catholics constituted a distinctive minority within Australia, characterized by a common Irish background, lower socio-economic status, and a strong sense of shared identity in a predominantly Protestant cultural and political establishment.

The pastoral strategy of the bishops focused on the establishment within each parish of a Catholic school financed and staffed solely from Catholic resources. A number of uniquely Australian religious orders developed with the particular mission of staffing Catholic educational institutions. This pattern remained until the large increase in immigration from predominantly Catholic countries after 1945.

During the decade 1951-1961, immigration came largely from strongly Catholic countries -- Italy, Malta, Yugoslavia, and Hungary. Consequently, the number of parishes rose from 943 in 1951 to 1,363 in 1976 -- an increase of 44 percent. The religious welfare of these migrants was the responsibility of the Federal Catholic Immigration Committee established in 1974. Currently, 147 priests from countries sending migrants to Australia, are employed as migrant chaplains. Two religious orders specialize in this work -- the Capuchin and Scalabrinian Fathers in South Australia and Victoria.

CURRENT STATUS

In terms of religious practice, 1981 Gallup Poll figures point to a relatively high level of church attendance by Roman Catholics.

Other studies show figures ranging from 29 percent to 60 percent for different areas within Australia.

Significant charismatic groups have grown up within the church; one estimate of the situation in 1975 suggests the involvement of 7,000 adults in prayer groups.

The church continues to grow. Its population is now characterized as being younger, more female, and migrants from non-English speaking countries. These changes create pressures on the administration of some parishes.

The real crisis for the church lies in the area of personnel. Between 1966 and 1976 the Catholic population increased by nearly 15 percent; during the same period the number of clerics and religious fell by almost 12 percent.

The decline in the numbers of both priests and religious is due to a decline in entry rates, and an increase in the rates of resignations and retirements. Over a quarter of all priests and 40 percent of the sisters are over 60 years of age.

Orthodox Churches

BRIEF HISTORY

While there were Orthodox immigrants to Australia during the 19th Century, no organized structure of Church life existed until 1924, when the Patriarch at Constantinople declared the Holy Metropolis (diocese) of Australia and New Zealand.

Almost every traditional Orthodox nation is represented in Australia. With immigration continuing, the established pattern of separate ethnic churches is strengthened by the arrival of newcomers. Orthodox Christians continue to grow and live out their faith mainly within respective ethnic communities, of which there are currently 16. The ethnic church with its particular language and culture forms the center of all aspects of community life for the migrants.

CURRENT CONCERNS

The significant problems facing the Orthodox churches are rooted in their ethnic strength. They have no local facilities for the training of clergy, and thus are dependent upon the national parent churches. More crucial is the problem of the children of migrants, who are brought up in Australian social and cultural values in school and through the communications media. This points to the potential for cultural clash and lack of continuity in passing on religious values and commitment, as worship services in Orthodox churches are still conducted almost exclusively in the language of the migrants.

COOPERATIVE AGENCY

On the level of inter-Orthodox cooperation and unity, a significant step was taken in 1979 with the formation of the Standing Conference of the Canonical Orthodox Churches in Australia (SCCOCA). A number of non-Canonical churches (e.g., Serbian Orthodox Church) remain outside this organization.

Anglican Church of Australia

BRIEF HISTORY

The Anglican Church of Australia traces its history to the founding of the first British settlement at Sydney in 1788. Its earliest clergy brought with them an awareness of being the established church back in England. The leaders of the Church of England during the formative years, most notably Bishop Broughton, took up the quest for a privileged place in Colonial society, particularly in terms of seeking government aid for clerical stipends, salaries for teachers, and for the building of schools and churches. Not succeeding, they took the responsibility for ministry to the whole community, which had to be funded out of voluntary giving -- a situation they were manifestly not used to.

The adjustment to the situation of being one of a number of denominations, rather than in a position of privilege, has been an ongoing element in the history of the Anglican Church since then.

CURRENT STATUS

In 1981, the Church of England in Australia changed its name to the Anglican Church of Australia. Through the years, census data indicates a decline in affiliation in the Anglican church.

The relative strengths of the different theological traditions within the Australian Church have not been fully documented. At best, estimates of the charismatic movement in the Anglican Church are just that. In 1975, the number of clergy involved was estimated to be 100 with 10,000 adults meeting in prayer groups.

There has been renewed activity among the three theological movements within the church. National Evangelical Anglican Conferences were held in 1972 and 1981; the formation or revival of groups concerned for a Catholic renewal within the Anglican Church has recently been reported, centered in Adelaide; charismatic influence is also widespread and crosses the Anglo-Catholic/Evangelical Divide.

Perhaps most significant has been the development of increased cooperation and understanding between these divergent groups. This was most evident in the preparation and widespread agreement on a new Australian Prayer Book with its wide range of contemporary services, published in 1976.

Congregational Union of Australia

The first Congregational Church in Australia was organized in 1829. However, it did not achieve any distinctive identity appealing to a broad base. Although achieving significant growth in South Australia during the 1960's, reaching 1.7 percent of the state population, affiliation dropped to 0.9 percent by 1976.

In 1976, 83 percent of Congregationalists voted to join the Presbyterian and Methodist Churches to form the Uniting Church, while a continuing number of congregations have since come together to form the Congregational Union of Australia. This association consists of 30 congregations with 1,500 members.

In the 1981 Census, 0.2 percent of the population still nominated themselves as Congregationalists.

Presbyterian Church of Australia

In 1809, settlers in Sydney formed the first Presbyterian Church in the country, though the first minister did not arrive until 1823. A dispute over whether state financial support should be accepted led to a division into two separate Synods in 1846. They were reunited in 1964. The Presbyterian church has been strongly Scottish in its membership and has drawn much of its strength from the cohesiveness of the community comprising it. A decline in adherence from 13 percent of the population in 1911 to seven percent in 1976 was due partially to the changing ethnic composition of Australia.

In 1976 about 75 percent voted in favor of joining the Uniting Church. However, 521 congregations with about 45,000 members (32 percent of church membership) opted to continue as the Presbyterian Church of Australia. This group was as a whole more theologically conservative than the congregations which went into Union.

In the 1981 Census, 4.4 percent of the population claimed adherence to the Presbyterian Church. The strength of the continuing denominational allegiance in this case is a good indicator of ethnic identity and its function as a reference point for social identity.

Methodist Church of Australasia

Church development during the 1830's and 1840's was largely due to the increasing number of migrants who were Methodists. During the gold rush of the 1850's, the Methodist circuit system was able to keep up with the rapid population movements, but the laity was also expected to take the initiative for evangelism in frontier areas. During the last half of the 19th century, the Methodist Church provides the only case of an Australian church growing substantially from an already significant base, without assistance from immigration. However, more recently there has been a drop in membership from 173,539 in 1967 to 154,670 in 1976. Traditionally strongest in South Australia, Methodism declined from 22.7 percent of the population in 1961 to 15.7 percent in 1976.

In 1976, 85 percent of the Methodists voted in favor of the Uniting Church.

There are some small continuing Methodist churches. Assuming 10 percent of membership at Union were involved in the "continuing" congregations, as in the case of the Congregationalists, this would place membership of these Methodist churches at 15,000. In the 1981 Census, 3.4 percent of the population continued to identify themselves as "Methodists," although no such denomination exists per se.

The small Wesleyan Church doubled in its membership in the three years following Union, but still only accounts for 350 members.

Uniting Church

This was formed in 1976 from the Methodist Church, Congregational Union of Australia and the Presbyterian Church of Australia.

It places a strong emphasis on its identity as an Australian Church and has also taken a strong and occasionally controversial stand on social issues such as aboriginal land rights, poverty, and nuclear disarmament.

In 1981, 4.9 percent of the population identified with the Uniting Church. The only area recording a membership increase for the churches involved in and arising out of Union was the Northern Territory.

Baptist Union Of Australia

The first Baptist congregation dates back to 1813. The Baptists have a small but distinct minority on the Australian religious scene, with membership remaining relatively stable at 1.3 percent of the population over the last 20 years. The church is slightly stronger in Tasmania (1.9 percent of the population) and South Australia (1.7 percent) than in the other states.

Churches of Christ in Australia

This denomination was founded in 1846. By 1975 it had 410 congregations, but between 1967 and 1979, overall membership declined by about 3,000. In 1981, it comprised 0.6 percent of the total population.

The Church's key problems seem to relate to the issues of identity (being able to differentiate itself from other small non-liturgical Protestant denominations), and dependence upon population growth. Growth in adherence from 1976 to 1981, according to Census figures, was 2.9 percent -- considerably less than population growth over the same period.

Lutheran Church of Australia

The Lutheran Church had its beginnings in Australia in 1838 among German immigrants. Early growth focused on Adelaide and the Barossa Valley (South Australia). Later, congregations sprang up in New South Wales (NSW), Queensland, and Victoria, largely as a result of migration from South Australia.

In 1846, because of doctrinal differences, the Church divided into the United Evangelical Lutheran Church in Australia and the Evangelical Lutheran Church of Australia. In 1966, the differences were resolved and the churches reunited, becoming the Lutheran Church of Australia.

Lutheran growth rate between 1976 and 1981 was 4.3 percent. In 1975, it had 751 congregations.

The Church remains largely concentrated in South Australia where five percent of the population are members, and in Queensland, where 2.2 percent are members. It comprised 1.4 percent of the total Australian population in 1981.

Pentecostal Churches

Although comprising only 0.5 percent of the population, in 1981, Pentecostal Churches grew 87.9 percent during the preceding five years. The fastest growing of the numerous Pentecostal groups were: Assemblies of God in Australia, 130 percent over a ten-year period, and the Apostolic Church, 40.9 percent over a ten-year period. Other Pentecostal Churches include Christian Revival Crusade, Full Gospel Church in Australia, International Church of the Four Square Gospel, National Revival Crusade, and the United Pentecostal Church.

Evidence on the source of growth is not readily available. Claims have been made by a number of pastors of fast-growing Pentecostal Churches that 60 percent of new members are from those who previously rarely attended church.

ECUMENICAL RELATIONSHIPS

The Australian Council of Churches (ACC) provides the major forum for ecumenical contact and cooperation. Member churches are:

The Anglican Church of Australia
The Uniting Church in Australia
The Federal Conference of the Churches of Christ
The Salvation Army - Eastern and Southern Territories
The Australian Yearly Meeting of the Religious Society of Friends
The Antiochan Orthodox Church
The Armenian Apostolic Church
The Coptic Orthodox Church
The Greek Archdiocese of Australia
The Romanian Orthodox Church

The Serbian Orthodox Church in Australia and New Zealand
The Syrian Orthodox Archdiocese of Australia
The Assyrian Church of the East

The Australian Episcopal Conference of the Roman Catholic
Church has observer status, as have a number of other churches,
including the Lutheran Church and the Assemblies of God in
Australia.

State Councils of Churches associated with the ACC exist in each
state:

NSW Ecumenical Council
Queensland Ecumenical Council
South Australian Council of Churches
Tasmanian Council of Churches
Western Australian Council of Churches
Victoria Council of Churches

The membership of these councils is in general broader than that of
the national body, e.g., in Tasmania, the Baptist and Catholic churches and the Revival Crusade hold membership.

Weaknesses of the Australian Council of Churches which are considered significant are the low level of the Roman Catholic and
Lutheran involvement, the almost total absence of Baptist involvement, the absence of any Russian Orthodox involvement, and the
retreat of the Pentecostal Churches after a period of contact during
the three years from 1966 to 1969.

Structure And Ministries

The ACC has a number of Commissions, mostly staffed on a voluntary basis, which deal with Church and Society, Education, Community Relations, and International Affairs. It is also involved in
relief and development through its Division of World Christian
Action, which participates in fund raising for overseas projects as
well as refugee resettlement within Australia. Further commitments
in this area include joint sponsorship with the Australian Episcopal
Conference of Action for World Development (a development
education program) and Force Ten (a joint ACC -- Australian
Catholic relief and development organization).

The ACC has had a particular concern over the years for the social
and political situation of the Aboriginals. It has been active in

sponsoring contact between Aboriginals, Africans and Black Americans, lobbying for Aboriginal land rights and bringing the attention of overseas churches to their situation. In 1981, for example, a World Council of Churches study team visited Australia to investigate the situation and to report their findings to the church overseas.

CHRISTIAN ACTIVITIES

Mass Evangelism

The most substantial efforts at mass or "crusade" evangelism have been those conducted by the Billy Graham Evangelistic Association in conjunction with the churches in all of the major urban areas and most of the regional centers throughout Australia in 1959 and 1968.

There have been other mass evangelism crusades including those by Oral Roberts, Leighton Ford -- in Melbourne and Tasmania -- and denominationally-oriented efforts such as "Tell Australia" and "Mission to the Nation" sponsored by the then-Methodist Church.

In the light of a changing climate of values and attitudes towards Christianity, a Commission on Evangelism in the evangelically-oriented Anglican diocese of Sydney in 1971 suggested that a decreasing emphasis be placed on such rallies. Since then, with the exception of the 1979 Billy Graham Crusade in Sydney, efforts at mass evangelism have been confined to regional and local areas.

Leighton Ford visited Sydney in 1985. Other examples of recent mass evangelism are "Mission Melbourne," a multi-denominational program, and "Cross Over Australia," a Baptist program.

Local Evangelism

Most denominations have departments at the State/Synod/Diocesan/Presbytery level concerned with encouraging evangelism at the level of the parish or individual congregation. Some churches have used training material in personal and visitation evangelism. Some occasional successes have been reported with home-based dialogue evangelism.

Within the last few years, seminars using American programs such as Evangelism Explosion, or more generally emphasizing Church growth principles, have become widespread, particularly in Churches of Christ, Baptist and evangelical Anglican Churches at a local level.

PERSON-ORIENTED EVANGELISM

Included in person-oriented evangelism are the following:

The work of Scripture Union missions in Holiday Evangelism; the Inter-School Christian Fellowship; the churches and interdenominational agencies' major program of outreach in the area of camping; and the Australian branch of the Prison Fellowship founded by Charles Colson.

For students, Student Life and Navigators have groups and staff on the major campuses. The Australian Fellowship of Evangelical Students (AFES) has 80 affiliate groups and 13 staff workers on university and higher education campuses. It also has a graduate fellowship concerned with Christian discipleship in the professions.

The umbrella organization representing a variety of Catholic student groups is the Tertiary Catholic Federation of Australia.

The Australian Student Christian Movement (ASCM) has active groups on a half dozen campuses. It is generally more liberal in theology and focuses on Christian social responsibility in the secular world.

The Summer Institute of Linguistics through its Australian Aborigines Branch is the major agency involved in translation of the Scriptures into Aboriginal languages. Seven other church agencies are involved frequently in cooperation with SIL.

Bible Reading

The Scripture Union of Australia is the major agency involved in the promotion of Bible reading. Explanatory notes and Bible discussion material for a wide range of age groups and literacy levels are prepared locally. Some materials are imported directly from Scripture Union in the United Kingdom. The State Branches of Scripture Union promotes these materials through Christian bookshops, local church representatives, and through school groups and camping programs.

Religious Press

The structure of the religious press varies among denominations.

The Roman Catholic Church has a series of diocesan newspapers plus specially focused magazines published by religious orders or lay groups. Among this latter group one of the most significant is *National Outlook* (circulation 12,000), a monthly which focuses on contemporary issues both in Australia and overseas from a Christian perspective.

The Uniting Church is served by a series of papers covering one or more States and published every two weeks.

The Anglican Church has two major independent weekly newspapers plus a series of diocesan magazines.

On Being, an independent monthly evangelical magazine with a concern for social issues and for evangelism within the specific contours of Australian society, has also been successful in establishing itself as an economically viable enterprise. (Circulation: 8,500).

Most church papers are subsidized, with the consequent tensions in editorial policy when dealing with controversial issues, either in or outside the denomination in question.

Specialist Christian scholarly publications originating within Australia include: *Journal of Christian Education* (Circulation: 1,200) and *Interchange: Papers on Biblical and Current Issues* (Circulation: 1,500).

Radio

There are three types of radio stations currently operating:

    (1)   The government-owned-and-funded Australian Broadcasting Commission (ABC), which is a national system with two urban and one country station. In reporting aspects of Australian life, ABC provides a number of religious programs representative of the life of the various churches and religious groups. These include direct broadcasting of church services and community hymn singing, documentary programs on religion and theology, and shorter commentary segments by religious leaders.

(2)   Commercial Stations. Three stations initially had
        church connections: 2CH and 2SM in Sydney and
        5KA in Adelaide. Because of pressure of ratings, these
        stations reduced their religious programming and the
        churches now have little if any influence on the sta-
        tions' programming. The Broadcasting Act compels all
        broadcasters to provide one hour of free time each
        week to the churches.

        Apart from clergy-staffed open-line programs, religious
        programming has generally been reduced to spots
        lasting from 30 seconds to two minutes, some five-
        minute items, and the occasional quarter-hour presen-
        tation. Christian impact via this medium is minimal.

(3)   Public Radio. CBA FM in Sydney broadcasts Christian
        programs geared to a general audience. A Tasmanian
        station is modeled on Christian FM stations in Amer-
        ica. Its programming consists of gospel messages, Bible
        readings, devotions, church services, etc., around the
        clock.

Television

More religious TV programming in Australia originates from the
British Broadcasting Corporation than from Australian sources. The
churches have one percent of program time on commercial TV
channels for religious programs. The various state branches of the
Christian Television Association (CTA), Anglican Television, and the
Catholic Communications Centre take advantage of this free time.

Being free, religious programs tend to be screened in periods least
disruptive to TV station economics, i.e., Sunday morning and late
Saturday night. Even groups that have bought their own time
(particularly for American electronic-church-style programs) still
seem to be restricted to Sunday morning.

Christian Education

As of 1981, 23 percent of all school pupils attended non-
government schools. Although the situation varied between States,
at the national level there had been a continuing increase in the
number of students attending non-government schools after 1976.

The Roman Catholic Church was the only church which had a substantial involvement in post-secondary education. It operated seven small colleges of advanced education, majoring in teacher training.

The Anglican Church had not been involved in educaton so closely nor on such a large. Its schools were run more independently and catered to those sections of the community higher on the socio-economic scale.

The same was largely true of the schools historically operated by the Methodist and Presbyterian churches -- now the Uniting and Continuing Presbyterian churches.

The only other churches that developed school systems are: (1) The Seventh-day Adventist Church, which in 1977 had 63 primary schools, 19 secondary schools plus a small College of Advanced Education; and (2) the Lutheran Church, which in 1971 had 26 primary day schools, four secondary schools and a college of advanced education, majoring in teacher education.

The significant growth in the five years after 1981 was in the area of small Christian schools operated by individual churches and groups of parents.

Theological Education

Only two universities offer theological degrees, Sydney University (Bachelor of Divinity, BD) and Flinders University (Bachelor of Theology, BTh). Queensland University offers a BA in which majors are possible in Biblical Studies and Theology. Macquarie University also offers a number of courses in Biblical History as part of a BA degree.

Fifty-eight institutions offer courses in Biblical studies and Theology. The majority of these are independent or interdenominational Bible Colleges representing a very wide range of theological positions. Most of them are not recognized as degree-granting bodies.

The remainder of the institutions are denominational in character, with their chief task being the preparation of students for the ordained ministry.

In three cities, Sydney, Melbourne and Adelaide, cooperation between these colleges has developed.

The most recent developments in theological education have focused on the needs of the laity. A wide variety of institutions and programs have been developed.

The Armidale diocese of the Anglican Church, a large rural diocese in northwestern NSW, has pioneered an extensive and successful Theological Education by Extension (TEE) program.

Resources for theological study and research within Australia are very limited. There are only 12 theological libraries within Australia that have holdings greater than 15,000 volumes.

Political Lobbying

There are three main areas where Church-related organizations or non-church run Christian organizations have been variously active in the lobbying process:

(1) Overseas aid and development;

(2) Social welfare, particularly issues of poverty and unemployment;

(3) Issues relating to personal morality, gambling, marriage laws, availability of abortions, pornography, sex education in schools.

Counselling

The Christian presence in industry has been slow to develop. The Interchurch Trade and Industry Mission, however, has a total of 20 full-time and 20 part-time chaplains involved in ministry to workers in the manufacturing industry Australia-wide.

Life Line is a round-the-clock telephone-counseling center with back-up services staffed by Christian lay people on a voluntary basis. It began operating in Sydney in 1963 as an initiative of the Rev. Alan Walker of the Central Methodist Mission.

This service has now spread to 150 cities in 12 countries. In Australia, a network of Life Line telephone ministries operates in 22 centers. Sydney has two telephone centers which handle over 40,000 calls per year.

Social Welfare Activity

There are few areas of welfare service in which church agencies are not active; for example, the Anglican Diocese of Sydney Home Mission Society, in 1981 employed 400 people and was involved in:

- Nursing homes for the aged
- Retirement villages
- Migrant resettlement
- Adoption
- Counselling
- Emergency assistance
- Thrift shops
- Children's homes
- Work co-operatives for long-term unemployed

An indication of the size of the operation of church-related agencies, for example, can be seen by looking at two of the Anglican agencies in Melbourne. The Mission of St. James and St. John had a budget in 1981-82 of $1,900,000; the Brotherhood of St. Lawrence in 1981 had 400 employees and a budget of $5,727,000.

A full-scale study of this aspect of the church's work still remains to be done. Though certain agencies like St. Vincent de Paul and the Salvation Army are household words, the extent of Christian caring and service is seldom realized by the community as a whole.

Non-Christian Religions

The three major non-Christian religious groups are: Buddhist -- 35,000; Jewish -- 62,000; and Muslim -- 77,000. These groups are characteristically ethnic in nature, e.g., Indo-Chinese refugees (Vietnamese, Cambodians, Laotians) with a Buddhist background; Turks and Middle Eastern immigrants who are largely Muslims. There are significant language and cultural barriers which have to be overcome if there is to be a culturally-sensitive Christian witness to these minority groups.

Chapter Three: *Melanesia:*

Fiji
New Caledonia
Papua New Guinea
Solomon Islands
Vanuatu

FIJI

Profile

NATURAL FEATURES: Land area: 18,376 sq. km; consisting of some 300 islands, islets. **Largest islands:** Viti Levu, Vanua Levu. **Terrain:** Mountainous; islands are volcanic in origin. **Climate:** Tropical maritime.

CAPITAL: Suva. **Population:** 71,000. **Major centers:** Lautoka, Ba, Nadi, Sigatoka, Nausori, Levuka, Savusavu, Labasa.

POPULATION: 677,000 (1985 est.). Fiji Indian (50 percent), Indigenous Fijians (45 percent), Europeans, Chinese, and other Pacific Islanders (5 percent). Indigenous Fijians are a mixture of Polynesian and Melanesians; Fiji Indians are descendants of Indian migrants of the 1800-1900's. Thirty-seven percent urban. **Annual growth rate:** (1985) 2.1 percent.

RELIGION: Christians: 50 percent. **Hindus:** 41 percent. **Muslims:** 8 percent. **Others:** 1 percent.

LANGUAGE AND LITERACY: English is the official language. **Other languages:** Fijian, Hindi, Urdu, Tamil. **Literacy rate:** 80 percent.

GOVERNMENT: Parliamentary democracy. **Executive:** Prime Minister and Cabinet. **Legislative:** Bicameral -- Senate and House of Representatives. **Judicial:** Supreme Court and other courts. Governor General appointed by British Monarch.

ECONOMY: Per Capita GDP: (1983) US $1690. **Annual growth rate:** 15.1 percent. **Natural resources:** timber, fish, gold, copper. **Agricultural products:** sugar, copra, bananas, ginger. **Industry:** sugar refinery, tourism, gold, lumber, small industrial and construction work.

Historical Background

Human settlement on Fiji dates back more than 3,000 years. Traditional Fijian culture has been based on a cycle of labor services, offerings, and exchange revolving around a chief at each level in the hierarchy of social groups. The "vanua," literally the land, formed the stable base for the many small federated or related communities. Inter-tribal wars were a relatively common occurrence in the culture.

In 1643, Abel Tasman, a Spaniard, sighted the Fiji Islands, but the first western visitor was Captain James Cook, an Englishman, who arrived in 1774. By the early 1800's, many overseas trading ships traded in Fiji for sandalwood, pearls, and beche-de-mer (*trepang* or edible sea cucumbers). Some traders also did "blackbirding" or kidnaping of workers for the plantations.

British influence became strong in Fiji in the 19th century, and the islands were ceded to Great Britain as a Crown Colony in 1874 by Ratu Cakobau, the leader of the ruling chiefs. Fiji remained a Crown Colony until independence was granted in 1970.

PEOPLE GROUPS

Fijian society can be subdivided by major population groups, such as Fijian, Indian, Chinese, European, part-European, and other Pacific Islanders (see Table 5 below). Each group is described in general terms by geographic location, occupation, and religious preference. The category of part-Europeans will not be described separately since this group tends to be dispersed throughout the other populations.

Fijians, who make up 45 percent of the total population, are predominately rural and involved in subsistence agriculture. Approximately 86 percent of the Fijian population lived in rural areas in 1966. Although there is some evidence of change, traditional social organization still follows strong kinship lines, with its patterns of communal ownership of land, consensus decision-making, and elaborate systems of exchange of goods and services. The continued participation of Fijians in this mode of livelihood is assured by laws which give them protection in their ownership of land. For these reasons Fijians have not become involved in commercial agricultural development programs.

However, the traditional patterns are gradually changing as many younger Fijians move into urban areas seeking the material rewards of wage-labor employment and business. Those Fijians not involved in subsistence agriculture claim a disproportionate percentage of senior civil servant and governmental positions, usually living in the larger urban areas, such as Suva. The Fijians are thoroughly Christianized, with most belonging to the Methodist Church.

Indians were first brought to Fiji in the late 1800's as indentured laborers to work on the cotton plantations, and later on sugar plantations. They have now become the largest sub-group in Fiji. In 1966, 80 percent of the Indians in Fiji were rural, but because of the laws protecting Fijian ownership of the land, most work on plantations or as tenant farmers.

In urban areas, Indians predominate in a number of occupations, such as merchants, traders, artisans, and lower-level professionals and clerks. In both rural and urban areas, Indians do not rely upon extended kinship networks, as do the Fijians, nor upon the structures of caste.

Generally, the population is internally organized on the basis of area of origin, religion, and language spoken at home, although the Indians are becoming more uniform in their usage of Hindi because of the influence of schools. Approximately 80 percent of the Indians are Hindu and 15 percent Muslim.

The small Chinese population is employed mainly in the area of commercial enterprise. Strong family ties and a sense of common ethnicity link members of this group. In 1966, 63.6 percent of the Chinese population was Christian, with most adhering to Roman Catholicism.

There are three main groups of Pacific Islanders in Fiji. Each of these groups resides on islands some distance from the major centers of commerce and political activity. These groups tend to follow their traditional patterns of life, relying heavily upon kinship and related obligations. The three groups are: Rotuma Islanders living on Rotuma, a dependency of Fiji; Micronesian Islanders who were moved from Ocean Island to the Fijian Island of Rabi because of drought and over-population; and Polynesians from Tuvalu (formerly the Ellice Islands) who were moved to Kioa for the same reasons as the Micronesians from Ocean Island. The members of these groups did not continue as Congregationals, but became Methodists instead.

Complicating the description of people groups in Fiji is the fairly rapid rate of urbanization. About a third of the Fijian population is immersed in an urban social system and under the direct influence of an urban lifestyle. This is causing significant shifts in Fijian social groupings. There is evidence that within Fijian urban society, new alignments of peoples, and perhaps eventually new definitions of people groups, are beginning to emerge. An embryonic class structure is developing within which people have commonly shared values and a sense of identity. It remains to be seen whether this new pattern of alignments will transcend ethnicity as an important determinant of social behavior and cultural values in Fiji.

TABLE 5

POPULATION OF FIJI BY ETHNICITY[1]

	1936	1956	1966	1976	1981
Fijian	97,651	148,134	202,176	259,932	290,496
Indian	85,002	169,403	240,960	292,896	326,346
Chinese	1,751	4,155	5,149	4,652	4,692
European	4,028	6,402	6,590	4,929	3,554
Part-European	4,574	7,810	9,670	10,276	11,128
Other Islanders	5,292	9,742	11,892	14,113	13,683
Other	78	91	173	1,270	490
Total	198,376	345,737	476,737	588,068	650,409

[1] Pacific Islands Yearbook, 1984: p. 83.

Socio-Political Conditions

Up to the time of independence in 1970, Fijian political structures were based on the traditional chieftain system and family or village groupings. Remnants of this system can still be seen in the Council of Chiefs, which advises the government on issues touching the ethnic Fijian people, their land, customs, and traditions. The Council is made up of chiefs, who are accorded great respect. Political allegiances tend be based on race, with the indigenous Fijians lining up with Prime Minister Ratu Sir Kamisese Mara's Alliance Party, and the Indians voting mainly with the National Federation Party.

In spite of political differences, there is general racial tolerance and harmony within Fiji. However, the traditional land tenure system, in which lands are kept inalienably under traditional communal ownership, is challenged by the Indian community, which has demanded a relaxation of the system. Unless some provision is made for more equitable land distribution, friction may develop over this issue in the future.

Economic Conditions

Of the almost 700,000 citizens of Fiji, more than half are less than 21 years old, making this the fastest growing segment of the population. Each year, there are 6,000 to 8,000 youth joining the 81,000 people in paid employment. As a consequence of the large number of unemployed youth and slow economic growth, unemployment rose to about 10 percent in the 1980's. One symptom of these economic problems is the rising crime rate in Suva among Fijian youth. Government policies now encourage new work force members to join the village economy rather than the urban market.

Sugar and copra for export are mainstays of the Fijian economy. Whereas the production of these and other agricultural products has increased roughly in proportion to the growing population, there are often adverse effects from shifts in the world market. Increasingly, there is pressure to develop tourism and manufacturing as more stable industries on which to build the future.

First Missionaries In Fiji

Christianity first came to Fiji in 1830, when three Tahitian missionaries were sent to the island of Oneata by the London Missionary Society. Five years later, David Cross and William Cargill of the Wesleyan Church established a mission base on Lakeba, and in the following years, missionaries were stationed at Rewa, Somoso-mo, and Viwa. The missions made little progress for the first 15 years, but when the Paramount Chief of Lau, the *Tui Nayau*, was converted in 1849, other chiefs and mass conversions quickly followed.

In each district in which the Wesleyans worked they were careful to integrate their mission structure with that of the indigenous culture, being particularly deferent to chieftain authority. This strategy contributed to the success of the mission, and by the 1870's, Fijian missionaries were being sent by the Wesleyans to evangelize Melanesia. Also, many among the younger Fijians were literate and could read the Fijian Bible in the Bauan dialect.

During the early period of Wesleyan work in Fiji, the Kingdom of Bau, centered on a small island off the eastern coast of Viti Levu, was ruled by Ratu Cakobau, Fiji's Paramount Chief. In 1854, as a result of intense effort and prayer by Wesleyan missionaries, Cakobau embraced Christianity. However, he did not give up his love of war. In his view, the eastern Fijian chiefs, even though fellow Christians, represented a threat to his power and influence because of their close association with the Tongans. He embarked on a series of "religious wars" that did not end until 1874, when Fiji was formally ceded to Great Britain by Ratu Cakobau and other leading chiefs.

Status of Christianity

For one and a half centuries, the churches in Fiji have experienced times of zeal and vigor, alternating with times of lethargy. The last 10 to 15 years have seen a steady movement toward the Bible and revivals, counteracting the influence of secularism and materialism. Today, virtually all native Fijians consider themselves Christian, and the country has become a center for South Pacific church activities.

According to the 1976 census, Christians comprised about 51 percent of the total population of Fiji. The Methodist Church is numerically the strongest with 220,000 members, followed by the Roman Catholic with 50,000 members. Muslims and Hindus comprise about 48 percent of the population. Other non-Christian religions include the Baha'is, Jehovah's Witnesses, and Mormons. Traditional religion has virtually disappeared, although it sometimes manifests itself in indigenous expressions of Christianity.

NATIONAL CHURCHES

The main churches operating in Fiji are listed with their population (1976) as follows:

Methodist	219,937
Roman Catholic	49,826
Anglican	5,756
Assemblies of God	7,188
Seventh-day Adventist	9,370
Presbyterian	619
Smaller churches:	7,264

(Baptist Bible Church, Brethren, Bethel Full Gospel Pentecostal, Congregational, Pentecostal, Churches of Christ, Salvation Army, South Sea Evangelical Mission, United Pentecostal, Free Church of Scotland. Also included are other religious bodies such as the Christadelphian, Church of God International-Armstrongism, Jehovah's Witness, and Mormons.)

Even before Fiji obtained its independence in 1970, most of the church personnel had largely become localized. In 1984, only a small number of overseas missionaries served in the churches. More recently, there has been a growing realization that although localization is the primary objective, the churches derive benefits from having links with Christian workers from other cultures. Church leaders would insist however that overseas workers should come in the spirit of openness, and with an attitude towards understanding the local culture. They should also learn to work and relate effectively with the people at different levels.

Wesleyan/Methodist

In the early part of the mission work in Fiji, the Methodists worked more closely with the indigenous Fijians than with other groups. Today, church ministries include work with Indian congregations in response to the change in the nation's ethnic makeup. Ministries served by the Methodists include those with the mixed European community which has emerged from Fijian and English relationship.

The Methodist church in Fiji and Rotuma celebrated its 150th anniversary in August, 1985. The focal themes in the celebration included a national thanksgiving for the coming of Christ to Fiji and for the work of the Church in building a peaceful nation. The

Church re-emphasized its continuing mission as it accepted the challenges of the 21st century.

Different groups within the Methodist Church are engaged in various ministries. Some of these are as follows:

EVANGELISM IN FIJIAN LANGUAGES

The Department of Evangelism produces monthly booklets for Bible reading, devotions and pamphlets on doctrine and Christian living, in Fijian.

YOUTH WORK

Ministries to children and young people continue to be a challenge for the Church both present and future. The involvement of the young people at various stages of their growing up is considered crucial in the life and work of the Church. A major concern at present is the increasing crime rate in urban areas where young people are involved. These youth have either drifted away or have left their homes in villages to flock to the urban areas. Training, counseling, and rehabilitation centers such as The Good Samaritan Inn are efforts to make youth appreciate the constructive ways of life in community settings.

The Youth Department has about 38,000 members. It produces literature for youth and Sunday schools. This department also runs development projects assisted by various non-governmental organizations in the 24 divisions of the church, including those on Rotuma and Rabi island.

OVERSEAS MISSIONS

Sending local missionaries overseas has been practiced by the Fijian church for over 100 years now. Starting in 1875, overseas mission work had been heavily financed by overseas boards. Recently, efforts were made to involve local people in sponsoring missionaries to be sent overseas. The officers of the mission board visited circuits and villages to discuss their role in mission and to encourage people to give generously to the mission work. A pledge system was instituted and has gotten a good response from the people. Taking pledges and gifts on Pentecost Sunday from every church in Fiji and Rotuma is a major source of income for missions.

Missionary families serve in Papua New Guinea, Northern Territory of Australia, Belize, Costa Rica, Panama, New Zealand and Great Britain.

WOMEN'S MINISTRIES AND FELLOWSHIP

Women's work with the church and missions dated back before the Fiji Government instituted social services. Women volunteers from the missions worked with the nursing programs in the villages.

In 1949 Mrs. S. G. Cowled started the Methodist Women's Fellowship. Women members became and have continued to be active in various ministries. These include the following: full support to the church work from village to conference level; support of evangelism in the church; small prayer and Bible study groups in local churches; hospital visitation; and community welfare work.

SOCIAL PROGRAMS

The Methodist Department of Christian Citizenship and Social Services is responsible for several programs. The Family Life program includes seminars, workshops, a family education program, and counseling services. Social rehabilitation provides prison chaplaincy work and rehabilitation among ex-prisoners and the "rootless" youth in the cities and towns. Community development creates employment in rural and urban areas offering training programs in logging, milling, boat building, furniture making, metal work and screen printing.

This department also produces literature on social issues. It formerly published the Methodist monthly, *Takai Ni Loloma*, in Fijian and English with a circulation of about 2,000. The original Methodist newspaper, *Ai Tukutuku Vakalotu*, ran for 70 years printing letters from Fijians in New Britain and Papua New Guinea and pulling together the scattered Fijian Church for mission support and unified social action.

EDUCATIONAL INSTITUTIONS

Today, the Church runs 25 educational institutions comprising 2 vocational/technical, 9 secondary, and 14 primary schools.

Roman Catholic Church

Marist missionaries began work in Fiji in 1844 after Methodism had been firmly established. A prefecture apostolic was organized in 1863. The main area of Catholic strength was on Taveuni and the adjacent part of Vanua Levu. The hierarchy was established in 1966 with diplomatic relations with the Vatican starting in 1978.

In 1985 about 57,000 of the Fijians or 8.5 percent of the population were Catholics. The Roman Catholics have also increased their ratio among the Fijians, mixed Europeans, and the Rotumans. Alan Tippett reported incidences of some Fijians with Methodist backgrounds turning to Roman Catholicism, and some Pacific Islanders with Roman Catholic backgrounds turning to Methodism. Mixed Europeans, Chinese, and part-Chinese Christians are predominantly Roman Catholic. In recent years, the church has made special efforts to establish contact with the Indian majority, and by 1974, 1.5 percent of the Indians were Catholics. Language study and contact through the bishops of India were initiated. A group of brothers from the Monfort Brothers of St. Gabriel arrived from India in 1973 and set up a Boy's Town in Fiji.

An indigenous archbishop heads the archdiocese of Fiji.

CHRISTIAN WORKERS

In 1986, the Catholic population totaled 57,000. There were 23 parishes and 1 mission in Fiji. Among the personnel were 17 diocesan priests and 73 other priests. Seminarians studying for diocesan and religious priesthood numbered 45. There were 54 religious brothers and 311 religious sisters.

RELIGIOUS ORDERS AND CHURCH ORGANIZATION

Major religious orders include the Columban Fathers, the Daughters of Our Lady of Compassion, Indian Missionary Society, the Marist Brothers, Marist Fathers, Marist Sisters, Missionary Sisters of the Society of Mary, Monfort Brothers of St. Gabriel, Sisters of Our Lady of Nazareth, Sisters of St. Joseph of Cluny, Daughters of Charity of St. Vincent de Paul, Christian Brothers and the Vincentian Fathers (Congregation of the Missions).

Among the church organizations are the Pastoral/Parish Council, Eucharistic Ministers, Confraternity of Christian Doctrine, Legion of Mary, Catholic Women's League, Blue Army of our Lady,

Pioneer Total Abstinence Association, Youth Club, Guild of Saint Stephen, Antioch Youth, Christian Mothers, Christian Family Movement.

CHRISTIAN MINISTRIES

The varied ministries of the Roman Catholic Church in Fiji focus on education, development and communication, youth apostolate, marriage encounters, Christian family movements, relief and charity, hospital and prison ministries.

EDUCATION AND TRAINING PROGRAMS

The comprehensive Catholic educational institutions are comprised of the following:

(1984)		Enrollment:
Primary Schools	40	9,837
Junior Secondary	6	982
Secondary	12	6,474
Teacher Training College	1	76
Catechists' Training Centers	8	154

Secondary schools include the Cathedral, Holy Family, Marist Brothers', St. Joseph's, St. Thomas', and Wairiki high schools. Tertiary institutions including Corpus Christi College, provide three-year training programs for primary school teachers; St. Bede's College in Savusavu; St. John's College in Levuka, Ovalau; and Xavier College in Namosau, Ba.

The Pacific Regional Seminary in Suva is sponsored by the Episcopal Conference of the Pacific and is a training center for priests for the South Pacific. The Marist Training Center in Taveuni is also a regional center run by the Marist Fathers for Oceania Province.

Other training centers include the Navesi Catechetical center run by the Archdiocese of Suva, the Marist Brothers' Novitiate, the Monfort Boys' Town sponsored by the Fiji Government in cooperation with the Monfort Brothers of St. Gabriel and the Archdiocese of Suva, the Nazareth Domestic Training Center and St. Teresa's Novitiate run by the Sisters of Our Lady of Nazareth.

CHARITABLE INSTITUTIONS

The following charitable institutions are in operation:

> Chanel Home of Compassion, for female invalids -- staffed by the Daughters of Our Lady of Compassion

> Father Law Home, for aged men -- staffed by the Sisters of Our Lady of Nazareth

> P. J. Twomey Memorial Hospital -- a government hospital for the treatment of   leprosy, staffed by the Missionary Sisters of the Society of Mary

> RA Maternity Hospital

> Crippled Children's Hostel -- owned and managed by the Fiji Crippled Children's Society and staffed by the Sisters of Our Lady of Nazareth

> Bethany Hostel for Girls -- run by the Sisters of Our Lady of Nazareth

Anglican Church

The Anglican Church of Fiji belongs to the diocese of Polynesia and is part of the Province of New Zealand. Its members are mostly Melanesians. The Anglican cathedral in Suva has many European members. It sponsors six primary schools and one secondary school. It runs an orphanage. It does not have an active literature program. Among the expressed needs of the local church is to train, assist, and encourage local writers to produce materials in English, Fijian, and Hindi for evangelism and cultural growth.

Students are trained for ordained ministry at St. John's Training Center. The students come from different parts of the Pacific.

Assemblies of God

The Assemblies of God came to Fiji in 1926 but made little impact prior to 1965. In 1976 there were about 7,000 adherents -- a large increase from 3,000 in 1966. The first converts of the first missionaries were mixed Europeans and Fiji Indians. The A/G (Assemblies of God) has a regular Bible School and operates a day school program that includes kindergarten, primary, intermediate, and high school. Today, it has 195 churches and outstations with more than 142 national workers and a Sunday school enrollment of nearly 6,000.

Fiji Gospel Churches

Known as "Brethren," this Christian group is growing in Fiji. The common rites of each assembly had been the gathering of a few in open homes to study the Bible and break bread. This practice continues today in centers where Brethren are found in fellowship.

Elders care for the members of the church. They set high standards of character and life; they are responsible for the administration of church activities; and they contribute leadership in evangelical organizations. In Fiji, this includes the Bible Society, Scripture Union, World Vision International, Christian Women's Convention International, Gideons International and Prison Fellowship.

Today, 17 Christian assemblies meet in such places as Suva Street, Samabula, Raiwai, Tacirua, Nausori, Sawani, Logani, Sigatoka, Nadi, Lautoka, Ba, Labasa, Savusavu, Taveuni and Korovou.

BRETHREN CHRISTIAN MINISTRIES

Outreach programs includes education, Bible study, Compassion Inc. cooperation, film ministry, and a cassette library. Bible studies are held in Hindi and Fijian.

The Fiji Gospel Film has about 30 films with gospel messages for youth and adults. The library loans films to all evangelical churches in Fiji and other parts of the South Pacific.

Gospel schools have about 12,000 students from preschoolers to high school. The schools are co-educational and multi-racial. Continued localization of the teaching staff, financing, program enrichment, and spiritual outreach are ongoing challenges for the assemblies.

Among the training sites for assembly leaders are the Coral Coast Bible School, the Discipleship Training Center in Sawani, the camps, and the outreach work of Compassion.

Salvation Army

The Salvation Army in Fiji is part of this worldwide Christian organization. It came to Fiji in 1973 through New Zealand. Its wholistic ministries emphasize evangelical, developmental, rehabilitation, vocational training, and relief work.

About 300 officers comprise its membership. Its leaders are both expatriates and nationals. Officers are trained through rigorous programs of community, vocational and rehabilitation tasks. The core workers -- mainly volunteers -- proclaim the gospel through community service projects.

To become an officer, an individual undergoes a one year training period of orientation and lessons; a residential course during the second year; and two years of probationary systems of examinations and practical work.

SOCIAL CONCERNS AND MINISTRIES

Current ministries address the needs of women in poverty, especially among the young Indian women. In addition to being poor, these women often come from broken families.

As are other Christian and social organizations in Fiji, the Salvation Army is concerned with the interlocking effects of social problems on the people. Family life problems, alcoholism, criminality, unemployment, urban migration are some of these pressing concerns.

The Salvation Army also has two training farms in a rural area 35 miles out of Suva. Young people with some social problems are trained in agriculture, fishing, poultry raising, carpentry and welding. Supervising the trainees are rehabilitation graduates themselves.

Housing and shelter are extended by the Salvation Army for people in trouble. A Girls' Home houses women too young to be sentenced in courts. They are given life-skill training and employment. In cooperation with the government's Women's Social Services, the Salvation Army also provides temporary shelter for women with difficulties. Another hostel takes in young men placed by the court for employment.

The Salvation Army also assists disaster victims through such programs as the Hurricane Relief Program. Housing repairs and rebuilding are extended to families in need of this kind of assistance.

The Salvation Army is a member of the Fiji Council of Churches. It also works closely with the Fiji Council of Social Services. Half of its budget is supported by assistance from New Zealand and Australia.

First Baptist Church

The First Baptist Church in Fiji is associated with the Southern Baptist Convention and the New Zealand Baptist Union. The first church was planted in Lautoka in 1973. In 1985 it had churches in Suva, Nadi, and Ba.

Grace Bible College offers a two-year program for the training of pastors. Its program is linked with the Southern Baptist Seminary in the Philippines and the Golden Gate Seminary in San Francisco. Opened in 1983, the college has about 11 full-time and 50 part-time students.

Among the church's outreach ministries are work with the students of the University of the South Pacific, pastoral work with 16 Korean families, and fellowships with some Chinese groups. An elder of the the Grace Baptist Church works for the Prison Fellowship.

COOPERATIVE CHRISTIAN AGENCIES

Fiji, because of its geographic location, has become the center of many regional and international agencies for the Pacific. Consequently it houses the secretariat of the Pacific Conference of Churches, the Pacific Theological College (Protestant), the Pacific Regional Seminary (Roman Catholic), and the CEPAC, the Catholic Episcopal Conference of the Pacific. (Described more fully in Chapter One).

The Fiji Council of Churches is the ecumenical council with seven members: the Methodist Church, Congregational Church, Presbyterian Church, Anglican Church, Roman Catholic, Salvation Army, and Baptist Mission Church. Founded in 1964, it had four original members. The Roman Catholic church joined in 1968. Their activities include the Week of Prayer for Christian Unity, Bible Week, a chaplaincy program in hospitals, prisons, and university; joint services, and projects such as low cost housing. It is also affiliated with the Pacific Conference of Churches.

The Evangelical Fellowships of Fiji is the local counterpart of Evangelical Alliances in other countries. Membership is on an individual basis rather than denominational. Its main objective is to keep the fire of the "evangel" burning and to encourage members through fellowship meetings and witnessing.

PARACHURCH GROUPS

The following operate in Fiji and the Pacific region as parachurch agencies: World Vision International (regional in scope); Bible Society in the South Pacific, Scripture Union, Child Evangelism Fellowship, Campus Crusade for Christ, Gideons International, and Pacific Students for Christ.

All these different agencies have a somewhat free but cohesive relationship so that many of them come together for fellowship and joint efforts as and when needed. They have worked together in undertakings such as the celebration of the Annual Bible Week, relief work during disasters, and Pastors' Conferences.

CHRISTIAN ACTIVITIES

Literature Distribution

Religious journalism has existed in Fiji since early in this century. Today, there are some church bookshops connected with major denominations. Two church printing presses publish materials in Pacific vernaculars and in English. There remains, however, a major lack of Christian literature in Fijian and Hindi.

Bible Translation

This is generally undertaken by the Bible Society of the South Pacific (BSSP). The BSSP is currently working on translations of scriptures into Rotuman and Fijian. The Summer Institute of Linguistics assists in some translation, but its main concentration of effort is on Papua New Guinea.

Social Concerns

Churches in Fiji are also active in the fight against crime, drugs, and related offenses. They run hospitals, orphanages, homes for disoriented young men and women, craft and agricultural schools. They have active programs for prison visitation and rehabilitation of ex-prisoners. Their efforts are sometimes hampered by lack of financing and trained personnel.

Broadcasting

Religious broadcasting in Fiji began with programming on station 2JV. Today, the Fiji Broadcasting Commission donates time for religious broadcasts. A Religious Advisory Committee allocates program time among the different denominations. This coordination is now undertaken by the Fiji Council of Churches.

Daily morning devotionals, worship on Sunday mornings, and church news on Sunday afternoons comprise the religious broadcasts. A program spot on Wednesdays invites questions from listeners. Separate programs are made for the English language station and the Fijian/Hindustani station. The latter is prepared by Fijian pastors and church people. Hindi broadcasting tends to be short, given the very small Christian community among this group.

Among the denominations participating in the broadcasts are the Methodist, Roman Catholic, Anglican, Congregational, Presbyterian, Assemblies of God, Fiji Gospel Churches, Salvation Army, Seventh-day Adventist, and Baptist churches.

EVANGELISM AMONG UNREACHED

The Indians in Fiji are largely unreached, with less than four percent of their number being identified as Christian. Among the Indians are numerous people groups, each with its own identity and special needs for ministry. The first group is made up of Indian Hindus, comprising 80 percent of the Indian population of Fiji. Within this group are a number of sub-groups differentiated from one another on the basis of area of origin in India or their Hindu sect. Traditionally, the Christian church in Fiji has based its evangelism strategy for Hindus on various types of educational programs, but this has led to little significant response on the part of the Indians. Since the late 1950's, however, there has been a shift in emphasis to more direct evangelism and presentation of the gospel. Although the new strategy has resulted in greater response, it also has come at a time when the Indian Hindu community has developed more internal organization and a stronger resistance to Christianity.

The second largest unreached people group in Fiji is made up of Indian Muslims. They constitute 15 percent of the Indian population and are divided into numerous factions, each of which zealously guards its individuality and separateness. The Muslim community as a whole, however, is united in respect to duties laid down by the laws of Islam and in its quest for separate political status and legal recognition of religious needs. A small portion of the Muslim population, the Ahmadyias, have a missionary orientation and have actively proselytized among the general population in Fiji. Each of the Muslims factions is closely organized, consistent in the practice of its faith, and intolerant toward those of other faiths, including Christians.

Fiji has undergone a high rate of urbanization, much of it centered in Suva. In the process, classes are emerging which cross ethnic lines. Signs point to a growing division between clerical/technical workers and unskilled or semi-skilled workers, and there is already a firm break between labor and management. It appears that occupation is becoming a major force in the shaping of social relations, even at the expense of ethnic divisions. It is not possible at this time to point with certainty to the existence of people groups in Suva based on class, but social forces are apparently moving the society to this point. It might very well be that a multi-ethnic, urban workers group will emerge with ministry and evangelism needs of its own.

Major Non-Christian Religion: Hinduism

HINDUISM AMONG INDIAN FIJIANS

Hinduism, an ancient Eastern religion, has a strong hold upon most of the Indian Fijians. About 80 percent of the Indian Fijians are Hindus while 15 percent are Muslims; 4 percent, Christians; and 1 percent, Sikhs.

The Indians who first came to Fiji included traders from northern parts of India -- the Lucknow and Benares area. Some were Gujarati traders. Others were indentured workers in the sugar plantations. They came mainly from Madras and Kerala. Their descendants now comprise the largest non-Fijian ethnic group within Fiji.

Family life and family religion are prominent elements among Hindus. Family prayer flags are raised year by year and Hindu priests come for devotion time. These traditional observances are important to Hindu families.

Hinduism has had a recent renaissance among the Indians. Celebration of traditional Hindu festivals have grown in popularity. Diwali, festival of light, is observed by the whole Hindu community and has become a public holiday in Fiji. Basic Hindu beliefs and practices are strong even though new and non-traditional elements in the culture have come about, such as the disappearance of caste, the increasing use of English, and the emancipation of women.

The Ramakrishna Mission, centered in Nadi, works for the renaissance of Hinduism although its influence has waned recently. This mission runs a large secondary school, the Shri Viveknanda High School in Nadi. It distributes literature on Hinduism.

The Hindu cult of Hari Khrishna has gained ground in Fiji, with a temple built in Lautoka for its adherents.

NEW CALEDONIA

Profile

NATURAL FEATURES: Land area: 19,013 sq. km. **Major island:** New Caledonia or Grand Terre. **Island groups:** Isle of Pines, Loyalty Islands (Ouvea, Lifou, Mare), Belep, Surprise, Huon and Chesterfield Islands. Grand Terre is continental with mineral deposits; terrain is mountainous with steep slopes in the east and some plains in the west. Other islands are raised coral formations.

CAPITAL: Noumea. **Population:** 85,000.

POPULATION: 153,000 (1985). Kanak, 43 percent; European, 37 percent; Wallisian, 8.4 percent, Polynesian, 3.8 percent, Indonesian, 3.6 percent, Vietnamese, 1.6 percent. **Annual growth rate:** 2.0 percent. **Urban:** 61 percent.

RELIGION: Christians: 90.6 percent. Catholics, 72.5 percent; Protestants, 18.1 percent. **Major Protestant denominations:** Evangelical Church of New Caledonia and Free Evangelical Church. **Muslims:** 4.0 percent. **Buddhists, Baha'is, tribal religionists:** 4.5 percent.

LANGUAGE: French, Melanesian-Polynesian dialects.

GOVERNMENT: Official name: Territory of New Caledonia and Dependencies, a French overseas Territory represented in French

Parliament by two Deputies and a Senator. It is administered by a French High Commissioner and since December 1984, by President of the Council of Government. **Legislature:** 42-member Territorial Assembly. In 1985, four Regions with corresponding Assemblies were created.

ECONOMY: Per capita GDP: (1982) US $4,500. **Mining industry:** nickel (world's third largest deposit), chrome, iron, manganese, cobalt and others. **Agricultural crops:** coffee, maize, wheat, vegetables. Extensive cattle grazing, some fishing and forestry, some food processing.

Melanesian-European Contact

Melanesians in New Caledonia are believed to be descendants of Papuans and Austronesians who migrated to the region in the Third Millenium B.C. Loyalty Islands had contacts with the Polynesian cultural area during this period.

The British Captain James Cook sighted New Caledonia in 1774; he named the island Caledonia, Latin for Scotland, because of the steep cliffs and tree-covered hills reminding him of Scotland. The British, however, did not settle on the island. Commerce and evangelism brought Europeans to New Caledonia. The initial years of contact included times of hostility.

EARLY MISSIONARIES

In 1840 and 1841 the London Missionary Society sent catechists from Samoa and Cook Islands to the Isle of Pines and to Touaourou on the main island. They did not succeed as they did in Mare and Lifou in the Loyalty Islands.

The Marist missionaries of the Roman Catholic Church came to the main island in 1843. They, too, suffered great difficulty in trying to convert the people to Christianity. However, they benefited from the protection of France's policy of supporting Roman Catholic missionary activity, especially when New Caledonia became a French colony in 1853.

FRENCH COLONIAL RULE

For decades the region served as a penal settlement, with as many as 40,000 French prisoners at one time. Thousands of these individuals, as well as guards, prison workers and missionaries, stayed on and settled after the penal settlement was disbanded.

Gradually, a population of New Caledonia-born Europeans emerged, the descendants of convicts, political detainees, and free settlers. These "Caldoches" were culturally French but regarded New Caledonia, rather than France, as their home.

After the abolition of the penal colony, the colonial administrators encouraged the migration of laborers from Asia and other parts of Oceania for cheap labor. These immigrants came from New Hebrides, now Vanuatu; China; Japan; and French Indochina. Most important in these groups were the indentured laborers from Vietnam and East Java in the Netherlands East Indies, now Indonesia.

RELATIONS WITH KANAKS

With few exceptions, Europeans had poor social relations with the native inhabitants. The indigenous Kanaks failed in a rebellion against the French authorities in 1878-79. The French authorities then instituted the *indigent*, an administrative system putting the Melanesians in about 50 districts or native reservations. A chief appointed by the Colonial Governor headed each reservation. Most of the chiefs lost their traditional prestige; many clans were separated from their ancestral lands. Disease and alcoholism reduced the population drastically, from 60,000 indigenous people in 1876 to 27,100 in 1921. This figure has only recently begun to climb.

ECONOMIC ENTERPRISES

The best land in the islands was owned by the European settlers. At first, they tried to grow rice, coffee, wheat and other agricultural products, using Kanak labor. These crops failed. At the turn of the century, they shifted from agriculture to raising cattle; vast acres of land were needed for pasture. Subsequently, mineral deposits were discovered: gold, copper ore, lead, zinc, chrome, and silver. But it was nickel in great quantity that brought prosperity to the islands. Through the years, New Caledonia became the world's leading supplier of this metal.

Ethnic Groupings

New Caledonia has a complex mixture of ethnicities and nationalities. The indigenous population of Melanesians comprises 42.6 percent of the 153,000 total. Known as Kanaks, they decreased in number in the early 1900's but in mid-century this trend reversed. They form a solitary people group distinguished by language, culture and historical-political processes from the rest of the population on New Caledonia.

The other major people group consists of Europeans, dominated by French settlers. They make up approximately 37.1 percent of the population and are united by ethnicity, political loyalties and a sense of common identity.

The discovery of nickel attracted migrants from France, Wallis Island, Tahiti, Java and Indochina. The Wallis Islanders came to New Caledonia when resources became scarce on Wallis Island. They have remained a relatively closed group and are separated from the original inhabitants of New Caledonia by mutual distrust.

Tahitians were drawn to New Caledonia by high wages associated with mining. They have tended to remain a separate community. Tahitians are noted for their desire to return to Tahiti once enough savings have been gathered.

There is also a small population of Javanese Muslims and a scattering of other Asians.

Complex Socio-Political Struggles

France has ruled New Caledonia for more than 130 years. Noumea, the capital, has developed very much like a French metropole. The struggle between the Europeans and the native Melanesians (or the Kanaks) is at the heart of the problem faced by France in dealing with the future of the territory; the Kanaks demand total independence. About 90 percent of the Melanesians support the Independence Front. In political matters, the non-Melanesians, Asians and Pacific Islanders tend to take the side of the Europeans.

The political struggle for independence or autonomy has been fierce in the past few years. Pro-independence parties include the Kanak Socialist National Liberation Front (FLNKS) and the moderate Kanak Socialist Liberation (LKS). Pro-status quo bodies include the European-dominated conservative Rassemblement pour la Calédonie dans la République (RPCR) and the extreme right-wing minority, the National Front.

Elections were held in New Caledonia in September 1985, pitting the indigenous Melanesian Kanaks seeking independence against the predominantly white immigrant community set on staying with France. Political parties opposed to independence, RPCR and the National Front won slightly less than 60 percent of the votes combined.

FLNKS won 28.5 percent, and the moderate Liberation Kanak Socialiste (LKS) 6.4 percent; the pro-independence vote was 35.2 percent.

New Caledonia has been divided into four regions; for each of these the latest elections chose a new Assembly. Legislative and executive powers previously held in a single territorial assembly are being devolved to these regions and enhanced. In the plans announced by French Prime Minister Laurent Fabius, each region constitutes a territorial congress. This congress is responsible to implement a referendum on independence for the colony -- possibly in close association with France in defense and security before the end of 1987.

The north region; which has about 19,000 inhabitants; has nine councilors; the center region has 25,000 inhabitants with nine councilors. The South region has 85,000 inhabitants including Noumea, the capital, with 21 councilors. The Loyalty Islands, with 15,500 inhabitants, has seven councilors.

Some sectors of the south region are not pleased with this grouping, inasmuch as these urban elements are lumped together and are comparatively underrepresented in the congress. On the other hand, the three bush regions (which include the bulk of the Kanak population) -- the north, the center and the Loyalty Islands -- are more heavily weighted. The regions also assume wide economic powers, including responsibility for development and education. They will also become responsible for land reform. It is in the three bush regions that the European and Melanesian cultures come into sharpest conflict over alienation of tribal lands by white farmers since French settlement in 1853.

Major players in the political arena are: Edgar Pisani, former Special Minister for New Caledonia; Jacques Chirac, former Prime

Minister, leader of RPCR; and Jean-Marie Tjibaou, leader of FLNKS (the Kanak party).

With the new congress and the regional presidents, the Kanaks will have an opening to begin work immediately on their policies of communal agriculture-based development, and replacement of French education with a Melanesian system. The FLNKS is oriented towards village-based communal values, usually with a strong streak of Christianity going through their traditional customs.

Major Economic Mainstay: Nickel Mining

New Caledonia has a well-developed mining sector that has brought prosperity to the country. Per capita GDP in 1983 was estimated at about US $6,600. However, the modern economy has not benefited people equally. In mid-1984, Noumea, having a predominantly European population, had a standard of living similar to that of cities in Western Europe, while in the interior where Melanesians predominate, underdevelopment persists despite government-supplied basic health and educational services.

The economic well-being of many residents of New Caledonia depends on the fluctuating demand for nickel. When prices are high, the region has jobs to offer and money flows freely. When demand is low and prices decline, hardships set in. Many laborers who left other islands, such as Wallis, in order to obtain jobs in New Caledonia, are forced to migrate elsewhere or to return to their homes, where conditions are generally worse.

Agriculture contributes only 3 percent to the GDP. Principal crops include corn, yams, taro, sorghum, potatoes, vegetables, and fruits. Many food items and basic commodities are imported. Cattle are raised in some flat areas in the west. It provides 60 percent of the demand for beef. Commercial fishing in 1984 remained relatively undeveloped, although the territory had tuna fishing agreements with United States and Japanese fishing firms.

Status Of Christianity

In 1980, 90.6 percent of the population professed to be Christians, divided between Catholics, 72.5 percent, and Protestants, 18.1 percent. Muslims constitute about 4 percent of the population. These are predominantly found among the Indonesians and Algerian Arabs. Comprising about 4.5 percent of the population are small groups of Buddhists, Baha'is, and adherents of tribal religions. Cargo cults from Vanuatu have had some influence with some groups.

The Protestants represent one-fourth of the population with approximately 30,000 followers. A schism in the main Protestant church occurred in 1958. The Evangelical Church of New Caledonia and Loyalty Islands, originating from the London Missionary Society and the Society of Evangelical Missions in Paris, became autonomous in 1960. It has 20,370 membership, with 120 parishes served by 70 pastors, and 150 deacons, mostly Melanesians. The Evangelical Church is a member of the Communaute Evangelique d'Action Apostolique (CEVAA) and of the Pacific Council of Churches.

The Free Evangelical Church, the other branch in the schism, has about 8,000 followers with approximately a dozen Melanesian pastors.

Membership in Christian denominations include the following:

Total Population	137,000
Roman Catholic Church	91,370
Evangelical Church	20,370
Free Evangelical Church	8,560
Assemblies of God	680
Seventh-day Adventist	650
Anglicans (one small congregation in Noumea) and others	260

Other religious bodies include Jehovah's Witnesses (620); Baha'is (320); Muslims (4,250); Church of Jesus Christ of Latter-Day Saints (Mormons) (530); Reorganized Church of Jesus Christ of Latter-Day Saints/Sanitos (320)

L'EGLISE CATHOLIQUE/CATHOLIC CHURCH

In 1985, there was one archdiocese in New Caledonia headed by an archbishop. It had 36 parishes. Among the church workers there were 11 diocesan priests, 54 religious, five seminarians, 62 brothers, 192 sisters, and 210 catechists. The catechists were mainly Melanesians and were responsible for teaching young catechumens.

The church operates primary and secondary schools. The Roman Catholic Church took a neutral position on the question of the political independence of New Caledonia.

The Archdiocese of Noumea is a member of the Catholic Episcopal Conference of the Pacific (CEPAC) and, through CEPAC, of the Pacific Conference of Churches. It also has two suffragans: one in Port Vila, Vanuatu; and the other in Wallis and Futuna.

L'EGLISE EVANGELIQUE/EVANGELICAL CHURCH

The Eglise Evangelique took the position of supporting the independence movement. It has become an influence for unity and has also warned of extremism. The church has also attempted to tie its Christian witness and theological foundations with the struggle for independence. It continues to discuss its own conception of the meaning of independence, of the essence of Kanak culture and civilization, and of the attitude which should be adopted by the Kanak to other ethnic groups, based on both the gospel and the traditional form of "accueil" (welcome) in Kanak culture.

The Evangelical Church sought the support of other churches throughout the region, including the Pacific Conference of Churches, in the issue of independence for New Caledonia. The latter group has expressed its full support.

In the November, 1984 elections, the leaders of the three major churches issued an ecumenical declaration calling for justice in the country, asking that all be reconciled in the true Christian spirit.

MAJOR CHURCH CONCERN

Unreached People Groups

Almost all of the Melanesian population belong to either Protestant or Roman Catholic churches. Likewise, the other Pacific Islanders are predominantly Christian. The large European population is nominally Roman Catholic, but in French Polynesia, actual participation in the church is marginal. There is a need for the development of effective models for evangelism and renewal for this people group.

There are a little more than 6,000 **Muslims** in New Caledonia. These are primarily from Java and use Javanese as a vernacular. There are significant cultural, linguistic and socio-political barriers which make it difficult for the churches in New Caledonia to reach out to the persons in this people group. An effective evangelistic outreach is needed to share the gospel of Jesus Christ with them.

PAPUA NEW GUINEA

Profile

NATURAL FEATURES: Land area: 461,700 sq. km. **Terrain:** Mountainous island. The eastern portion of the main island is Papua New Guinea and the western half is the Indonesian province of Irian Jaya; the nation also includes the Bismarck Archipelago, with New Britain, New Ireland and Manus; Bougainville and Buka Islands; the Admiralty Islands; and Nukumanu (Tasman).

CAPITAL: Port Moresby. **Population:** 122,700 (1983). **Other cities:** Lae, Madang, Rabaul.

POPULATION: 3,400,000 (1986 est.). **Annual growth rate:** 2.6 percent. **Ethnic groups:** New Guinean, Papuan -- 78 percent; New Guinean, Melanesians -- 20 percent; Anglo-Australian -- 2 percent; Chinese -- 0.3 percent; others -- 0.1 percent. **Urban:** 13 percent.

RELIGION: Christians: two-thirds of the population, at least nominally; Roman Catholics, 974,000 (1984); Lutherans and other Protestants; 320,000. **Traditionalists and non-Christians:** magico-religious beliefs.

LANGUAGES AND LITERACY: About 700-800 languages. Tok Pigin (Melanesian Pidgin English), and Hiri Police Motu are linguas franca. English is the national language. **Literacy:** 32 percent.

GOVERNMENT: Parliamentary democracy. Independent state since 1975 within the British Commonwealth. Prime Minister, head of government. **Subdivision:** 19 Provinces and the national capital district.

ECONOMY: Per capita GDP: (1985) US $900. **Annual growth rate** (1970-1980): 2.5 percent. **Agricultural crops** (35 percent of GDP): coffee, cocoa, copra, palm oil, tea, rubber. **Industries:** copper and gold mining, timber, manufacturing and food processing. **Monetary unit:** kina (1 kina = US $1.05 in 1985).

Papua New Guinea Under Colonial Rule

The people of Papua New Guinea had no written history before the coming of the Europeans. The evidence of their oral history, however, indicates that most of the peoples were on the islands long before they were "discovered" in 1545. It was not until the 1870's that the Western nations took an interest in this area.

At first, the northern portion was under the control of Germany, and the southern portion under Great Britain. Britain put the southern territory, renamed Papua, under the administration of the Australians in 1901. After World War I, both the Territory of Papua and the Trust Territory of New Guinea were placed under Australian administration by the League of Nations.

With the exception of a short period during the World War II when part of New Guinea was occupied by Japanese forces, Papua New Guinea remained under this system until 1973. The Australians granted internal self-government on December 1, 1973, and full independence on September 16, 1975, when Papua New Guinea then became a State within the British Commonwealth.

PEOPLE GROUPS

The estimated population of Papua New Guinea in 1986 was 3,400,000. The population is generally scattered evenly throughout the country, with more concentration in the highland provinces. The population in the central province, which includes the capital city of Port Moresby, was estimated in 1980 at 275,900.

The indigenous people of Papua New Guinea are considered Melanesians. Some ethnologists make a distinction between the Papuan-type people, who tend to inhabit the interior, and the Melanesian people, who settle along the coasts and on the offshore islands. Some of the people on the offshore islands are of Micronesian or Polynesian blood. The expatriate population of Papua New Guinea was more than 47,000 in 1971; since independence, this number has dwindled to around 29,000 in 1980. A small number of Chinese also live in New Guinea.

Outside of Australia, Papua New Guinea is the largest country in the South Pacific. It is also the most complex in terms of ethnicity. Approximately 78 percent of its population are Papuans who live in the interior regions of New Guinea and the larger islands. Another 20 percent are Melanesians who live on the coasts and offshore islands. Among these two native populations, there are over 700 distinct languages and many more identifiable people groups.

Papua New Guinea has experienced drastic changes. One of the primary forces affecting the social and cultural makeup of the population is urbanization. Approximately 13 percent of the population of Papua New Guinea now lives in cities. The two largest urban areas are Lae and Port Moresby. Although ethnicity remains an important cultural force, there is evidence of the emergence of people groups based upon class, among those persons who have been in cities for a greater length of time. One can expect that new people groups will form with time in Papua New Guinea cities.

Socio-Political Conditions

Papua New Guinea has a parliamentary system of government. The 109-member Parliament elects the majority party's leader as Prime Minister, having executive authority together with the National Executive Council. Suffrage is universal, but voting is done voluntarily. The country is divided into 19 districts for local government. Major political parties include Pangu Pati, the Melanesian Alliance, the National Party, the United Party, and the People's Progress Party.

Relations between the government in Port Moresby and the Indonesian government have been sensitive on the matter of the Irian Jayan refugees along their common border. About 11,000 refugees have camped in Papua New Guinea. Irian Jayans, who are pre-dominantly Melanesians, opposed in vain their annexation to Indonesia. About 80 percent of the Irian Jayan population of 1.2 million live in the remote highlands, where many tribes still adhere to stone-age culture and resist outside influence, particularly of non-Melanesian origin.

Economic Activities

Subsistence agriculture is the occupation of the majority of the population. Commercial crops, coffee, tea, copra, and cocoa are the major exports. The small amount of manufacturing is mostly for local consumption, although a few industries have begun to export limited amounts of their products. The mining industry, particularly copper and gold, produces considerable export earnings. Exploration is under way for oil and natural gas, but no large fields have yet been found. The timber industry has also become a major exporter in recent years.

Papua New Guinea receives a large portion of its budget in economic aid from Australia.

Status Of Christianity

Mission Impact

The Christian churches and missions in Papua New Guinea have had a tremendous influence in the development of the country, particularly in helping to unite the many tribes and clans into one people. Christian missions have been working in the country for over 100 years. Church growth has taken place since the coming of the missionaries, but major movement into the church has occurred in the last 35 years. Many heavily-populated areas of the highlands of Papua New Guinea opened to missions only after the 1950's.

The coastal areas have higher percentages of Christians, with a fairly even distribution in the rest of the country. Much medical and educational work carried out by the churches and missions in their early days was subsidized by the Australia administration. After independence in 1975, such assistance continued. Cooperation exists between the churches and the government, particularly in the fields of education, medicine, and economic development. Many of the national Parliamentarians are Christians.

There were approximately 1,600 foreign missionaries serving in Papua New Guinea on June 30, 1980, a ratio of approximately one missionary per 2,000 people. With the present rate of church growth, some indications show the nation will be totally Christian by 1990. However, the churches have grave concerns about the nurture and organization of the Church and the nominalism of most of the Christians.

FROM MISSIONS TO NATIONAL CHURCHES

The Christian community in Papua New Guinea has grown over the last 35 years. People have usually come into the church in groups and have preserved their local society. Church growth will continue, although at a lower rate, because the great majority of people have already become Christians. Many of the churches are beginning to view their task more in terms of the wider needs of the Southeast Pacific and Southeast Asia.

TABLE 6

PAPUA NEW GUINEA CHURCH STATISTICS

Church Name	Year Work Begun	Worship Places	Church Membership	Adults	Data Year
Anglican Church of PNG	1891	276	150,000	---	1980
Apostolic Christian Church	1960	25	5,000	1,250	1970
Apostolic Church Mission	1954	194	17,000	10,000	1970
Assemblies of God	1948	270	20,000	1,250	1970
Assoc. of Baptist for World Evangelism	1967	---	1,000	500	1970
Bamu River Mission	1936	14	2,000	92	1970
Baptist Bible Fellowship International	1961	---	150	100	1970
Baptist Union of PNG	1949	400	32,700	60	1984
Bible Missionary Church	---	21	3,000	500	1970
Bethel Pentecostal Temple	1948	120	40,000	20,000	1970

Church Name	Year Work Begun	Worship Places	Church Membership	Adults	Data Year
Christian Brethren	1955	40	15,220	7,000	1970
Christian Revival Crusade	1963	23	2,000	500	1970
Church of the Nazarene	1955	34	3,000	1,000	1970
Church of Christ in Christian Union	1963	86	9,200	5,000	1970
Churches of Christ Mission	1958	---	7,000	3,000	1970
Evangelical Bible Mission	1948	85	2,000	1,000	1970
Evangelical Church of Papua	1931	154	30,000	14,000	1985
Ev. Lutheran Church of PNG	1886	2,023	500,000	---	1980
Four Square Gospel Church	1955	179	20,000	12,394	1970
Faith Mission	---	---	8,730	4,000	1970
Greek Orthodox Church	---	1	200	100	1970
Gutnuis Lutheran Church (formerly Wabag)	1948	365	60,000	---	1980
Independent Chris. Miss. Soc.	1956	7	3,000	1,000	1970
Kwato Church	1917	---	4,000	2,400	1970
Manus Evangelical Church	1914	34	4,000	2,500	1970
National Revival Church Miss.	---	---	500	200	1970
New Guinea Gospel Mission	1960	---	1,000	500	1970
New Tribes Mission	1949	100	10,000	7,000	1970
Pentecostal Church	1968	11	850	70	1970
Roman Catholic Church	1844	19	974,000	--	1984
Salvation Army	1956	60	1,500	50	1984
South Sea Evangelical Church	1882	77	7,500	75	1984

Church Name	Year Work Begun	Worship Places	Church Membership	Adults	Data Year
Sovereign Grace Baptist Miss.	---	---	3,000	1,500	1970
Swiss Evangelical Brotherhood Mission	---	---	7,000	3,000	1970
United Church in PNG and Solomon Islands	1871	2,082	380,800	---	1980
Wesleyan Church	1961	37	5,000	802	1970
Worldwide Missions 1970		1971	---	7,000	3,000
Other Protestant Denominations	---	---	5,000	2,000	1970

(Excluding cultist churches, e.g. Paliau Church in Manus.)

Of the estimated total Christian population of 2,500,000 in 1982, 51 percent are Protestant and Anglican, 31 percent Roman Catholic, 7.5 percent indigenous religious, and 7.5 percent non-committed. See Table 7 for further statistical breakdown.

NATIONAL CHURCHES

Roman Catholic Church

BRIEF HISTORY OF MISSIONS

Marists began evangelism work in 1844, but did not have initial success. In 1885 French Sacred Heart Fathers began mission work in the south coast of Papua, on Yule Island about 70 miles from Port Moresby. Originally confined by a government policy to work only in this area, the missionaries later pushed into the rugged interior, where they contacted the widely scattered but vigorous indigenous people. They worked particularly with the Meko people. By 1914, they began work in Port Moresby; in 1926, they established a mission in Samarai, and later in Dobu.

In the northern part of the island, missionaries from the Society of the Divine Word from Germany came when the territory was annexed by that country in 1895. They centered their work at Alexishafen near Madang, where they established institutions and buildings. They expanded later to the north coast and up the great Sepik River.

Meanwhile, German missionaries of the Sacred Heart Mission established their work on the Bismarck Archipelago, centered at Vunapope, near Rabaul. Their mission expanded throughout the archipelago and Manus. They worked with the Tolai people, among others. The Roman Catholics in these parts of the island became stronger than those in southern part. The missions purchased lands and built large plantations, which eventually provided major support for their operations.

The Roman Catholic mission did not join the Country Conference in 1890. This conference, called by the British government, decided areas in which missions could work. Unlike the work of the London Missionary Society, the Anglicans, and the Methodists, the Roman Catholic missionaries did not utilize Pacific Islander missionaries mainly because local leadership had not been developed as much by the European clergy.

All Catholic churches are part of the one church centered in Rome and headed by the Pope. In 1966, the Roman Catholic Church in Papua New Guinea obtained provincial status with centers in Madang, Port Moresby, and Rabaul. As was true for many island churches during the 1960's and 1970's, the Roman Catholic Church moved from a mission to become a more national church. From 1972 to 1975, 200,000 members of the church made a self-study examining the life of the church. From this convention of the National Catholic Assembly came the National Catholic Council which was composed mainly of lay people who became active advisers and workers in the church.

More recently, a large increase in membership was noted after the visit of Pope John Paul II in 1984.

MEMBERSHIP

The estimated total number of adherents of the Roman Catholic Church in 1984 was 974,000, making it the largest single church in Papua New Guinea. Its membership is represented in most areas of the country, but most concentrations are found in New Britain, East and West Sepik provinces, North Solomons, and New Ireland. It is also represented in all urban areas. The Roman Catholic Church has 19 dioceses. About 50 percent of the members attend church regularly.

CHURCH WORKERS

By the end of 1984, it had a total of 4,545 workers serving in evangelism, health, education, and administration.

The Roman Catholic Church had 503 priests and 1,500 men and women, both nationals and expatriates, working in other areas of the ministry. Over 50 percent of these are missionaries. Fifty men are national priests, and about 600 men and women are nationals doing other religious activities in the Church. Another 500 workers are expatriates.

Most higher education positions in seminaries and other leadership positions are held by expatriate missionaries, with part-time catechists and lay helpers who are both nationals and expatriates.

EDUCATION AND TRAINING

The Roman Catholic Societies, in the post-war period, stressed the training of indigenous leaders. A small group of local priests had been ordained. This indigenizing emphasis remains strong, but much remains to be done. The Catholic Church continues to provide its vigorous training programs to train and educate national leaders. Some have become outspoken Christian politicians and administrators in both national and provincial politics. The present Archbishop is a national.

By the end of 1984, the church had 453 primary schools, 79 tertiary schools and four theological colleges in Papua New Guinea. It has 22 hospitals and provides other social services.

AFFILIATIONS

The Roman Catholic Church of Papua New Guinea is associated with the Roman Catholic Church in The Vatican in Rome. It is part of this church and is financially dependent on overseas churches and organizations. It aims to be independent financially in the future.

CONCERNS

The Church identifies the following as important issues needing to be addressed: evangelism, unemployment, youth problems, alcoholism, and movement of people to towns.

Lutheran

The Lutheran Church entered Papua New Guinea in 1886 under the auspices of the Neuendettelsau Mission Society from Bavaria. The missionaries were soon joined by others from the Rhenish Missionary Society, then the largest on the European continent. Neuendettelsau began its work in the Finschhafen area, and the Rhenish Mission in the Madang area. Under the guidance of pioneer missionaries, the missions trained Papuan Christians to become missionaries to other people groups. Instead of working with individuals, they concentrated on the tribal structure of the New Guinea people and endeavored to win groups of single units. This work has been fulfilled, and now the Evangelical Lutheran Church of Papua New Guinea constitutes the largest Protestant group and is one of the largest mission churches in the world.

Established in 1956, the Evangelical Lutheran Church of Papua New Guinea became fully autonomous in 1976. It has continued to grow rapidly, particularly through all the highlands, having an estimated 500,000 adherents in 1980. To date, there are over 3,000 full-time workers in the church serving in evangelistic, educational, and medical programs. About 500 overseas workers are in its mission program.

The Missouri Synod Lutheran Mission began work in the Enga Province in 1948. As a result the Wabag Lutheran Church, was established in 1963. This church is now known as the Gutnius Lutheran Church. It presently has a baptized membership of about 60,000, with a total Christian community of about 60,000. As with other Lutheran work in Papua New Guinea, indigenous Christians have been involved with the work of evangelization from the beginning. It has a local staff of 450, supplemented by 70 overseas personnel, to carry out each program in evangelization, medical and economic development.

From the Australian Lutheran missionary activity the Siassi Lutheran Church developed. It joined the Evangelical Lutheran Church of Papua New Guinea in 1976. The Lutheran churches, cooperate through the Council of the Lutheran Churches of Papua New Guinea.

United Church

The United Church of Papua New Guinea and the Solomon Islands was formed by union in 1968 of the Papua Ekalesia, the United Synod of the Methodist Church in Melanesia, and the Union Church in Port Moresby. The Papua Ekalesia, formed in 1962, included the church initiated by the London Missionary Society and the Kwato Extension Association. The Presbyterian Church of New Zealand came in to assist later.

In addition the United Church brought together the work of the Methodist Missionary Society which began in the island of New Britain in 1874 and in Papua in 1890. The Methodists decided in 1966 not to form their own church.

Like the development of the other churches, the work of the mission forming the United Church progressed slowly until after the second World War. This church had an actual membership of 272,000 with 380,800 in their community of adherents. Most of the work of the United Church is carried out in four areas of Papua New Guinea: the Island of New Britain, the Gulf and Central District of Papua, the Milne Bay District and the Southern Highlands.

The United Church has developed strong New Guinea leadership and has placed its total program in the hands of local Christians. Each region of the church has a New Guinea bishop at its head, and the present moderator is also from New Guinea. The United Church accounts for approximately 15 percent of the Christian community of Papua New Guinea. Today, the United Church remains the most localized major church.

Anglican Church

Anglican work began in Papua in 1891 at Dogura in the Milne Bay Province on the northeast coast. Upon the insistence of the administrator of Papua, the Anglican, Methodist, and the London Missionary Society agreed to a division of territory for their mission endeavors.

The Anglican Church was assigned the areas now known as the Northern Province. To this date, the major area of Anglican influence is in this province, although it has spread to other centers in Papua New Guinea. The Diocese of Papua New Guinea was established in 1898, and was a missionary diocese of the Church of

England in Australia until the formation in 1977 of an autonomous Anglican province, the Church of the Province of Papua New Guinea, with five dioceses.

Presently, the Anglican Church serves 150,000 adherents. The indigenization of the priesthood is being encouraged. Today, two of the five bishops are Papua New Guineans. The Anglican community accounts for over 5 percent of the Christian population.

Baptist Union of Papua New Guinea

MISSION HISTORY

The Australian Baptist Missionary Society started its work in Papua New Guinea in 1949. It established its mission in two fields, one in Enga in the Western Highland Province, and the other in Telefomin and Tekin areas of the Upper Sepik.

THE ENGA FIELD

The Baptist Mission started its work at Bayer River where the first baptism took place in 1956. The church was formed a month later. C. P. Mildred Tinsley Hospital opened that same year and a nursing training program was soon developed.

In 1964, the Enga church commenced its own missionary work in the Wapi, among the Pinais and Pinales. Meanwhile, Mt. Hagen Baptist Church was constituted in May 1963, and Lae Church in 1972, to meet the needs of members who moved out of their areas to the towns for employment or higher education.

TELEFOMIN/TEKIN FIELDS

The Baptist work in Telefomin in West Sepik Province started in 1951. The first baptism took place in 1959, marking the establishment of the local church in Telefomin, expanding later into the valleys of Eliptaman, then to Tifalmin, Feramin, and Miyanmin Valley. The main thrust came through the Bible School at Telefomin started by Rev. Gil McArthur and Don Doull.

The mission also initiated educational and medical work. It started the first girls' school at Bayer River for the Highland Regions in 1958. In 1968, the Baptist Bible School opened in Pinyapaisa, later moving to Kwia.

CLINICS

Medical work at Telefomin began in 1961 and grew into a large nursing training program.

MEMBERSHIP

The Baptist Union of Papua New Guinea (BUPNG) has 400 churches with 32,700 baptized members; 400 national pastors and 37 expatriate missionaries.

CHURCH ACTIVITIES

Most of the church activities are geared towards including varying peoples and tribes of many different language groups and backgrounds. Worship songs are in local languages; some urban churches use pidgin hymns or translation of English hymns. There are English services for the English-speaking expatriates and for some nationals in the towns.

The church spends most of its time on evangelism and nurturing church growth, and less on social ministry. Occasionally, it participates in government-sponsored programs working with medical groups, youth and community programs. It has a Prison Fellowship program in Mt. Hagen.

As a church, BUPNG identifies the following issues needing to be addressed: evangelism, youth problems, loss of traditional values, movement of people to urban centers, and discipleship. It also plans to send Papua New Guinean missionaries overseas, particularly to Australia and Indonesia. It expects to establish an urban ministry training center in Port Moresby.

AFFILIATIONS

BUPNG is an associate member of the Australian Baptist Missionary Society, the Baptist World Alliance, and Asian Baptist Fellowship. It is a member of the Evangelical Alliance and Melanesian Council of Churches; and an affiliate member of the Churches Medical Council of Papua New Guinea.

Salvation Army

The Salvation Army, whose officers first came to Papua New Guinea in 1956, still has a comparatively small membership. Besides evangelization, it provides an extensive welfare program. It has approximately 60 different centers with 1,500 fully-committed members. Many villagers attend worship services, but are as yet to be confirmed soldiers. It has 101 full-time ranking officers and 52 part-time officers, more than half of whom are Papua New Guineans; 35 are expatriates. There is no basic role difference between the national and expatriate Army officers. The Salvation Army is international, and appointments are given according to the suitability of persons.

SOCIAL MINISTRIES

The Salvation Army has hostels and hospitals as a part of its social ministry. The hostel and hospital buildings are partly subsidized by the government.

FUNDING

About 80 percent of the total operation costs of the Salvation Army are generated from within Papua New Guinea. It receives about 20 percent from its territorial headquarters in Sydney, Australia. Its budget in 1984 for social and pastoral work was approximately K900,000.

LEADERSHIP AND DECISION-MAKING

The central church organization of the Salvation Army has wide controls, but local decisions are usually made within the local framework. Most of the leadership positions are held by local people, and as such, continual leadership training is given to them.

AFFILIATION

The Salvation Army is a member of the Melanesian Council of Churches. It also serves in the various committees of different Christian movements in the country.

South Sea Evangelical Church of Papua New Guinea

HISTORICAL BACKGROUND

The South Sea Evangelical Church of Papua New Guinea is the result of the work of an interdenominational mission called South Sea Evangelical Mission. Historically, its work is traced back to 1882 with Florence Young, who started an evangelistic outreach to the Melanesians on her brother's sugarcane plantation in Queensland, Australia.

The workers, or "Kanaks," were on three-year contracts to cut and process sugarcane, after which they had the option of being repatriated. Florence Young started a school for them on Sundays teaching them about Christ and to read as well. The Sunday School was successful and expanded to evening class in 1885. The first Kanaka baptism was reported in 1886. The work continued to grow; Florence Young enlisted the help of some of her friends, expanding the work to cover 10,000 imported laborers from Melanesian Islands on the Queensland plantations. The Queensland Kanaka Mission (QKM) was founded as an interdenominational mission, totally supported by offerings.

In 1889, another mission staff carried on the work when Florence Young left for China with the China Inland Mission. After 25 years, the Mission reported 19 missionaries at 11 mission centers and some 2,484 baptized converts.

More detailed accounts of the growth of this church is found in the Solomon Islands "National Churches" section.

Evangelical Church of Papua

HISTORY

The Evangelical Church of Papua (ECP) has its roots in the Papuan coast near the mouth of the Fly River. In 1931, the first Unevangelized Fields Mission (UFM) began work amongst the Fly River peoples, centering primarily in the Gogodala tribe. In 1940, UFM missionaries entered the Suki area of the Middle Fly. WWII forced the retreat of the UFM missionaries to their homelands of Australia and New Zealand.

After the end of World War II, UFM missionaries returned to the Fly River area to continue their task; this included church planting, medical work, education and development. During the 20 years from 1945-1965, the work of UFM spread throughout the Western Province and the Southern Highland. This expansion was the joint work of both national and expatriate missionaries.

The UFM missionaries represented many Protestant denominations from their homelands. In July 1966, the Evangelical Church of

Papua (ECP) was established out of the work of UFM. The church was truly indigenous from its inception.

CHURCH GROWTH

The church and mission have worked together in spreading the gospel in the Western and Southern Highland Provinces. In 1970 the mission changed its name to the Asia Pacific Christian Mission (APCM) in order better to represent its work. During this period, the mission began the process of integrating into the ECP. In 1983, the full integration of ECP and APCM was accepted.

In 1975 the church's membership and adherence was estimated at 13,500; in 1985 it was 30,000. The growth rate for the decade was 66.3 percent.

This growth trend is expected to continue at approximately the same rate for the next decade. In some areas, the growth rate may be more due to high receptivity, especially in the urban areas and the unreached tribal work (currently numbering six tribes).

MINISTRIES

The ECP works with more than 35 tribal groups in the Western Province, the Southern Highlands, and the capital city, Port Moresby.

The urban work is heterogeneous in nature, with many distinct tribal groups represented. The rural work is more homogeneous in nature and focuses on geographic regions, primarily using the vernacular language of the specific people.

In 1985 ECP had 250 ordained and commissioned clergy and pastors. Thirty-one missionaries engaged in church ministries such as training and health education.

MAJOR CHRISTIAN PROGRAMS AND ACTIVITIES

Evangelistic Outreach

Evangelism continues to be one of the major concerns of the churches. Not only are they engaged in constant outreach to those who have still not heard the gospel, they are continually attempting to encourage renewal among Christians. Specialized ministries have been developed by many of the churches to reach people in urban situations and mines. In some instances, it necessitates a "tent-making" ministry, where the church places a qualified Christian in a position to witness to other people working in the same area. Chaplains have been placed by many of the churches at government schools, particularly high schools and tertiary institutions. The churches feel a particular need to make sure that the young people are well versed in the scripture and know the Lord Jesus Christ.

Individual churches, independent fellowship and missionary agencies continually emphasize evangelistic work. In some of the major urban centers, these outreaches are cooperative. It is recognized by most of the churches that the changing urban situation calls for special ministry, both to the Christian and to the non-believer.

In recent years, several crusades and rallies have been held in Papua New Guinea which, combined with the use of literature, have attempted to rekindle an interest in Christianity in those who have become indifferent. It should be pointed out, however, that large attendance at these rallies and crusades does not indicate a true interest in Christianity; often they are viewed as entertainment.

Many attempts are made by the churches to keep in contact with students, particularly in the secondary education system.

Overseas churches have been lending qualified educational staff to the government, particularly in secondary and tertiary education. By working with the government system, individual Christians are given a good opportunity to witness to their faith.

Literature Production

Many churches and missions are engaged in literature production, distribution and literacy work. Until the coming of Christian missions, none of the languages of Papua New Guinea had been reduced to writing. It was only after missionaries had accomplished this that people could be taught to read and literature could be produced. Much emphasis in recent years has been placed on the development of literature in Melanesian Pidgin and simple English. Literacy programs in Melanesian Pidgin have been developed by Kristen Press Inc. The Summer Institute of Linguistics focuses on vernacular literacy. Adult literacy is still low, although it is growing every year.

Bible correspondence courses and Bible readings have been prepared specifically for students in high school. These are available both in

Melanesian Pidgin and in English. No statistics are available on the use of these courses.

Most of the major churches publish Christian periodicals and newspapers; however, since many of these are published in local languages, the distribution is limited. Christian literature in Wantok is produced by the Roman Catholic Church, but aimed at the entire Christian community. Kristen Press, Inc., runs periodic training courses for Christian writers. Literature is one of the ways in which the Christian church can have an impact on the entire national population.

Bible Translation And Distribution

Bible translation has been carried on by the various mission groups, the British and Foreign Bible Society, now the Bible Society of Papua New Guinea, and, since 1956, the Summer Institute of Linguistics (Wycliffe Bible Translators). Of the 700 to 800 known languages in Papua New Guinea, a relatively small percentage have scripture. One of the major tasks of the church is providing more of the people with the scriptures translated in their own language.

In February 1969, the New Testament in Melanesian Pidgin was published by the Bible Society. Now in its third edition, some 70,000 copies have been distributed throughout Papua New Guinea. Translation of the Old Testament has been going on for some years, with portions available only recently.

As the church and government combine to encourage literacy, there will be a much greater demand for scripture and scripture portions; e.g., translation is being done in at least 90 different Papua New Guinea languages. The United Bible Society reports the following distribution in 1984:

Bibles	27,975
New Testaments	64,718
Portions	70,302
Selections	130,074
Totals:	293,069

Additionally, the Scripture Union Notes are well distributed throughout all high schools with Scripture Union Fellowships.

Education

THEOLOGICAL

There are about 20 theological colleges and seminaries in Papua New Guinea which are members of the Melanesian Association of Theological Schools. Six offer degree level work. There are also many small Bible schools and individual training programs carried out by the churches. Currently, there is no union seminary.

Many of the training programs are designed for people with little formal education. The major emphasis is in preparing individuals for service in the local congregations. A good start has been made in Theological Education by Extension; but because of the lack of formal education for many people, this program has yet to be widely accepted.

CHRISTIAN

The Christian churches and missions have long been involved in education. Approximately 60 percent of all pupils in educational institutions receive their instruction through church or mission schools. In addition, many Christian educators serve on both national and local education boards for education in Papua New Guinea.

The Christian churches are involved in primary, secondary, vocational and teacher education. There is no distinctly Christian university, although the churches support many programs at the University of Papua New Guinea and the University of Technology.

Most Christian schools and teachers have become a part of the National Education Service, which was established by the government in order to guarantee more equitable distribution of education and educational funds. Due to the large number of Christian teachers also teaching in government schools, Christian principles are found throughout the education system.

Social Concerns

From the very beginning of the Christian mission in Papua New Guinea, the ministries of service and proclamation had to work together. The majority of people are subsistence farmers with many needs, in terms of health, agricultural development, economic development, community development and literacy training.

RELIEF ASSISTANCE

Christian churches have been leading in the assistance programs to people affected by natural calamities such as severe storms, drought and floods. In 1983, with the cooperation of Christian missions, the government engaged in a flood-relief program for several thousand people in Lae, Papua New Guinea, and for over 10,000 refugees; funds for this program were supplied by various Christian mission agencies throughout the world. The food distribution on the local level was carried out by Christian missionaries and local workers.

URBAN COUNSELING

The Christian churches have begun bringing counseling services and other assistance to people who have left their homes to settle in urban areas. Because of Papua's long history of rural living, many problems arise for the urbanites. The churches are attempting to find ways to serve them, such as giving assistance to unwed mothers and mothers of young children who have been deserted by their husbands. In addition, concerted attempts are made to reach the youths in these urban areas who are being affected by the trauma of modernization.

MEDICAL WORK

As in the field of education, the Christian missions serve more of the people medically than do the government medical services. Many of the best hospitals are church supported.

Medical work, particularly in the area of community health developed by the churches, is now also being undertaken by the Public Health Department. Many opportunities are available for Christian medical workers to serve their country and church.

Many of the rural medical works are in rugged and isolated areas accessible only by air, necessitating many smaller strips being built by missionaries for medical supplies to be brought in by Mission Aviation Fellowship (M.A.F.) planes.

The Christian church has several training schools for medical workers, one of which includes a Registered Nurse program. Only the government, through the University of Papua New Guinea, has the facilities to train physicians.

COOPERATIVE AGENCIES

There are two major bodies of church cooperation in Papua New Guinea -- the Melanesian Council of Churches and the Evangelical Alliance. The Melanesian Council of Churches is the larger of the two, and is made up of the following:

- Anglican Church of Papua New Guinea and the Solomon Islands
- The Roman Catholic Church
- Evangelical Lutheran Church of Papua New Guinea
- Gutnius Lutheran Church of Papua New Guinea
- Salvation Army
- United Church in Papua New Guinea and the Solomon Islands
- Western Highlands Baptist Union Inc.

Associate Members

- Bible Society of Papua New Guinea
- Kristen Press
- Scripture Union
- Churches' Council for Media Coordination
- Melanesian Institute for Pastoral and Socio-Economic Service
- Melanesian Association of Theological Schools
- Churches' Medical Council
- Lifeline
- Church of the Nazarene
- Mission Aviation Fellowship
- National YWCA
- Summer Institute of Linguistics
- Churches' Education Council

The Evangelical Alliance of Papua New Guinea brings together the majority of the faith missions working in New Guinea. The largest of these is the Asian Pacific Christian Mission (formerly Unevangelized Field Mission), which began work in Papua in 1932.

FOREIGN MISSIONS

The history of Christian mission has been presented under the heading of each national church. At present, there are about 80 separate agencies working in this country. Most of the leadership roles are being taken over by the national church leaders, and the number of missionaries has been reduced to approximately 1,600. This excludes operations of such organizations as the Mission Aviation Fellowship, the YMCA, Wycliffe Bible Translators, and other service organizations. Of these overseas missionaries, 1,100 are engaged in administrative or commercial activities. The missionary force has been very important in the development of the country, not only as far as its churches are concerned, but also in the development of the wider community. Many overseas churches have provided specialists in medicine and education to aid the government. For the foreseeable future, the missionary will continue to serve both the Church and the community in Papua New Guinea.

Three major organizations serve in a special way for most of the missions in Papua New Guinea. They are: the Wycliffe Bible Translators, who entered New Guinea in 1956, and are mainly concerned with Scripture translation; the Mission Aviation Fellowship, which provides air transportation for the majority of Protestant missions; and the Christian Radio Missionary Fellowship, which has established a radio communication network for most of the Protestant churches. Among them, these three service organizations field more than 500 workers in Papua New Guinea. They are not included in the totals of workers as listed.

Many of the larger churches have begun to recall some of their overseas personnel as the total missionary staff continues to decrease. The developing churches are asking for specialist help in particular areas only where they do not provide the training themselves. In recent years, missionary groups from smaller church bodies in America have entered Papua New Guinea in great numbers; at present their major emphasis seems to be on witnessing to and winning over members of the established churches. This is one of the difficulties the churches are facing in Papua New Guinea.

The missionary community, however, is an international one. Mission societies from the U.S.A., Great Britain, Australia, New Zealand, Federal Republic of Germany, Canada, the Netherlands and Switzerland work in Papua New Guinea. In addition, missionaries come from Belgium, France, Italy and Poland. The largest number of overseas missionaries are British Commonwealth nationals (Australia, New Zealand, Great Britain) followed by Americans.

As the national churches themselves begin to take up the full task of the Church in this land, they are also being challenged to send their own missionaries to the remote areas of P.N.G. to win their own isolated countrymen to Christ.

MAJOR CHURCH CONCERN

Unreached People Groups

Papua New Guinea has seen rapid acceptance of the Christian gospel in people groups contacted by outsiders since World War II. Any list of unreached people groups among the **Papuan or Melanesian populations** would be outmoded almost as fast it is published. Yet, there are still a few people groups which have been resistant to the gospel; some who have shown initial acceptance and then become involved in a nativistic "cargo cult"; and some who have not been contacted with the message of Jesus Christ.

It is commonly noted that the Church in Papua New Guinea is village-based and has not been effective in attracting the attention of migrants to the city. Accordingly, as new people groups are formed as a result of forces of change in the city, it is likely that many will exist which are not being reached by the church. This is an area which needs focused research.

SOLOMON ISLANDS

Profile

NATURAL FEATURES: Land area: 28,530 sq. km. It consists of a double chain of six large islands and numerous small ones. **Major islands:** Guadalcanal, Choiseul, New Georgia, Santa Isabel, Malaita and San Cristobal. These islands are rugged, mountainous and with limited coastal plains. Outer islands are raised coral reefs or coral atolls.

CAPITAL: Honiara on Guadalcanal. **Population:** 20,000.

POPULATION: 300,000 (1985). **Annual growth rate:** 3.1 percent. Nearly half of population is under 14 years old. **Ethnic groups:** Melanesians -- 94 percent; Polynesians -- 4.0 percent; Micronesian -- 1.5 percent; European and Chinese 0.5 percent; 10 percent urban.

RELIGION: Christians: 95 percent. Church of Melanesia-Anglican, 35 percent; Roman Catholic, 18 percent; South Sea Evangelical, 16 percent; United Church, 11 percent; Seventh-day Adventists, 10 percent. **Traditional animists:** 5.0 percent, in the isolated interiors.

LANGUAGE: English-official; Pidgin and many local dialects. **Literacy rate:** 13 percent.

GOVERNMENT: Independent democracy, a member of the British Commonwealth. **Head of state:** British Monarch represented by the Governor-General. **Executive:** Prime Minister and Cabinet. **Legislative:** Parliament with 38 members. **Judicial:** High, magistrate and local courts.

ECONOMY: Per Capita GDP: (1983) US $603. **Economic sources:** fish, agriculture and forestry resources. **Products:** coconut and oil palm. Bauxite reserves on Rennell and Waghena; phosphate in Bellona.

Historical Notes

The Solomon Islands is comprised of a large number of islands, which prior to Western colonization were politically and culturally distinct. Spanish explorer Mendana called the islands the Solomons because he thought they were the lost islands of King Solomon. Today, there are 87 different vernacular languages which often are mutually unintelligible. Pidgin and English are universally used and act to bring down barriers to communication and interaction.

There has been a growing urbanization in the Solomon Islands. The largest urban center is Honiara, with a population of about 20,000. It is too soon to tell if a distinct urban way of life is developing in such a way that would cause the emergence of new people groups.

People Groups

Approximately 93 percent of the population of about 300,000 could be classified as Solomoni Melanesians. This population is almost all Christian. On the eastern fringes of the Solomon Islands are peoples which are classified as Polynesian in physical type, language and life-style. They too, are almost all Christian. In the interiors of the larger islands are found Solomon Island Papuans. They are isolated from the rest of the population in the Solomon Islands, speak a language akin to Papuan languages in Papua New Guinea and are outside the mainstream of Solomon Island society.

Other populations in the Solomon Islands include a community of Gilbertese (I-Kiribati), who were moved to the Solomon Islands to escape acute land shortages and the hardships of drought; a small population of Chinese; a number of Fijians; and a small European population.

Socio-Political Conditions

The society of the Solomon Islands is divided into numerous linguistic and cultural groupings. However, larger social identities are forged by regional or island groupings. Christianity, education, and the growing dependence of the people on the central government for a variety of social services have also united the divergent groups. At the same time, the government supports cultural movements emphasizing the value of traditional customs of the major groups.

The extended family is the common basis of social organization. Descent lines can be patrilineal, matrilineal, or both. Patrilineal descent lines predominate on Malaita, Guadalcanal, Makira, and Choiseul. Matrilineal descent lines are common on Santa Isabel and in the Santa Cruz Islands. Land and material wealth are indicators of social status; leadership in the community is conferred to the "big man" -- one who gives the most successful feast -- or by virtue of skills, not heredity.

Melanesian groups have careful delineation of taboos and roles for each sex; the separation of the sexes, however, does not mean subordination of one to the other. The Polynesians, on the other hand, tend to follow a patrilineal system. Social organization is hierarchical and hereditary.

Traditional custom, called "*Kastom*" in Pidgin English, has been used as a rallying point of the indigenous people and government people. An all-purpose ideology that can mean different things to different people, it was first used during the Marching Rule, a Populist political movement begun in Malaita after World War II. For some, "*Kastom*" is a political symbol against incursion of Western religious and economic ideologies; for others, it is used as a symbol of national identity and as a way to legitimize themselves to the common people.

With a 13 percent literacy rate, the Solomons has the lowest in the whole Asia-Pacific region. Only 65 percent of the children get a primary education and only 35 percent go to secondary schools. The 3.1 population growth rate is also alarming.

Economic Conditions

The economy is a mixture of subsistence farming, fishing and some modern activities. In 1985 only 10 percent of the population was in organized employment. The cash economy contributes about 65 percent to the GDP, supplies exports and helps pay for imports and government services. Subsistence economy provides food, housing, and local village services.

The Solomon Islands has underdeveloped mineral resources such as copper, lead, zinc, silver, nickel, cobalt and gold. The forested hills also contain valuable tropical hardwood.

In 1984, the Solomons had a trade surplus for the first time. Income from copra and palm oil was a major contributor.

An incident concerning an American tuna fishing vessel off the coast of Santa Isabel led to an embargo of the sale of fish from the Solomons to the U.S. Fish exports account for a third of the country's export earnings. The country has fishing agreements with the Japanese Taiyo Fishery Company.

History Of Mission

The first Europeans to land in the Solomons and stay for a length of time were a group of Marist Catholic priests who founded a mission on Makira in 1845. The mission failed when many of the priests died because of diseases and attacks by the local population. Two groups of Marist missionaries later came in 1898 and 1899. The group from Fiji, at that time another British colony, settled in South Solomons. The missionaries first stayed in small islands then moved on to Guadacanal, where they won the majority of the people to Catholicism. However, they did not develop indigenous leadership at that time. The other group of Marists, from Samoa, established the mission in Bougainville, North Solomons. Their vigorous training of catechists enabled them to develop quickly a strong indigenous priesthood. Two vicariates formed from these two movements of Catholic missions in the Solomons.

The Anglican mission known as Melanesian Mission operated in New Hebrides (now Vanuatu), Banks, Santa Cruz, and the Solomon Islands in the mid-1800's. George Selwyn, the first Anglican bishop of New Zealand, visited and cultivated friendships with leaders of these areas. He invited these leaders to send young men to train in the Anglican center in Norfolk Island. Later, the Diocese of Melanesia was established in 1861. The training center was moved from Norfolk Island to Siota on Nggela (Central Solomons) in 1919. Anglicans worked with the Nggela and Ysabel people. The Melanesian Brotherhood emerged from the Melanesian mission in

1925. This became the largest and most effective indigenous religious order for men in all of the Pacific Islands at that time. Ini Kopuria founded the group.

Methodists entered Bougainville in 1917. Their main work, however, was centered in Western Solomons, in New Georgia, Villa Lavella, Kolombangara and Choiseul. Their work in educating the local people was considered highly successful.

The South Sea Evangelical Mission started from the work of Florence Young, who ministered to Solomons laborers in Queensland. After the laborers' repatriation, Young followed them and established the missions center in Malaita. This became the largest mission in the island.

Meanwhile, Seventh-day Adventist missionaries from America and Australasia arrived in 1914 and established their work in New Georgia. Their work spread later to Rennell and Bellona Islands in the Western Solomons.

All of these early missions pioneered the establishment of primary education among the people. They also opened hospitals and did medical work in the 1920's and 1930's.

Status Of Christianity

In 1985, more than 95 percent of the population professed to be Christians. About a third of the people belonged to the Church of Melanesia (Anglican); almost 20 percent were Roman Catholics. The South Sea Evangelical Church had about 16 percent of the population, mainly in the eastern and northern islands. The United Church, a union of Methodists and Congregationalists, had 11 percent, particularly in Western Province. Seventh-day Adventists comprised one-tenth of the population, while indigenous and marginal Protestant churches, such as Jehovah's Witnesses (JW), constituted the rest of the Christian community. (NOTE: JW is tabulated in census data as "quasi-Christian"). About 5 percent of the population are tribal religionists, including those who belong to the so-called cargo cults. The tribal religionists live mostly in the isolated interior regions.

There are three major Protestant churches in the Solomon Islands, namely: the South Sea Evangelical Church, United Church, and the Seventh-day Adventist. The three churches together sponsor over 170 primary schools, three secondary schools, four hospitals, one maternity hospital, nine clinics, a vocational school, and various development projects and publications.

NATIONAL CHURCHES

Church of the Province of Melanesia (Anglican)

The Anglican Church was formed as the Province of Melanesia in 1975. Formerly a missionary diocese of the Church of the Province of New Zealand, it was the largest church with 40,000 membership in 1970. It is strongest in the Eastern Islands, Santa Isabel, Malaita, Guadalcanal and San Cristobal.

The church membership includes about 50 percent youth, 25 percent men and 25 percent women. It has five bishops, including the archbishop, and over 300 ministers. Among the 20 missionaries, three are expatriates. The church members come from different ethnic and language groups. English, Pidgin English, and appropriate dialects are used during the worship services. Hymns are found in these different languages. Worship format has long been patterned after the western model, although some indigenized adaptations have occurred.

Local church decisions are made by the congregation, the pastors and deacons. Even though leadership training is given only occasionally, local people assume leadership positions.

The church is affiliated with hospitals and theological colleges, maintaining over 100 primary schools, a secondary school, and a teacher-training college. Many schools have been handed over to the government. Medical and social services institutions include two hospitals, one clinic, a leprosarium, and several community centers.

The church is a member of the Anglican Consultation Council, the Pacific Conference of Churches and the South Pacific Anglican Community.

The church is financially independent as it receives overseas income from land it owns in New Zealand. It provides and maintains all church buildings. Church giving for missionary and social work ranges from one to five percent of its annual budget. Occasionally, the church participates in government-promoted programs. Among its ministries are those in Christian citizenship and responsibility training. Individual churches support denominational social ministries.

Roman Catholic Church

Marist priests first established a mission in the Solomons in 1845. They failed due to hostility and hardships. In 1897, a prefecture was established which was elevated to vicariate in 1912. Since 1962, it has been divided into two dioceses: the Diocese of Auki and the Diocese of Honiara. The church has approximately 39,000 adherents composed of 35 percent youth, 32 percent women and 33 percent men, with members coming from different language and ethnic groups. Church membership is increasing mainly due to new births; new converts comprise about nine percent of the members. Church attendance is fairly regular.

The Archdiocese of Honiara has 19 priests, while Auki has eight. Seventeen of the priests are missionaries and ten are nationals. Catechists number 325. Pope John Paul II visited the Solomon Islands in 1984.

The church runs five hospitals, five primary schools, one secondary school and a training center for local Sisters. The church provides buildings for itself, sometimes with a subsidy from the government. About 60 percent of the churches' budget comes from overseas assistance. Allocation for missionary and social work ranges from five to ten percent of the churches' income. Church services during the Mass are in English, with some hymns in the local language.

Among the issues identified by the church as crucial and needing to be addressed are divorce, youth problems, unemployment, movement of people to urban areas, and loss of traditional values.

South Sea Evangelical Church (SSEC)

The South Sea Evangelical Mission founded the South Sea Evangelical Church in the Solomon Islands. Historically, it originated from the mission to the islanders who were in Queensland, Australia as sugar plantation workers in 1882. The Queensland Kanaka Mission of Australia established an outreach mission in Malaita in 1904. This mission became known as the South Sea Evangelical Mission. The South Sea Evangelical Church was established in 1964 and became fully independent in 1975.

The SSEC has 349 churches, its membership of 36,000 being composed of 30 percent youth, 35 percent women and 35 percent men. Up to 95 percent of the church members attend church services regularly, while 90 percent of the children go to Sunday school. A weekly house and Bible fellowship is conducted on weekdays. The membership continues to grow, as revival experiences empower the church through outreach work and open-air crusades. Church worship services, hymns and literature are in the local language, English or Pidgin English.

The church has 414 pastors and missionaries. Twenty-six expatriate missionaries are with SSEC, some of whom serve as teachers, agriculturalists, and pastor trainers. National workers number 380; 12 are ordained ministers, the rest are lay pastors. Part-time workers include many village pastors. Church leadership both local and central is in the hands of nationals. Church discipline is the responsibility of the local church itself.

The SSEC has one clinic, one tertiary school, one theological college, six Bible schools and one Bible vocational institute. Soon to be established are a new theological college, Bible school and three Bible vocational institutes. The Church is a member of the Evangelical Alliance of the South Pacific.

Among the Christian activities led by organizations within the church are pastoral training, Bible schooling, evangelism and vocational training. Singing and evangelistic teams have done outreach work in Papua New Guinea and Vanuatu in seven open-air crusades.

While an independent church, SSEC still receives some financial assistance from the South Sea Evangelical Mission body in Australia. About 10 percent of its budget comes from overseas and 90 percent from the Solomon Island churches. From 5 to 10 percent of the church budget goes to missionary and social work.

The SSEC identified the following as crucial issues facing the church: alcoholism, divorce, youth problems, movement of people to towns and the need for evangelism. The church has also been teaching Christian citizenship and responsibility in the different communities, with local churches supporting this denominational social ministry.

The United Church

The United Church in the Solomon Islands is part of the United Church of Papua New Guinea (see section on "National Churches" under Papua New Guinea in this same chapter).

The United Church is a union of Methodist and Congregationalists. It is found in all parts of the Solomons but it is strongest in the Western Island Province. It has 400 churches with 20,000 members. Sixty percent of the members are adults while 40 percent are comprised of young people. About 60 percent of the members attend church regularly; 20 percent of the children attend Sunday schools; and 30 percent of the membership are involved in mid-week Bible fellowship. Church membership is said to be on the rise because of church confirmation classes and renewal meetings.

The church has 38 ministers, 30 of whom are nationals. The expatriate ministers teach in Bible schools and act as advisors in the national churches. Nationals occupy leadership positions.

The church has 11 primary schools, one hospital, and three clinics. It also operates a theological college and Bible colleges. Leadership training among the workers has been conducted. Local and national church leadership is indigenous.

Among the concerns of the church are evangelism, discipleship, unemployment among the people, heavy migration to towns, and loss of traditional values.

The church receives about 30 percent of its budget from overseas and 70 percent from within the national church. About 20 percent of its annual budget goes to missionary and social work. The United Church began its own mission field in the early 1980's in Guadalcanal.

The church is an affiliate member of the Solomon Islands Christian Association (SICA), the Melanesia Council of Churches, and the World Council of Churches.

Seventh-day Adventist

The Seventh-day Adventist (SDA) work in the Solomons began in 1914. Rev. G. E. Jones started the work among the Western Islanders, which then spread in the islands through the national missionaries. They are present at Rennell and Bellona while about 9 percent of their work is concentrated in New Georgia.

The SDA has 120 churches with a membership of 12,000. Its membership consists of 80 percent youth, 10 percent men and 10 percent women. Up to 90 percent of the members attend Sabbath regularly, and between 65 percent and 80 percent of the children go to Sabbath schools. On mid-week days, about 50 percent of the church members are involved in Bible studies or house fellowship. New members are gained through vigorous evangelistic programs, while some old members drop out.

The SDA church has 339 pastors, ministers, and missionaries. Church leadership is basically in the hands of the nationals, while the expatriates work in special areas as advisers, administrators and teachers. Evangelists and pastors also serve as part-time church workers.

The SDA works with one hospital, 45 primary schools, and a lay training school in Malaita. It uses theological colleges and Bible schools of other denominations in Papua New Guinea.

The worldwide SDA church contributes 30 percent of its budget to the national church in the Solomons. Seventy percent comes from within the Islands' SDA churches. All its buildings are provided by the church, with some subsidies from the worldwide church. Missionary and social work is funded by the Western Pacific SDA body and the Solomon Island Church Administration. Its current annual budget is $350,000. The church has a regular plan for social ministry and it often participates in government-promoted programs with discretion. The local church often supports the denominational social ministry.

The SDA Church of Solomon Islands is a direct member of the worldwide Seventh-day Adventist Church body. It is an observer in the Solomon Island Christian Association.

Among the issues confronting the church are evangelism, discipleship, youth problems, movement of people to towns, and unemployment problems. The church started its own mission field in the early 1980's. Bible students, pastors, and trainees serve as missionaries.

Assemblies of God

In 1971 Fijian missionaries established The Assemblies of God church in the Solomons. It has about 1,000 members today, composed of 50 percent youth, 30 percent women and 20 percent men, with 14 churches. About 80 percent of the members attend Sunday church services regularly, with 25 percent of the children going to Sunday schools. About 30 percent are also involved in mid-week Bible studies and home fellowship. Church membership is increasing, mainly due to continuous evangelistic programs, youth activities, and leadership training. There is still a great lack of trained national leaders to fill responsible positions.

Pidgin English and the local language are used in most of the activities in the church with hymns sung in English.

The church has 14 pastors with six assistants, and 15 ministers, two of whom are missionaries from the United States. Missionaries serve as advisors and directors of correspondence training and as Bible school teachers. Three pastors and two evangelists serve as part-time church workers.

The Assemblies of God is affiliated with a Bible college in Honiara. The church maintains contact with all Assemblies of God bodies throughout the world. It is a direct member of the worldwide Assemblies of God body, and of the Evangelical Alliance of the South Pacific.

The church's total budget comes from the churches in the islands. About 6 percent of its income is devoted to missionary and social work, with a budget in 1984 of $16,000.

Among its major activities and programs are the following: evangelistic outreach work, Bible school, leadership courses with an emphasis on good citizenship.

INTERDENOMINATIONAL AGENCIES

The Solomon Islands Christian Association is the major interdenominational body in the islands. Its members include the Anglican, Roman Catholic, and United Churches. The Solomon Islands

Region of the United Church is also a member of the Melanesian Council of Churches.

CHRISTIAN ACTIVITIES

Education

The Anglican and Catholic churches pioneered in establishing schools in the islands at the end of the 19th century. Today, major denominations operate their own schools at different levels, including Bible schools and a theological college. (See major churches above for descriptions of their educational programs.)

Broadcasting

Radio broadcast time is given by the government to the different churches. This time is shared, as the churches alternate their broadcast time. On Sunday, there is a 15-minute devotional, 30 minutes of hymn singing, and 15 minute news program. Each weekday morning there is a five-minute devotional. The Christian Broadcasting Service in Banz, Papua New Guinea, produces materials for broadcasting in the Solomon Islands. The Roman Catholic Church is a member of the regional broadcast group called UNDA.

VANUATU

Profile

NATURAL FEATURES: **Land area:** 12,189 sq. km. A chain of several islands, the most important being Espiritu Santo, and about 70 small islands. The large islands are mountainous; the smaller islands are coral atolls; all are within the hurricane zone.

CAPITAL: Port Vila on Efate Island.

POPULATION: 130,000 (1985). Vanuatuans of Melanesian descent -- 92 percent; Non-Vanuatuans (Europeans, Vietnamese, Chinese, and other Pacific Islanders) -- 8.0 percent. **Annual growth rate:** 4.2 percent (1975/80). **Urban:** 18 percent.

RELIGION: **Christians:** 84 percent. **"Cargo Cults:"** 12 percent. **Animist:** 4 percent.

LANGUAGE AND LITERACY: Bislama (Ni-Vanuatu Pidgin), French, English. Over 100 others. **Adult literacy:** 60 percent.

GOVERNMENT: Parliamentary form; President is head of state. **Executive:** Prime Minister. **Legislative:** 39-member Parliament. **Judicial:** Supreme Court with Chief Justice and three judges. National Council of Chiefs is advisory to the government on matters of culture and tradition.

ECONOMY: Per capita GDP: (1979) US $.48. **Main industries:** copra, frozen fish, seafoods, beef, some tourism, and previously, manganese mining. Most people are engaged in subsistence agriculture.

Historical Background

The Western World first became aware of Vanuatu in the early 17th century through the writings of the Spanish explorer, De Quiros. In 1774, Captain Cook charted Vanuatu, then the New Hebrides, opening up the area to joint colonization by France and Britain. In 1914, the two countries signed a protocol to establish a condominium.

The two colonial powers established dual administrative systems in education, health services, immigration, and national security. This has created a number of difficulties for the newly independent government. The task is further complicated by traditional tribal customs and a firmly established land tenure system.

People Groups

The original inhabitants are Melanesians, who speak over 100 indigenous languages. Among the population of Vanuatu are numerous people groups, most of whom are Christian. Outsiders include Europeans (primarily French), Polynesians, Micronesians from Kiribati, Fijians, and a very small populations of Vietnamese and Chinese.

Ni-Vanuatu, the people of Vanuatu, have long lived in small villages isolated from one another by jungles or oceans. Most have lived self-sufficiently and found little need to communicate with distant, sometimes hostile neighbors.

Urbanization has been concentrated in Port Vila and Espiritu Santo. Approximately 18 percent of the population can now be classified as urban.

Socio-Political Conditions

There is no uniform culture in Vanuatu. Languages, dances, songs, games, food, and agricultural practices vary from village to village, from family to family. Because of the numerous (over 110) spoken languages, *Bislama*, a Pidgin English, serves as the lingua franca.

About 50 percent of the total population is under 15 years of age. The smaller islands are the more densely populated; in other areas communal ownership of the land tends to limit full utilization.

A British-French condominium existed in Vanuatu until independence in 1980. The Vanua'aku Party, led by Father Walter Lini, an Anglican priest, played an important role in the struggle for independence. Lini became the country's first prime minister, a position which he still holds. Vanuatu has been active politically and diplomatically in its pursuit of a non-aligned status.

Economic Conditions

The climate and soil of Vanuatu are favorable for the development of agriculture and livestock husbandry; however, only copra has been exploited as an important cash crop. Timber is available in the forests. Vanuatu has no significant mineral resources. Manganese deposits, which were formerly mined, have now been depleted. There are abundant marine resources in the country's 200-mile exclusive economic zone offshore, but except for a Japanese frozen fish plant at Palakula, there is no large-scale development of fisheries. Fishing rights have been negotiated by USSR with the Vanuatu government.

History Of Missions

Christianity, in the form of Protestantism, was established in Vanuatu nearly a century and a half ago with the arrival of the first missionaries. Conversions were widespread, although the most significant increases came during the years after 1930 through the work of indigenous Christian evangelists, helped by resident European missionaries.

The Presbyterian Church of Vanuatu, the largest denomination, traces its growth to the movement of local and foreign missionaries in the 1850's northward from the southernmost island of Aneityum to the more populous islands in the central part of the chain. From the 1870's to the 1920's, Presbyterian-trained evangelists were sent in a steady stream from the island of Nguna, north of Port Vila, the present capital, to the north-central islands, where most Presbyterians are found today.

Meanwhile, Anglican mission enclaves on Banks and Torres Islands in the north served as a base for the southward spread of the Anglican Church of Melanesia. There was little encroachment of the Anglicans and Presbyterians on each other's territory, as the two churches continued to support the ideal of denominational comity.

Status Of Christianity

Vanuatu's independence grew out of a desire to create a national community based on Christian principles. This relationship between nationalism and Christianity continues to be a dominant concern both for government leaders and for church people. Ordained clergy led the independence movement and continue to hold key positions in government. Vanuatu remains a nation with an extremely high proportion of practicing Christian adherence and one in which Christianity plays a major part in the life of the people.

NATIONAL CHURCHES

The major churches in Vanuatu include:

DENOMINATION	% OF POPULATION	ADHERENCE
Presbyterian Church	40	45,000
Roman Catholic	16	18,000
Anglican Church	14	16,000
Churches of Christ	5	3,500
Apostolic Church	1	1,000
Seventh Day Adventists	5	4,000
Assemblies of God	2	2,000
Free-Evangelical	1	1,500

In addition to these nine churches shown in the table, there are a number of small Christian groups within the country. Non-Christian groups include Jehovah's Witnesses, Baha'is, and Animists. There are several forms of "Cargo Cults" with about 14,000 adherents.

Presbyterian Church

About 40 percent of the Vanuatu population adheres to the Presbyterian Church. The membership is found throughout the islands, especially in those areas where the Presbyterian missions have operated since the 1800's. Originally, separate Presbyterian mission agencies sent missionaries to Vanuatu from New Zealand, New South Wales, Victoria, and Tasmania. A mission of note is the John Paton Fund operated out of Britain. Paton was a renowned and gifted writer-missionary in Vanuatu. Other missionaries came from Scotland, Canada, and South Australia. Their work was difficult and slow.

The Presbyterians worked in the southern islands. By the 20th century, all these islands, except Tanna, were Christianized. Their mission then extended to the north where the population was larger -- in Santo, Malekula, and Ambrym. The missionaries tended to be strict with the local people; they were slow in developing indigenous ministers at the beginning.

Throughout their history in Vanuatu, the Presbyterian missions were heavily involved in the poltical development of the country. In 1870-1880, they tried to encourage Great Britain and Australia to assume control of the country, not France. When the British-French condominium was signed in 1906, the missionaries worked for the betterment of the working conditions of laborers in the plantations.

By 1948, the Presbyterian Church of New Hebrides was inaugurated. The foreign missionaries became advisors to the governing body, the General Assembly. In 1970, the Presbyterian Church acted as moderator and executive officer of the Synod in Vanuatu. The church also participated vigorously in the independence movement in Vanuatu in the 1970's.

The church ministries include extensive educational and medical work. The missions originated the establishment of primary schools in the villages. Today, the church still runs secondary schools.

Roman Catholic Church

The Roman Catholic Church in Vanuatu, comprising 16 percent of the population, has also seen rapid growth in this century, after a comparatively late start. The first prefecture was not established in the islands until 1901. Thereafter, Roman Catholic growth went hand in hand with the expansion of French influence under the joint British-French sovereignty. There have been attempts to foster harmonious Protestant-Catholic relations dating back to the mid-1960's; the church is a full member of the Vanuatu Christian Council.

The Columban Mission succeeded the Marist fathers in their work on Tanna. (Tanna is the island de-Christianized by the John Frum "Cargo Cult," which is still strong there today.) The Columban fathers found most of the ground work done already with church buildings and two parishes and a strong community with a legacy of goodwill. The Columban Mission was sent by the Fiji church as missionary outreach to Vanuatu. Where they operate in Tanna, the mission tries to bridge "custom belief" in Christian faith.

Many of the Christians there are still practicing "custom beliefs," adhering mainly to animism and mysterious beliefs. The people believe in sacred stones which they claim God uses to make their yams and vegetables grow. It is also part of the "custom belief" that every person has special charisma, some for healing or prophesy, others with power to control nature.

The Catholic school system works in cooperation with the public school system. They both use the same text books, and the government pays the teachers' salaries. Each Catholic school is controlled locally by a School Committee just as are the public schools. Teachers are appointed to the various mission schools after consultation between the Ministry of Education and the Catholic Education Secretary. Emphasis is on the missions' prayer services and religious instructions. Four new areas have opened up in the area since 1980. Two are fully eucharistic communities.

Church of Melanesia (Anglican)

This church is the product of the earlier work of the Melanesian Mission that also operated in the Solomon Islands. It originally started at the Banks Group in the north. In its comity agreement with the Presbyterians in 1881, the mission expanded in three areas: Aoba, Maewo, and Pentecost.

Today, the church has its own bishop and accounts for a 14 percent membership among the Ni-Vanuatus. It continues to be linked with the wider Province of Melanesia. It has also strong education and medical ministries in some parts of the islands.

Churches of Christ

This church began in the north-central island of Pentecost, through the efforts of a recruited Vanuatuan laborer, who had been converted while working in the sugarcane fields of Australia. He became an evangelist upon his return home at the turn of the century. Foreign missionaries of the Churches of Christ played a key role as evangelists during the 1920's and 1930's, but local leadership has continued to be influential in the denomination.

As a Pentecostal body without an extensive central organization, these churches tend to be independent and have strong Ni-Vanuatu leadership. About 5 percent of the population belongs to this church.

Others

The Seventh-day Adventist Church (SDA) and the small Assemblies of God Church have undergone significant rapid growth in recent years. The SDA has a long history of contact in Vanuatu and claims five percent membership among the population.

CHRISTIAN ACTIVITIES

Scripture and Bible Translation

Bible translation is an important task facing the major churches in Vanuatu. The complete Bible has been translated into only two indigenous languages. The New Testament is available in Tanna and Futuna. World Bible Translation (WBT) teams are presently involved in nine projects. The Bible Society in the South Pacific, together with the Vanuatu Christian Council is currently translating the whole Bible in *Bislama*. The New Testament has been completed and is now in use.

Youth Ministry

Campus Crusade for Christ works with students of high school age. The organization reports that Pacific youth demonstrate a great hunger for Christ. Campus Crusade works in several high schools, the newest of which is the Matevulu School on Espiritu Santo.

MAJOR CONCERNS

One of the major concerns of the church in Vanuatu at both the local and the national level is the trend toward religious pluralism and ways of dealing with it. Within the nation, the ideal of one village, one church still remains strong, and there is a strong sentiment to limit religious freedom to those groups willing to cooperate in the Vanuatu Christian Council.

A second concern is that worldly values are replacing the more traditional Christian values in Vanuatu society. Many church people see a rise of secular influences in such things as the upsurge in tourism and the new opportunities for advanced university education. At the same time, however, both the church leaders and many church members want to see their nation and their local villages gain the benefits promised by modern development, provided that that these are shared fairly in a Christian manner.

With the coming of independence, national reconciliation was a major priority. The Ni-Vanuatuans found that it was not an easy task to establish a new national government after 80 years of condominium rule. However, by building on a strong base of Christianity and the widely shared Melanesian culture, the authority of the national government has been accepted in virtually every part of Vanuatu.

Unreached People Groups

Among the Melanesian population, there has been a small, but significant movement away from Christianity toward traditional or syncretic practices in Vanuatu. The best known movement is a cargo cult, the **John Frum movement**. A second, smaller movement is the **Nagramel movement**, found on Espiritu Santo. Both movements draw persons together into a cohesive whole in such a way that a strong sense of identity is created. The process produces distinct people groups in need of evangelization. Thus far, the churches on Vanuatu have not been able to mount an effective evangelism program.

Cargo Cults and the reversion to paganism that they represent have posed major problems in Vanuatu during the past 40 years. The more significant indigenous syncretic religion, the John Frum movement, is located chiefly in the once predominantly Presbyterian island of Tanna in the south. This cult grew during World War II when the islanders were overwhelmed by the amount of material possessions they saw arriving with the Allied soldiers. The much smaller syncretic cargo cult, called the Nagramel movement, attracted international attention when it was manipulated into attempted secession by foreign adventurers at the time of Vanuatu's independence.

Europeans make up about 5 percent of the population, all professing Christianity. The degree to which they are practicing Christians is not known.

The small **Vietnamese and Chinese populations** do not have significant percentages of Christians among them. No known evangelistic outreach exists.

Chapter Four: *Micronesia:*

Federated States of Micronesia --
Yap, Truk, Pohnpei, Kosrae

Guam
Kiribati
Marshall Islands
Northern Mariana Islands
Republic of Belau (Palau)

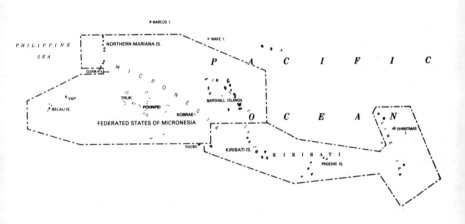

FEDERATED STATES OF MICRONESIA

Profile

NATURAL FEATURES: The islands of Truk, Pohnpei, Yap, and Kosrae are volcanic types of islands. Soil supports all types of tropical plants. Fish and marine life abound in the waters around the islands.

CAPITAL: Kolonia on Pohnpei. **Population:** 5,549 (1980).

POPULATION: 76,100 (1980 est). **People groups:** Micronesians, Polynesians, Filipinos, American expatriates. Truk: 37,488; Pohnpei (formerly Ponape): 22,081; Yap: 8,100; Kosrae: 5,491.

RELIGION: Christians: 90 percent. **Others:** Jehovah's Witnesses, Church of Jesus Christ of Latter-Day Saints (Mormons).

LANGUAGES: Yapese, Ulithian, Woleaian, Trukese, Pohnpeian, and Kosrean, all Malayo-Polynesian languages. English is the official language.

GOVERNMENT: Self-governing Federated States in "Free Association" with the United States. **Executive:** President. **Legislative:** Senate. **Judiciary:** Supreme and lower courts.

ECONOMY: Major funding comes from the United States. **Main industries:** agriculture and fishing. **Major exports:** coconut products, fish, fruits and vegetables.

Historical Background

Recent archaeological evidence indicates that some islands in this group have been inhabited since 2000 B.C. Initial settlements appear to have been made by migrants from Southeast Asia. The diggings are still in progress and not all of the findings have been analyzed. The major part of this work is being done on Yap, Pohnpei, and Nukuoro.

The first European visitors were probably those sailing with the Portuguese explorers. In 1525, they found themselves on what we now believe are Yap and Ulithi.

SPANISH INFLUENCES

Another significant visit was by the Spanish in 1686. Francisco Lazeano was blown off course on his voyage to the Philippine Islands. This event resulted in the naming of the island of Yap "La Carolina" after the Spanish King Charles II. In time, the title of the Carolines was given to the whole group.

In the 18th century, Spain had the most "interests" in the Carolines. No official declaration of the Islands' political status vis-a-vis Spain was made at that time. Gradually, other European states came to the Islands. British contacts were made in the 1790's when ships sailed through from Australia on their way to China. German trading ships also came to the area.

In the late 19th century, Britain and Germany challenged Spain's claim to the Carolines. The issue was finally submitted to Pope Leo XIII for arbitration. In 1885, he decided in favor of Spain, which took immediate steps to establish a governing presence in the Caroline Islands. Germany also received trading, fishing, and refueling rights in the Pope's decision.

GERMAN ADMINISTRATION

The Islands came under German administration after Spain's 1898 defeat in the Spanish-American War. World War I brought Japanese occupation to the area in 1914; this occupation was both military and civilian. After the League of Nations gave Japan a mandate to rule in 1921, they brought in agricultural, health, and infrastructure improvements. During World War II, the area was used primarily as fortifications from which to fight the war in the Pacific.

UNITED STATES TRUSTEESHIP

When the war ended, the United Nations declared the Caroline Islands part of the Trust Territory of the Pacific Islands. They were thus placed under the jurisdiction of the United States.

The United States' trusteeship of the islands accelerated in the 1960's and 1970's to bring about economic development with the stated purpose of developing self-sufficiency in the area. The political status is also evolving into a more independent one with the Islands now in "Free Association" with the United States since the signing of the 1982 "Compact."

People Groups

The people of the Federated States of Micronesia are classified as Micronesians despite distinct historical and cultural differences among the islander groups. Those of the outlying islands of Kapin-gamarangi and Nukuoro in Pohnpei are considered Polynesians. In addition, small populations of Filipinos and other expatriates live in the Federated States of Micronesia.

The people groups are defined as much by geography as by separate languages and cultures. Yet new people groups are emerging in the midst of larger groups. An example of this is the group of people who can be described as pan-Micronesian. The American era ushered in this formation since people now work for the civil government and move frequently from island to island in response to job changes. These people associate primarily with other civil service employees. They are educated in the American schools and they identify with each other as fellow members of this group.

Socio-Political Conditions

Original social forms which existed before European intervention are still maintained in certain areas with little modification. A matrilineal structure which was well developed on Kosrae has since been replaced by a patrilineal system. This was transmitted and expanded by the Yapese, who created an "empire-like" structure based upon this form. Old patterns are still in evidence on all the islands except the outlying, Kapingamarangi and Nukuoro.

Traditional patterns and lifestyles are in direct conflict with new ones introduced or superimposed by contact with the United States. Although improved agriculture, aquaculture, health and education are now available, so are fast foods, beer, and television. An over-dependency on non-local products and lifestyles are seen as dangerous to plans for greater self-sufficiency in this area.

The capital city of the Federated States of Micronesia is Kolonia on the island of Pohnpei. However, work has begun to rebuild the government offices on a new site southwest of the city. The total cost of $5 million will be paid by the United States.

The Federated States of Micronesia are in an era of transition. In 1979 the Caroline Island districts of Yap, Truk, Pohnpei, and Kosrae became the self-governing Federated States of Micronesia, thus forming a new relationship with the United States. The United States' Trusteeship has not been totally terminated but is being gradually diminished, as the new Island State takes on more responsibility for its own governance. The trusteeship should end in late 1986.

The Compact of Free Association was signed in 1982; this sent United Nations observers to oversee a popular vote concerning the acceptance of the new status between these Islands and the United States. It would grant full responsibility for the State's internal governing and most external relations as well. Certain economic assistance services and programs would be given by the United States in exchange for a guarantee that the Islands would not be used militarily by any other nation.

Currently, the Federated States of Micronesia's government consists of a President and Vice President, both elected from among the four State Senators elected for four years. There are ten other State Senators elected for two years each. The National Judicial Branch is a Supreme Court led by the Chief Justice.

Economic Conditions

The United States government provides over 90 percent of the money needed to meet the budget of the Federated States of Micronesia (F.S.M.) government. It employs an estimated 60 to 70 percent of the total wage earners of the Federated States of Micronesia.

Other workers on the islands are involved in farming, copra production, fishing, and local handicrafts. Few of these positions result in actual wages.

The major exports from these islands include coconut products, fish, fruit, and vegetables.

Barter and local ancient currencies (like the stone money of Yap) are still used, along with U.S. dollars. The value of stone currency and other similar forms of currency is determined by its age and history. One of the most highly-valued modern items for barter is American beer.

Both agriculture and aquaculture-development activities are planned by the government. Tourism is also a growing source of income. Visitors come mostly from the U.S. and Japan.

History Of Missions

ROMAN CATHOLIC MISSIONS

The 1885 Papal decision that the Caroline Islands belonged to Spain moved the Catholic Church to install Spanish Capuchins as representatives of the Spanish church. But in 1898, when Germany took over the Islands, the church replaced them with Germans of the Minor Capuchin Order.

Although the spread of the church was not rapid, the Caroline Islands vicariate was established in 1905. Six years later, it was extended to include the Mariana Islands.

The American branch of the Society of Jesus took over from the Spanish Jesuits after World War II, and was later joined by the Maryknoll and Mercedarian Sisters.

The Marianas were separated from the vicariate in 1946; two years later, the area was entrusted to the New York Province of the Society of Jesus. Early in 1980, it was elevated to a diocese, the Diocese of Caroline-Marshall Islands.

Rev. Francis Hezel, Director of the Micronesian Seminar for the Catholic Church, is currently writing the complete histories of the

100 years of the Catholic Church on Yap, Pohnpei, and Truk. He had already completed the first two histories in early 1986.

ABCFM/HAWAIIAN MISSIONARIES

The first group of Protestant missionaries arrived in the island group in 1852. The plan for this first outreach was to form a partnership of missionaries from the American Board of Commissioners for Foreign Missions (Boston) and from among the pastors of the Hawaiian church.

Over the next years both Hawaiian and New England missionaries met with successes and defeats -- the successes of lives won for the Kingdom, and the defeats of ill health and even death of many of their numbers.

Most of the early mission work was carried out by resident missionaries on the Islands of Pohnpei and Kosrae. Ill health and cultural conflict with the New England missionaries prevented the Hawaiian missionaries from easing the cultural impact of the New Englanders' gospel message. No attempt was made to incorporate local forms of worship or music. However, translation of the Bible was a priority with the New England missionaries.

After 12 years of work, the two "pillars" of the mission work in the Carolines, Albert Sturges (on Pohnpei) and Benjamin Snow (on Kosrae) had baptized 157 people. After 22 years of outside mission presence, the Church on Pohnpei became a "sending church." Its first missionaries went to the Mortlock Islands in the Truk group of Islands, west of Pohnpei.

LIEBENZELL MISSION/JAPANESE MISSION

German administration came to the Islands after Spain's defeat in 1898, and the missions took on a more German flavor. The American missionaries by mutual agreement turned over their work on Truk and the islands farther west to the Liebenzell Mission; the Americans continued to lead the work on Kosrae, Pohnpei and half of Truk.

Another shift of governing power under the League of Nations mandate naming Japan as protector of the area caused a return of the American missionaries. Also, through the intervention of the Pope, the Spanish Society of Jesus took over from the Capuchins of Germany. The Protestant Church of Japan also sent missionaries to

Pohnpei and Truk. Liebenzell missionaries returned to help the Japanese outreach to Belau after 1927.

The pre-World War II years saw a significant change in the attitudes of Japan toward the contribution of the Church in Micronesia. More and more, the resources of the Islands were dedicated to preparing Japan to make war. These "resources" included the people themselves, who were often used as laborers to build fortifications.

The Japanese missionaries were called back to Japan, and once war broke out, American missionaries were also recalled. Spanish and German missionaries were allowed to stay but many were killed or died from mistreatment; the continuation of an organized mission effort was impossible.

Due to the involvement of Americans in this area during World War II and after the U.S. Trusteeship was established by the U.N., American missions to Micronesia increased significantly after 1945. The American branch of Liebenzell devoted itself to the western part of the Carolines, and the American Board of Commissioners for Foreign Missions took responsibility for the eastern islands.

Status Of Christianity

More than 90 percent of the population of the Federated States of Micronesia profess Christianity. There remains, however, a strong undercurrent of influence from their original, indigenous religions, which includes both reliance upon magicians and on deceased family members for protection from spirits and the dangers of daily life.

Nominalism is also believed to be a problem among the Christians of this society, Christianized over 100 years ago.

ROMAN CATHOLIC CHURCH

The Caroline-Marshall Islands Diocese had 1,804 infant baptisms and 177 converts, for a total of 1,981 baptisms in 1984. The total Catholic population of the Diocese of Caroline-Marshall Islands was 46,912 as of early 1986.

In 1984, there were 7,128 students under Catholic instruction, and a total of 141 Catholic teachers in the diocese.

The five men and women's religious communities - Society of Jesus, Maryknoll Sisters, Mercedarian Missionaries, School Sisters of Notre Dame, Sisters of Mary -- had a total of 46 representatives in the Caroline-Marshall Islands Diocese. Thirty-six of these are missionaries from the United States.

PROTESTANT CHURCHES

The Protestant Church of East Truk and the United Church of Christ in Pohnpei are both churches originating from the American Board of Commissioners for Foreign Missions, now the United Church Board. The United Church of Christ in Pohnpei, although the older of the two (begun in 1852), had only 10,000 affiliates, while the Protestant Church of East Truk (begun in 1885) had 15,000 in 1982.

A relative "late comer" to the area, the Assemblies of God began its work in Micronesia in 1960. The work on Pohnpei and Truk consisted of eight missionaries, five credentialed ministers and two lay workers in 1984-85. These laborers had produced churches and three outstations attended by 142 baptized members and 304 "other believers" as of 1985.

Church Activities

MISSION GROUPS

Today, there are seven foreign missionaries as well as 76 indigenous pastors, evangelists and "Bible women" and the Micronesian Institute of Biblical Studies on Truk is also run by Liebenzell.

Yap Islands have five long-term foreign missionaries from Liebenzell Mission. In 1982, there were 2,000 affiliated participants in the Protestant Church in the Caroline Islands established by this mission.

BROADCASTING

Both Catholic and Protestant broadcasting is done in the area. Yap, Truk, and Ponape's government stations give free time for religious broadcasting. Roman Catholic programming of educational and religious content is heard over those stations. The FEBC programs, broadcast since 1977 from Saipan in the Mariana Islands, are received in the Federated States of Micronesia.

The Bible Society of Micronesia was officially incorporated in 1983, although the local office was formed in 1971.

A recent accomplishment in the Federated States of Micronesia was a translation workshop conducted on Yap through the United Bible Society. The translation of the Old Testament into Yapese is nearing completion. Bible translations into Pohnpeian and Trukese have been completed by local and missionary translators.

Thus far, Bible and scripture distribution has been a responsibility of the local church. The geographic constraints of the area make distribution slow.

Other Religions

Truk and Pohnpei also had three active congregations of Jehovah's Witnesses; about 1,000 individuals were listed as "Memorial Attenders" in the January 1985 worldwide report.

The Church of Jesus Christ of Latter-Day Saints (Mormons) listed their total membership in the F.S.M. as 838.

GUAM

Profile

NATURAL FEATURES: Land area: 549 sq. km. Island is of volcanic origin, with coral and limestone plateaus; the southern part is hilly. **Highest elevation:** Mount Lamlam. **Natural Harbor:** Apra Harbor, where U.S. Naval Base is located.

CAPITAL: Agana. **Population:** 106,000.

POPULATION: 112,000 (1982 est.). Approximately, 22,000 - military personnel and dependents of U.S. Defense Department. **Ethnic groups:** Chamorros (48 percent), Filipinos (20 percent), Caucasian (24 percent). **Other cultural influences:** Japan, Korea, China, Mexico, Polynesia and Micronesia. **Urban pop.:** 40 percent.

RELIGION: Christians: 97 percent. Roman Catholic - 93 percent. **Other denominations:** Episcopalian, Baptist, Seventh-day Adventists. **Others:** Jewish, Church of Jesus Christ of Latter-Day Saints (Mormons), Baha'is, and Jehovah's Witnesses.

LANGUAGES: English, Chamorro, Japanese, Filipino.

GOVERNMENT: Unincorporated territory of the United States; Guamanians are U.S. citizens but do not vote in national elections. **Executive:** Governor. **Legislative:** Unicameral Legislature with 21 elected Senators. **Judiciary:** District and Superior Courts with rights of appeals in the U.S. Supreme Court.

ECONOMY: GNP per capita: (1980) US $7,200. Main revenues come from the military base -- Air Force and Navy. **Main industries:** manufacturing and tourism. **Major exports:** fruits, vegetables, and fish.

Historical Background

Evidence of the original Guamanian people date back to 1320 B.C. Both a pre-Latte and a Latte culture existed. (See Northern Mariana Islands section of this book for further information on Latte culture.)

The Chamorros indigenous to Guam were living in a matrilineally-organized culture, with established hierarchies of nobles, bourgeois, and commoners when Magellan led the first Spanish expedition there, in 1521.

Guam was officially declared a possession of Spain in 1565 by Miguel Lopez de Legaspi. In the 17th century, it came to be a regular stop on the Spanish route between Mexico and the Philippines. Almost simultaneously with this increased interest by the Spanish, the Chamorros attempted to rid themselves of the Spanish. After 35,000 Chamorros were killed and, after years of warfare, the remaining 5,000 were finally brought into submission under Spanish rule.

From 1695 to 1898, Guam continued as a possession of Spain. When the Spanish-American war was won by the United States, Spain turned the Island over to the U.S. It has been a part of the U.S. ever since, except for approximately 2-1/2 years during World War II, when it was occupied by the Japanese military.

A U.S. Navy Administration governed the Island from 1946 to 1950, when an Organic Act incorporated Guam as a U.S. Territory. All inhabitants became American citizens.

People Groups

Guam's population is ethnically and socially heterogeneous. The largest people group is the Chamorro, or Guamanian (48 percent). The definition of being Chamorro is difficult to establish on the basis of language use, cultural values or behavior. Legally, anyone resident in Guam prior to 1944 is a Chamorro. The second major sub-population is made up by the 24 percent of the population which is United States military personnel or dependents. Filipinos make up 20 percent of the population and are forming a fast growing, cohesive community. Other populations are foreign workers, predominantly Korean.

Guam is one of the most heavily urbanized areas of the South Pacific. Approximately 40 percent of the Guamanian population lived in urban areas in 1980; most are found in and around Agana. Adding to the effects of urbanization is the heavy tourist industry, which has created thousands of jobs. These forces, along with the continued presence of a large United States military body, act to cause new social and cultural groupings. This has not been studied from the perspective of people groups. Possible people groups of importance, however, include the urban work force, the youth subculture centered on surfing, types of music, and possible drug use and the large numbers of tourists that annually pass through Guam.

Socio-Political Conditions

Guam is officially an unincorporated Territory of the United States. The Organic Act of Guam enacted in 1950, and since amended, defines this interrelationship. However, there are indications that this may change. In 1982, a popular vote made it clear that the majority wish to reform Guam into a Commonwealth. Negotiations are in progress.

Until further decisions are made, however, the current form of government includes a popularly-elected governor, a 21-member unicameral legislature, and a District Court, whose judge is appointed by the United States president.

The close relationship of Guam with the United States government has been both positive and negative. Although its population has U.S. citizenship, the U.S. Federal regulations governing its communications systems, shipping and immigration have not always been consistent. The FCC (Federal Communications Commission) treats Guam as a "foreign country;" the Federal Maritime Commission sees Guam as a part of the United States. Likewise, visa regulations indicate that the State Department views it as part of the mainland. There have always been perfectly logical reasons for these seeming contradictions, usually monetary; however, the overall impact on the Guamanians has been to perpetuate the feelings of "second-class citizenship," or, at least, of feeling that they are second-class in the eyes of the U.S. government.

The culture has been greatly affected and influenced by the Island's close relationship with the United States, but efforts are being made to preserve all elements possible of the Chamorro origins. The language itself has been declared the second official language and it is taught in all elementary schools.

Attendance at either public or private school is compulsory for ages six to 16. Most of the students attend the public school system.

Post-high school learning opportunities also exist. Two business colleges, a community college, and the University of Guam offer a variety of courses. Most post-high school training is given to teachers and nurses for the Island.

Economic Conditions

The U.S. Naval Station, communications installation and Strategic Air Command base situated on one-third of the island of Guam provide employment for approximately 20 percent of its population. Of the Chamorros themselves, over half are employees of the local or federal governments.

The second-largest economic base is tourism. Of the $150 million brought in by tourists, most (up to 84 percent) is from Japanese visitors. Both agriculture and fishing are seen as having potential for expansion; conditions are favorable, but have not yet been fully realized. Small-scale manufacturing is growing as an economic activity on the Island. Other primary economic activities are oil refining, rock and concrete production, clothing manufacture, and food processing.

Along with Nauru, Guam is one of the richest of the small island countries in the Pacific.

Status Of Christianity

ROMAN CATHOLIC MISSIONS/CHURCH

Brief History

The first Catholic Jesuit missionary came to Guam via the Philippines in 1668 at the command of Mariana, the mother of Charles II,

King of Spain. The Island chain of which Guam was then considered a part, was renamed the Mariana Islands.

The first year of the mission work was spectacularly "successful" and 13,000 were baptized. However, when the church insisted on such cultural changes as the abolition of ancestor cults and other integral parts of social life among the Chamorros, they objected violently.

Both on Guam and the other Mariana Islands armed battles were fought in which Catholic missionaries, as well as Chamorro, Mexican, and Filipino soldiers, were killed. By the end of these wars in 1694, it was estimated that only five percent of the original Chamorros population survived.

The strong influence of the Catholic Church and its presence in the form of Spanish priests continued through the 19th century, when the other islands of Micronesia came under German administration. Guam was the only one of the Mariana Islands which did not have German Capuchins brought in to replace the Spanish priests. The influence of the Philippine church was also evident in Guam and the Marianas. Guam was a regular stop for ships traveling between the Philippines and Mexico. Many settlers arrived from the Philippines and intermarried with the remaining Chamorro peoples. The Catholic church is described as having a "traditional Philippine-style" of Christianity.

Except for 2-1/2 years during World War II, when Japanese occupation troops expelled all but the two indigenous priests on Guam, the Island and the church have functioned under the U.S. government. The Catholic Church established Guam under the Capuchins in 1911. In 1946, the rest of the Mariana Islands were also included.

Current Status

In 1984 the area became an Archdiocese with the Diocese of Caroline-Marshall Island as its suffragan. One year later, the Marianas were also made a suffragan of the Agana Archdiocese as the Diocese of Chalan Kanoa, headquartered in Saipan.

Religious Workers

Both Capuchin and Jesuit fathers serve on Guam. Seven women's religious communities are also represented: Carmelite Nuns, Good

Shepherd Sisters, Religious Missionaries of St. Dominic, Franciscan Sisters of Perpetual Adoration, Religious Sisters of Mercy, Mercedarian Missionaries of Berriz, and School Sisters of St. Mary.

In 1986, a total of 47 priests and 138 sisters served Catholic members of 26 parishes in the Archdiocese of Agana. The first indigenous Micronesian bishop was ordained in 1970 to serve on Guam.

PROTESTANT MISSIONS/CHURCH

The Protestant church has a much more recent history and less extensive work than the Catholic Church on Guam. The major denominations with presences on the Island have all begun their work in this century.

The Assemblies of God began work on Guam in 1960. They listed 600 baptized members and three churches in 1984.

Starting work on Guam in 1961, the Southern Baptists had three churches with 450 members in 1984. Many members of these three churches are U.S. military personnel and their families.

General Baptists' work, begun in 1911, became indigenous and self supporting by 1972. In early 1986, it had four congregations with 330 members.

Other Protestant Churches include the Episcopal Church in Micronesia, which has administrative offices in Tumon Bay (under the jurisdiction of the presiding bishop in New York); the Church of God, both Anderson and Cleveland; the Christian Reformed Church; Church of Christ and Churches of Christ; the Conservative Baptists; and Pacific Ocean Mission. Liebenzell Mission works among students at the University of Guam.

Many of the members of other Protestant denominations are American military families or non-Guamanians.

CHRISTIAN ACTIVITIES

Local Evangelism

Campus Crusade for Christ began their ministry on Guam in 1975, continuing in 1981 with a full-time staff at the University of Guam and an "Athletes in Action" program. Child Evangelism Fellowship also had a ministry presence in 1981.

Broadcasting

Trans-World Radio established a station on Guam in the mid-1970's; local radio and TV stations both broadcast weekly Roman Catholic programs. In 1984, Christian radio programs were first broadcast in Chamorro through the work of the Southern Baptists.

Bible Translation

The United Bible Society distributes scriptures in Micronesia in Chamorro.

SOCIAL CONCERNS

Unreached People

Christianity is strongly established in Guam. Traditional religious forms have disappeared. With the rapid urbanization in Guam, however, ministry needs have changed. Urbanization has weakened the Pacific-style, village-based church. This has led to a lesser influence of Christianity in the urban areas of Agana. The effectiveness of the church in reaching some of the above mentioned possible people groups needs to be investigated.

There are approximately 9,000 **Koreans** living on Guam and working as laborers in the construction industry and elsewhere. They have brought with them a form of animistic/shamanistic practice which seems to have taken root. Although churches have begun to reach out to them, the Korean population forms an unreached people group in need of ministry.

Guam is a tourist destination for a large number of Japanese persons, most of whom are not Christian. **Japanese tourists and business travelers** make up a transient unreached peoples group. Although they are only on Guam for a short length of time, a ministry like the Waikiki Beach Chaplaincy designed for the Japanese could be an effective form of outreach.

Other Religions

Jehovah's Witnesses claimed 690 "memorial attenders" in their one congregation on Guam in 1984. The Church of Jesus Christ of Latter-Day Saints (Mormons) had 764 members.

KIRIBATI

Profile

NATURAL FEATURES: Total land area: 719 sq. km. Comprised of 33 atolls, in three principal groups: Gilbert Islands, Phoenix Islands, Line Islands, and Banaba.

CAPITAL: Bairiki on Tarawa Atoll.

POPULATION: 65,000 (1985); **Annual growth rate:** 1.6 percent. **Ethnic groups:** Micronesians, 92 percent; Polynesians, 2.5 percent; mixed Micronesians and Polynesians, 4.5 percent; and European and Chinese, 1.0 percent. **Urban:** 36 percent.

RELIGION: Christians: 95 percent. Roman Catholics, 48 percent; Protestants, 47 percent. **Major Denomination:** Gilbert Islands Protestant Church. **Others:** Baha'i, Church of Jesus Christ of Latter-Day Saints (Mormons).

LANGUAGE AND LITERACY: I-Kiribati. English is used in official communications. **Literacy rate:** 95 percent.

GOVERNMENT: A democratic republic with a President, known as Beritatenti, who is the head of state and the head of the government. **Legislative:** Unicameral House of Assembly known as Maneaba ni Maungatebu with 35 members.

ECONOMY: **Per capita GDP:** (1982) US $412. Subsistence agriculture and fishing. Phosphate mining on Banaba Island ceased after resource had been depleted. Dollar remittances come from I-Kiribati seamen serving on ships of other nations.

Commercial Interests In The Gilberts: Historical Notes

Kiribati (pronounced Ke're'bas) used to be known as the Gilbert Islands. Kiribati is the closest translation of the word Gilberts. Tungaru is the traditional name, used in precolonial times. The name Gilbert Islands was given to the group by the Russian hydrographer, A. I. Krusenstern, in the 1820's in honor of Capt. Thomas Gilbert who had explored the area in the late 18th century.

The first Europeans came to the Islands around 1840. Whalers, traders, and beachcombers came to trade, and some to settle. Some beachcombers became traders and agents for firms in Australia, Germany and the United States. Coconut oil and copra were primary commodities. Between 1860 and 1870, slave traders raided the islands for laborers in the guano mines of Peru and the sugar and coffee plantations in Fiji, Hawaii, Tahiti, and Queensland (Australia).

In 1892, the United Kingdom established a Protectorate over the 16 atolls of the Gilbert Islands and the Ellice Islands (now Tuvalu). The Fiji-based Western Pacific High Commission administered the two groups. In 1900, it annexed the phosphate-rich island of Banaba (formerly Ocean Island). Kirimati (Christmas Island) and others were added through the years. The Gilberts became a Crown Colony in 1916.

Tarawa Atoll became the scene of one of the fiercest battles between Japan and the United States during World War II.

After a referendum in 1975, the former Ellice Islands became the new state of Tuvalu. Gilbert was renamed Kiribati, having internal self-government in 1977; it became independent in 1979.

Phosphate mining in Banaba ceased after the exhaustion of deposits. Banabans were resettled in Rabi, a Fiji island, and sought compensation from those who benefited from phosphate mining.

The I-Kiribati People

Gilbertese people are locally known as I-Kiribati. They are believed to have originated from an admixture of Polynesian and indigenous inhabitants. They are of Micronesian descent and speak one common language in the islands.

The family occupies a central role in I-Kiribati society. The concept of reciprocity, known locally as "bubuti" provides an informal support system for people in the network.

Kiribati is remarkably homogeneous in terms of ethnicity. Over 96 percent of the population are I-Kiribati, or Gilbertese; another 2.5 percent are from other islands in the Pacific. Non-Pacific islanders only make up 1.0 percent of the population; neither of the two non-I-Kiribati populations forms a cohesive people group.

The people are very much influenced by the sea surrounding them, and are skilled in fishing and in making and sailing canoes. A marine training school operates in Tarawa; hundreds of Kiribati men are crew members on ships from other nations.

Socio-Political Conditions

For all its remoteness, Kiribati is of strategic importance to the United States and the Soviet Union, lying in the middle of lines of communication between Hawaii and Australia and New Zealand. The Islands are important to the Soviets, who test long-range missiles in the area between Hawaii and Kiribati.

After independence in 1979, Britain reduced its economic aid to the country. Thus, there have been pressures on the resource-poor country to look for other sources of assistance. It finally negotiated a fishing agreement with the Soviets, in which the latter is permitted to fish in their waters and to have onshore access to the country.

Contact with foreign values and a desire for material goods have increased, sometimes causing crime.

Economic Conditions

The people of Kiribati live mainly through subsistence agriculture and fishing. Copra, tuna, and sales of postage stamps through philatelic agencies are the only significant sources of income. Australia, Japan, the United States, and the European Community provide some aid; still, the government faces economic difficulties. The islands are far apart, and communication is inadequate and expensive. Health, education, communications, and law-enforcement services are spread thin among the tiny populations in the islands.

A cash economy exists in South Tarawa. Its rising population pressure has brought about dependence on imported foods.

About 1,000 Kiribati men work on overseas merchant ships, mostly West German. Their remittances to their families help the nation's economy.

Tourism is planned for the outlying Kirimati (formerly Christmas Island) near Hawaii. Attractions include a bird sanctuary for about 16 million birds of different varieties and deep-sea fishing. However, lack of accommodations and transportation remain major problems.

American And European Missions: Brief Historical Overview

The American Board of Commissioners for Foreign Missions (ABCFM) pioneered missionary work in Kiribati in 1856, concentrating its efforts on the northern islands. The London Missionary Society (LMS) commenced its work about the same time in the southern parts of the group. In 1917, the two mission bodies agreed that ABCFM hand over all its work to the LMS.

The first Protestant missionary, the Rev. Hiram Bingham of the American Board of Commissioners for Foreign Missions, established a mission in Abiang in 1857. He spread Christianity throughout the northern islands with the assistance of Hawaiian pastors. Meanwhile, the missionaries of the London Missionary Society had established missions in the southern Ellice Islands, now Tuvalu. They came northward in the 1870's. The Rev. S. J. Whitmee and some Samoan pastors went to Arorae, Tamana, Onotoa, and Beru. Their missionary work was not as successful as their work in the south.

The Roman Catholic missionaries were more successful in these northern islands. The priests of the Sacred Heart order began their work in 1888, using Nonouti as their first station.

Other missionary groups gained adherents after World War II. These groups include the Seventh-day Adventist Church; Church of God; The Church of Jesus Christ of Latter-Day Saints (Mormons) and the Baha'i Faith.

Status Of Christianity

The Christian religion plays a major role in the national life of Kiribati. In mid-1980's, about 95 percent of the population professed to be Christians. About 31,000 were Protestants, and 33,000 Roman Catholics. The latter are concentrated mainly on the five northern islands.

About 5.7 percent of the population is evangelical. Other churches include those of the Church of God and the Seventh-day Adventists.

KIRIBATI PROTESTANT CHURCH

Originating as a London Missionary Society (LMS) Congregational Mission church, this is the largest Protestant church in Kiribati today. It had 11,000 members in 1985. However, this once-strong Congregational Church is losing members and pastors to other Protestant groups, the Roman Catholics, Baha'is, and Church of Jesus Christ of Latter-Day Saints (Mormons).

Considering the limited number of highly-qualified ministers, the issue of sending missionaries to other parts of the world is minimal. The church still cries out for more qualified local ministers to meet the present-day needs of Kiribati. However, the church did start to send local missionaries in 1981; two of its ministers work with the Pacific Council of Churches based in Suva, Fiji.

ROMAN CATHOLIC CHURCH

French missionaries of the Sacred Heart began work in the Islands in 1888. A vicariate for the islands was organized in 1897. The hierarchy was established in 1966.

With a total population of 65,000 in 1985, Roman Catholic adherents numbered 33,000. Among the religious workers were a bishop for the diocese, 16 priests, six seminarians, five brothers, and 56 sisters. There were 24 parishes in the islands.

The diocese includes Kiribati, the neighboring countries of Nauru, Tuvalu, and two of the Phoenix Islands.

CHURCH OF GOD

An evangelical church, the Church of God, is growing, and new workers are being trained for advanced Bible School.

COOPERATIVE AGENCIES

As yet, there is no National Council of Churches in Kiribati. The two main bodies of the Kiribati Protestant Church and the Roman Catholic Church have worked together occasionally on some projects, such as their combined efforts in the establishment of the Seamen's Hostel.

CHRISTIAN ACTIVITIES

Education

The field of education is one of the areas where foreign missionaries' assistance is reportedly needed. The Council for World Mission (CWM) has helped by sending foreign teachers. However, this has slowed down because of high costs. It is more difficult to hire secondary school teachers to teach in church-run schools since their counterparts in the government-run schools are better paid.

Bible Translation and Distribution

A decade after the first missionaries arrived in Kiribati, the Kiribati Bible was produced. Both the Old and the New Testaments were translated. Work is being done at present to revise the vernacular translations.

Literature

The Roman Catholic Church publishes a monthly newsletter with a circulation of 2,000. Its title is *Te Itoi ni Kiribati*. The Protestant Churches publish *Te kaotan te ota*, a monthly newspaper.

Broadcasting

In 1983, there were an estimated 10,000 radio receivers. Radio Kiribati broadcasts programs in I-Kiribati and English. Both

Catholics and Protestants support important education programs focusing on public-information projects.

SOCIAL CONCERNS

Kiribati has undergone a substantial degree of urbanization; almost 36 percent of its population live in the urban areas of Tarawa. Yet, there is no evidence of an emergence of an urban identity or significant boundaries between those living in urban areas and those living in more rural parts of the country. Urbanization has not yet resulted in the formation of new people groups.

The Catholic Bishop of Tarawa has been outspoken in his concern over increasing population pressure. He hopes New Zealand or Australia might be encouraged to accept I-Kiribati immigrants.

MARSHALL ISLANDS

Profile

NATURAL FEATURES: The group contains 1,156 islands of varying sizes; two are inhabited. Distributed mostly in two chains: the Ratak or "Sunrise" in the east; and the Ralik or "Sunset" in the west. Kwajalein, in the "Sunset" chain, has the world's largest lagoon.

CAPITAL: Majuro. **Population:** 12,747 (1985).

POPULATION: 34,923 (1985), mainly Micronesians.

RELIGION: Christians: 94 percent. Protestants, 30,000; Roman Catholics, 3,000 (Approx). **Major Denominations:** United Church of Christ, Roman Catholic, Assemblies of God. **Others:** Jehovah's Witnesses, Church of Jesus Christ of Latter-Day Saints (Mormons).

LANGUAGES: English; Marshallese dialects.

GOVERNMENT: Self-governing in free association with the United States. **Executive:** President. **Legislative:** local legislatures. **Judiciary:** Supreme Court.

ECONOMY: Small scale industries: handicrafts, fish processing, copra processing. Some agricultural products such as taro, yam, and vegetables. Major funding comes from the United States.

Brief Historical Background

It is believed that like the other peoples of Micronesia, the Marshallese originally migrated to these Islands from Southeast Asia. Another possible route of migration was north through the Tuvalu-Kiribati chain of islands. No date for these early settlements is known.

European sailors first contacted the island farthest north in the group, Taongi, in 1526. Other Spanish explorers followed on an irregular basis over the next 42 years.

The next Europeans, British this time, did not arrive until 1767. It was a chance encounter with the Islands that was not repeated until 1788, when two other British sea captains came through on their way from Australia to China. One of these two was Captain John Marshall, whose name is now used for this group.

Russian explorers came next and conducted extensive surveys in the early 19th century. American whalers and missionaries also came at this time; the former to take away resources and the latter to provide them.

GERMAN ADMINISTRATION

German economic interests began to grow in the copra and shells that the Islands provided. In 1886, the Marshalls became a German protectorate. Their administrative policy was generally to utilize the existing social structures and to rule through the Island chiefs with only minimal interference.

JAPANESE ADMINISTRATION

With the outbreak of World War II, Japan occupied the Marshall Islands, having been given a League of Nations mandate for this arrangement in 1920. As in the other areas of Micronesia which the Japanese administered between the two World Wars, the interest began as economic and ended as military.

Some of the Marshalls were used as military fortifications by the Japanese during World War II. These were the first of the Japanese territories to be captured by the Allies during the War.

U.S. TRUST TERRITORY

U.S. nuclear testing began on Bikini in 1946. The Marshall Islands came under U.S. administration as a part of the Trust Territory of the Pacific Islands in 1947. Further nuclear testing was done on Eniwetok in the 1950's and early 1960's. Multi-million dollar clean-up programs are in progress now, including the building of a huge concrete cover over radioactive materials on Eniwetok that will remain radioactive for an estimated 25,000 years.

In 1979, the Marshall Islands voted to become a self-governing republic in free association with the United States.

People Groups

In 1985, 34,923 people lived on the Marshall Islands. The indigenous peoples among this number are classified as Micronesian; they are lighter skinned and more Polynesian looking than other peoples of western Micronesia.

The original society of these islands was organized under chieftains, and status was determined by kinship grouping. The social relationships were organized matrilineally.

The Marshallese language has two variations: The "Sunset" Islanders speak one variety and the "Sunrise" Islanders another. Each of these groups is able to understand the other's variation.

Socio-Political Conditions

Many Marshall Islanders both suffer and benefit from the scientific discoveries made in this century. Their way of life and social fabric have been forever changed by their relationship with the United States.

Military testing of nuclear weapons in the late 1940's through the early 1960's and missile weaponry tests in the present day have necessitated population shifts. Along with the social and psychological disruption of leaving their homes, there have been health problems associated with exposure to radioactivity. The U.S. government is making efforts to compensate people who have been affected by these military moves.

American cultural influence is felt particularly in the centers of population like the capital city, Majuro, and on Kwajalein. The children of all Marshall Islands are required to attend school from age six to 14 and to finish, at least, primary education. School curricula include instruction in both Marshallese and English for the early years, and in English for the secondary.

The benefits of modern medicine have insured better health to these traditionally vigorous people. Except for one private clinic, the government is the sole provider of health services.

Since May 1, 1979, the Marshall Islands have had a Constitution which will lead them eventually to a self-governing republic. Many of the provisions of this document are based on the traditional system of rule by hereditary chiefs forming the Council of Iroij. This system is now combined with a parliamentary-style elective process to provide for a president and legislature. The judiciary branch is headed by the Supreme Court.

This system is already in operation: the Islands will govern themselves while maintaining a "Free Association" with the United States as approved by the U.S. Congress.

Economic Conditions

The United States Government is the source of at least three-quarters of the cash income of the Marshall Islands. This funding is used for government operations and large scale development. Other income from the U.S. is in payment for use of the Kwajalein Lagoon for missile testing, as well as for social programs to relieve the overcrowding caused when the Islanders were moved from Kwajalein to Ebeye.

The greatest income from the private-sector source is from copra production. Coconut oil and a few "*trocas*" shells are also exported.

Efforts are underway to develop and improve existing agriculture, fishing, and tourism as sources of income.

Status Of Christianity

CATHOLIC MISSIONS/CHURCH

German Catholic missions worked in the Marshall Islands during the German administration of these Islands. The Order of the Sacred Heart came in 1899. They eventually made notable contributions to the education system and additions to the body of translated materials.

There are now Catholic churches on Ebeye, Majuro and Kwajalein; the churches are a part of the Diocese of Caroline-Marshall Islands, established in 1980. There are eight American Catholic workers on the Marshalls representing the Society of Jesus and the Maryknoll Sisters.

The number of Catholics in 1983 was 3,087; this was approximately eight percent of the total population.

PROTESTANT MISSIONS/CHURCHES

In 1858, the first American Board Missionaries were assigned to Ebon, one of the most southern of the Marshall Islands. Two of these couples served as missionaries in the Caroline Islands and later extended their work to the Marshalls.

The Marshall Islanders themselves requested other missionaries to be sent. At first, Americans were sent to fill the need. Later, through frequent visits to Hawaii and the training center of Lahainaluna Seminary by Benjamin Snow, a missionary supervisor, Hawaiian missionaries were assigned to the Marshall Islands.

The first of seven Hawaiian couples to arrive in the Marshalls were Debora and Hezekiah Aea. Through their work, along with the others who joined them, a Church was established that truly reflected the Marshallese culture. It was often cited as one of the finest missionary efforts to allow local church growth along patterns appropriate to the people for whom it was established.

With local candidates trained as pastors, the Marshall Islands' Church was soon able to direct its own spiritual life. Even through the years of political intervention from other nations -- Germany, Japan, and the United States -- it has been able to maintain itself and thrive.

In the early 20th century, an Australian, Carl Heine, with his Micronesian wife became notable converts in the Marshallese church. After he became a dedicated Christian, he and his family after him made significant contributions of service to the Church.

The German Liebenzell missionaries continued in the Marshalls after their work in the western Carolines was turned over to its American branch. However, during and after World War I, Japan expelled all the Germans; Japan offered missionaries as replacements, but the Marshallese church did not want them.

The United Church of Christ in the Marshall Islands, resulting from the American Board Misson work, had 10,000 (plus) affiliates and 88 congregations in mid-1980. The Assemblies of God had 5,100 "baptized believers" and 5,000 "other believers" in 19 churches served by two missionaries and 27 credentialed ministers in 1984.

CHRISTIAN ACTIVITIES

Broadcasting

The Marshall Islands' government gives free time on its radio stations for religious broadcasting. Catholic educational and religious programming are aired, and the FEBC broadcasting from Saipan in the Mariana Islands can also be received in the Marshalls.

Bible Translation

The United Bible Society established an office in Micronesia in 1971 and was incorporated in 1983. A Marshallese translation of the complete Bible was finished in 1982.

Other Religions

In 1985, Jehovah's Witnesses had 876 "memorial attenders" in the Marshall Islands. The Church of Jesus Christ of Latter-Day Saints (Mormons) claimed a membership of 1,142.

NAURU

Profile

NATURAL FEATURES: Land area: 21 sq. km. **Terrain:** A single coral island, four-fifths of which is phosphate rock. **Climate:** Tropical; dry season -- March to October, wet season -- November to February.

ADMINISTRATIVE CENTER: Yaren District.

POPULATION: 8,400 (1982 estimate) **Annual growth:** 1.3 percent. **People groups:** Nauruans (60 percent), other Pacific Islanders - Tuvalu, Kiribati (24 percent), Chinese (8.0 percent), Australians, New Zealanders (6.0 percent), Fijians (2.0 percent).

RELIGION: Christians: 82.7 percent. **Major Denominations:** Nauruan Congregational Church, 39.2 percent; Roman Catholic, 27.5 percent; Anglicans, 3.0 percent; Evangelicals, 1.9 percent. **Others:** Chinese folk religion, 8.4 percent; Buddhists, 1.7 percent; Baha'i, 1.6 percent. **Non-religious:** 6.0 percent.

LANGUAGE AND LITERACY: Nauruan, English. One hundred percent literacy.

GOVERNMENT: Independent republic, an associate member of the British Commonwealth. The President is the head of state and de facto prime minister. Unicameral parliament includes 18 members elected for three years. Judiciary is composed of Supreme, District, and Family Courts.

ECONOMY: Per capita annual income: (1985) US $23,400. **Main exports:** phosphates.

Historical Background

The early Nauru islanders belonged to 12 clans who spoke different dialects. The first European contact was in 1798 by the British, but it was in the 1830's that many outsiders came to Nauru. Beachcombers from whaling ships began settling on the island, influencing the Nauruans for the worst. Severe and widespread clan warfare broke out. In 1888, Germany claimed the island and ended the conflicts. Only 1,300 islanders were left.

Phosphate was discovered in 1898 and mining began in 1906. Nauru became a trusteeship of Great Britain, Australia and New Zealand when Germany lost control of the island in World War I.

In 1964, resettlement of the Nauruans to Curtis Island off the Queensland coast was proposed due to the progressive exhaustion of the island's phosphate deposits. The people elected to stay. The British granted independence to Nauru on January 31, 1968. Local control of the phosphate industry was established in 1970.

Socio-Political Conditions

Nauru is an anomaly in the Pacific. It is an island nation quickly being consumed by phosphate mining. Its population is 60 percent Nauru, 24 percent other Pacific Islanders (including 20 percent from Kiribati), 8 percent Chinese, 6 percent Caucasian and 2 percent Fijian. The native Nauruans live in scattered settlements along the fringes of the island. There are no established communities for non-Nauruans, most of whom are engaged in the mining industry and live in workers' dormitories. Income from the mining industry has created wealth, at least temporarily.

The Constitution provides for a parliamentary type of government with citizenship limited to those of Nauruan and Pacific Islander descent. Since independence in 1960, traditional political leaders have been elected to office, although the trend since 1978 is for younger and better-educated men to replace the older leaders. The present head of state or Chief of Nauru, is Hammer De Roburt. He has been elected to that position four times.

There are no organized political parties in Nauru. Education is free and compulsory between the ages of 6 and 16, and the literacy rate is about 100 percent. The government provides an extensive welfare system for the people.

Economic Conditions

Nauru, due to its phosphate deposits, has a large per capita income, which it receives as royalties from the Nauruan Phosphate Corporation (NPC). These revenues are shared among the government (50 percent), the Nauruan landowners (through a royalties long-term trust fund), and the Nauru local government council. However, at the present rate of production, the phosphate will only last until the year 2000. The government's economic policy is to invest the phosphate revenues in long-term trust funds, real estate, shipping, and fishing in the South Pacific, mostly in Australia, so that the Nauruans will have a source of income after the mine is depleted.

NPC hires laborers from Hong Kong, Kiribati, Tuvalu and recently a few from the Philippines.

Mission History

Tabuia, a Kiribati missionary, evangelized Nauru between 1888 and 1899, without direct oversight by a foreign missionary.

In 1899, Philip A. Delaporte, a missionary with the American Board of Commissioners for Foreign Missions (ABCFM) and the Central Union Church in Honolulu, came to Nauru. His sponsor was William Harris, a beachcomber who settled in the island in 1842 and who married several local women. In 1902, Fr. Alois Kayser from Alsace arrived as a Roman Catholic Sacred Heart Missionary. He and Delaporte become rival experts on Nauruan life and customs and the Church.

A few years after Nauru came under British rule in 1914, the London Missionary Society took over missionary responsibility for the island, with the result that a majority of Nauruans became Protestant. Religious literature was translated into Nauruan as early as the first decade of this century; scripture portions were translated in 1902, the New Testament in 1907, and the whole Bible in 1918.

Miners came to Nauru from other parts of the South Pacific, and the need for a local church was met by Samoan, Kiribati, and Tuvalu pastors.

Status Of Christianity

A majority of the Nauruans are Christians. They adhere mainly to the Congregational Church, which comprises 39 percent of the Christians in the country. An additional 28 percent are Roman Catholics, while a small percent are Anglicans. The Evangelicals comprise about 2 percent of the population.

NAURUAN PROTESTANT CHURCH

The dominant church, the Nauruan Protestant Church, was begun by Congregationalist missionaries of the London Missionary Society (LMS) in 1917.

Church life is said to have ebbed recently because of the relative wealth of the people and an increasing emphasis on materialism.

ROMAN CATHOLIC CHURCH

This church is part of the Diocese of Tarawa, Nauru and Funafuti with headquarters in Kiribati. In 1972, one resident priest and four sisters worked in Nauru. The church has an educational program consisting of Kayser College and primary and secondary schools, for which it receives staff aid. In addition to Nauruans, some Chinese and Filipino mine workers attend the Roman Catholic church.

ANGLICAN CHURCH

Served by a visiting clergy, the Anglican Church is one of the smallest in Nauru. It is part of the diocese of Polynesia, which in turn is part of the Church of the Province of New Zealand and the South Pacific Anglican Council (SPAC).

OTHER CHURCHES

Kiribati Protestant Church and the Tuvalu Location Church are small churches established to meet the needs of mine workers from other South Pacific countries. The churches have their own national pastors.

The Nauru Independent Church (Pentecostal) was established in recent years and has undergone rapid growth.

CHRISTIAN AGENCIES

The Bible Society of the South Pacific has a committee in Nauru for the distribution of religious materials for use in churches and in schools. The Central Pacific Bookshop is an active distribution center.

While there is no formal ecumenical agency, relations among Protestants, Roman Catholics, and Anglicans are said to be casual and friendly.

MAJOR CONCERN

Unreached People Groups

The **Chinese** population constitutes the one clear unreached people group on the island, but there is little evidence of focused outreach to them by the churches in Nauru.

Non-Christian Religion

The Chinese mine workers on Nauru adhere mainly to folk religion and Buddhism, although some have abandoned their religion and are now classed as non-religious.

The Baha'is are established in Nauru. In 1973, they had three religious centers.

NORTHERN MARIANA ISLANDS

Profile

NATURAL FEATURES: Land area: 471 sq. km. Sixteen islands, total; 14 are inhabited. Saipan and Tinian are most important islands. Northern islands are volcanic with some coral and limestone; southern islands have grassy pastureland and thick forests.

CAPITAL: Saipan. **Population:** 15,000 (1983).

POPULATION: 19,635 (1985). **Ethnic groups:** Chamorros.

RELIGION: Christians: 99 percent (est.). **Major denominations:** Roman Catholic, 71 percent; General Baptist, Seventh-day Adventist, Assemblies of God. **Other:** Church of Jesus Christ of Latter-Day Saints (Mormons).

LANGUAGE AND LITERACY: English, Chamorro, Carolinian, Japanese.

GOVERNMENT: Self-governing Commonwealth. **Executive:** Governor. **Legislative:** Bicameral (Senate and House of Representatives). **Judicial:** Part of the U.S. Ninth Circuit Court of Appeals. It has a District Court and a Commonwealth Trial Court.

ECONOMY: **Gross Island Product** (GIP, 1982): US $165 million. **Industries:** small scale handicraft; fish processing; copra processing; tourism.

Historical Background

COLONIAL ADMINISTRATION

The Mariana Islands' cultures thus far studied are the pre-Latte and Latte. "Latte" refers to the mushroom-shaped stone which was characteristically associated with important sites and houses. It is still closely linked with Chamorro ethnic identity today.

The Chamorros possibly migrated to these Islands from Malaysia, the Philippines, and Indonesia. Their origins are not entirely certain, but are closely linked with Southeast Asia. A unique aspect of their culture among the ancient peoples of Oceania is their ability to grow and cultivate rice.

Europeans first came to the Island chain in 1521 on an expedition with Ferdinand Magellan. In 1668, a Spanish priest renamed the islands "The Marianas" in honor of Mariana of Austria, mother of Charles II and widow of Phillip IV of Spain.

The Spanish continued their contact with the Mariana Islands on their trade route between Mexico and the Philippines. They also claimed it as a possession until 1899, when as a result of their defeat in the Spanish-American War, they decided to sell it to Germany.

The German rule ended in 1914, when Japan took over the Islands during World War I. The ensuing 30 years of Japanese occupation was a positive time at the outset, with much development of the infrastructure and agricultural methods. Sugar production and its by-products, molasses and alcoholic drinks distilled from molasses, became a significant part of the economy. The years of World War II saw a buildup of Japanese military and the eventual destruction of their bases by the United States.

The Americans built military bases on Saipan and Tinian; it was from Tinian that U.S. military planes took off to drop atomic bombs on Hiroshima and Nagasaki. After World War II, the United Nations included these Islands in the Trust Territory of the Pacific Islands, which came under the jurisdiction of the United States.

Socio-Political Conditions

Although the new constitution did not come into actual effect until 1978, the Northern Mariana Islands began a new political relationship with the United States in 1976. The Islands have entered into a Commonwealth status, paralleling the agreements that the U.S. has with Guam, Puerto Rico, the Virgin Islands, the District of Columbia, and American Samoa.

Unique aspects of the agreement provide the U.S. with 50-year leases, with option for renewal, on areas of the Islands to be used as military bases. The U.S. would also be required to provide defense for the Marianas' area. It also guarantees the right to a republican form of self-government, including separate legislative, executive, and judicial branches, plus financial supports for that government. Almost 80 percent of the voters endorsed this agreement.

A relatively low death rate and a high birth rate have resulted in a comparatively young population on the Northern Marianas. Almost one-half of the inhabitants are estimated to be under 15 years old.

Although the initial school enrollment figures are high, only half of the children enrolled actually graduate from high school. At least one-quarter of those who do finish secondary school go on to higher institutions. There is a two-year teachers' college on the Islands; all other students must leave the Islands for further study.

Overall, the adult literacy rate is quite high. Both Chamorro and Carolinian languages are taught, along with English. Programs also exist to preserve the original culture of the Islands.

Economic Conditions

The three southern islands of Saipan, Rota, and Tinian are the economic center of the Northern Mariana Islands. Because of the intense fighting during World War II, many of the development measures brought by the Japanese were destroyed. Flourishing sugar plantations on all three islands were not replanted after the War's end.

The main sources of income for the Islands are agriculture, especially growing vegetables such as coconuts, breadfruit, tomatoes for export; fishing; meat and milk production; small businesses; and tourism.

The tourist industry is especially flourishing. It brings in millions of dollars each year from Japan and the United States. Although Saipan draws most of the tourists, Tinian and Rota are improving their airstrips and have many natural attractions to recommend them to visitors. Deep-sea fishing and Micronesian historical sites, as well as fine beaches, can be found in and around Tinian. Rota's archaeological digs and natural caves are believed to have been lived in by Chamorros during the Spanish rule.

Although great economic strides have been made in recent years since the declaration of Commonwealth status, the United States is still providing millions of dollars annually to the Northern Marianas. The funds are grants-in-aid for large-scale improvements and development. The islands had an 11.4 percent unemployment rate in 1984.

People Groups

Of the estimated 19,635 people in 1985 on the Northern Mariana Islands, the majority claim Chamorro ethnic heritage; the Chamorro were the original ancient inhabitants.

There has been intermixture with other peoples, due both to migration and to foreign rule. The Spanish actually removed the population of the Islands in the early days of its rule in an attempt to quell their rebelliousness. "Migration" to the islands of the Caroline group and the eventual return of these individuals with their new families has created a significant Carolinian minority. Intermarriage of individuals from countries ruling the Islands as well as from the military of those countries, has added Spanish, German, Japanese, Filipino, Mexican, and Korean characteristics to the peoples living there.

A mix of cultural and social patterns has also resulted. The original matrilineal social structure has been replaced by a patrilineal form. This was probably due to the influence of the Spanish and their introduction of a new religion, Roman Catholic Christianity. Some remnant of the matrilineal organization still exists in Carolinian communities in the Saipan area.

The extended family is still the center of life for Chamorros. Land is owned by the family and worked by all. Decisions are made in common among the family members in councils.

Status Of Christianity

ROMAN CATHOLIC CHURCH/MISSIONS

The history of the Roman Catholic Church and missions in the Mariana Islands parallels that in Guam, until the elevation of this Church to the Diocese of Chalan Kanoa in early 1985.

There is one religious community of men represented in the Mariana Islands: the Capuchins, and two of women; Mercedarians and the Third Order of St. Frances of Mary Immaculate. Two men and approximately 12 women serve the Islands through these orders.

An estimated 14,000 Roman Catholic believers worship in nine parishes in the Marianas.

The bishop of the diocese is an indigenous priest; this is seen as part of a larger goal of indigenization for the entire Micronesian Catholic Church.

See also the "Catholic History/Missions" section for Guam in this same chapter.

PROTESTANT CHURCH/MISSION

The General Baptist denomination was the first Protestant group to begin work in the Northern Marianas. It established a congregation on Saipan in 1947. At one point it had nine ethnic groups and seven language groups represented, as well as several Protestant denominations. Its 1986 membership was about 350.

Eventually, groups developed their own congregational meetings. There are now two independent Baptist groups as well as a Seventh-day Adventist church and a new Assemblies of God church.

CHRISTIAN ACTIVITIES

The Far Eastern Broadcasting Corporation (FEBC) began work in the late 1970's on Saipan; its broadcasts are heard throughout Southeast Asia as well as in Micronesia.

The General Baptists in joint cooperation with the Roman Catholics and other denominations on Saipan have a Bible distribution program.

Both Youth With a Mission and Teen Challenge work among the young people of the Island.

The Catholic Church has an elementary school on Saipan as do the General Baptists.

Other Religion

The Church of Jesus Christ of Latter-Day Saints (Mormons) has built a church structure recently, projected to house 200 to 300 worshipers. Currently, the congregation numbers between 30 and 40 individuals.

REPUBLIC OF BELAU
(PALAU)

Profile

NATURAL FEATURES: Land area: 170 sq. mi. with 200 to 300 islands, part of the Caroline Islands archipelago. Four major islands comprise the Belau cluster including the largest, Babelthuap.

CAPITAL: Koror. **Population:** 7,585.

POPULATION: (1985) 14,800.

RELIGION: Major denominations: Roman Catholic, 40 percent, Liebenzell Mission, Seventh-day Adventist, Assemblies of God. **Other:** Jehovah's Witness.

LANGUAGE: Belauan dialects, English.

GOVERNMENT: Self-governing with free association with the United States. **Executive:** President. **Legislative:** Olbiil Era Kellau, the Chamorro legislature. **Judicial:** Supreme and Lower Courts.

ECONOMY: Main industries: small-scale handicrafts, fish processing, bottling, copra processing, bananas and boat building. Small mineral deposits exist. Tourism. **Main crops:** coconut, taro, breadfruit, bananas, yam, sweet potatoes, vegetables.

Historical Background

Because of its geographic proximity to Southeast Asia, the Belau cluster is believed to be the first among the Micronesian Islands to have been settled by immigrants. These inhabitants probably arrived from the Philippines or Indonesia.

Explorers from Spain first "discovered" Belau in 1710. As part of the Caroline Islands, Belau was included in Pope Leo XIII's Declaration placing them under Spain's protectorate in 1885. In 1899, the Islands went with the other Carolines when Spain sold them to Germany, and again, when Japan occupied them from 1914 to the end of World War II. Finally, Belau became part of the Trust Territory of the Pacific Islands assigned to the United States for administrative responsibility in 1947.

People Groups

About 14,800 people lived on the eight permanently-inhabited islands of Belau in 1985. The indigenous peoples probably came from an inter-mixture of Filipino and Indonesian emigrants as well as Polynesian and Melanesian settlers.

The Belauan language is closer in form to Indonesian languages than to the languages spoken in other parts of Micronesia. This is seen as partial confirmation of the peoples' Asian origins.

Family bonds are considered very important by the Belauans. Land and money (some ancient bead money is still used) are owned by the kinship group, and these groups are determined by matrilineal relationships. Although the responsibilities of men in a matrilineal society are to their sister's children instead of their wives, they are becoming more anxious to leave inheritances to their own children. Women, however, see this move as weakening their assurance of the support which is guaranteed by the old system and are hesitant to change the social patterns.

In general, the Belauan people are viewed by others as being both intelligent and articulate with a great sense of the joy of competition. The administration of the Trust Territory of the Pacific Islands has had representation from Belau that far outweighs the expectations based on their small population, and some believe these characteristics are the reason.

Two government-funded projects will further preserve the Belauan culture. Following an archaeological dig on the island of Babelthuap, a report was prepared based on oral traditions and dig findings that reconstructs life at the site. Other oral traditions and histories are also being systematically recorded and cataloged. The 14 elders being interviewed for the second of the two projects have been certified as "Living National Treasures." These oral folk histories were previously recorded on carved boards which combined graphic and communication skills to reproduce the important cultural information of the Belauan people.

Socio-Political Conditions

After the 1979 ratification of its Constitution, Belau became a self-governing Republic on the first day of 1981. The provisions of this document outline a government with the executive branch including both a Cabinet and a 16-member Council of Chiefs; a Chamorro legislative branch and a judiciary branch. The 16 states of Belau have similar governments of popularly elected or appointed public offices, but also include the traditional local chief in the modern system.

A "sticking point" for this new government is in its relationship to the United States. The Belauan Constitution includes a ban on hazardous wastes or nuclear weapons within its borders and up to a 200-mile ocean limit. The next move on the question of U.S. involvement in the area is pending a decision by the United States Congress to resolve the conflicting terms of the Belauan Constitution and the Compact of Free Association being requested by U.S. negotiators.

The government provides the majority of healthcare services for the Islands. A new National Hospital is planned; but thus far the existing hospital facilities and staff can provide only primary care for the Islanders. Serious cases are usually taken to Guam or Hawaii.

Education is compulsory through high school in Belau, with both private and public schools involved in this process. The number of islanders involved in college or university study is a comparatively high one in area.

Economic Conditions

Along with the re-negotiations of Belau's political status, vis-a-vis the United States, go its economic relations with that country. The U.S. Congress is linking its consideration of these crucial issues together. Belau has been operating at a deficit within a budget that had normally been funded up to 77 percent by the U.S.

However, development of Belau's agricultural and aquacultural resources is underway. Japan, in particular, is offering assistance for both of these plans. Other private foreign sources are investing in the potential tourist trade. Also, Belau's proximity to the Southeast Asian shipping routes makes it an ideal location to be developed into a major port complex.

Status Of Christianity

CATHOLIC CHURCH/MISSIONS

The largest and oldest (since 1891) Christian work on Belau is that of the Roman Catholic Church. The Spanish presence on the Caroline Islands, of which Belau was one until it declared itself a self-governing entity in 1981, brought Spanish priests and missionaries.

When Germany took over the Carolines from Spain in 1899, German Capuchins replaced the Spanish priests. One of its most notable impacts on Belauan society was the abolition of institutional warfare and concubinage. A restructuring of culture and other reforms followed these.

Belau is a part of the Diocese of Caroline-Marshall Islands. Its membership was 6,294, or approximately 40 percent of the population, in 1983.

PROTESTANT CHURCH/MISSIONS

The Protestant mission work on Belau dates to 1929 upon the arrival of a Liebenzell missionary couple, the Langes, and a Trukese Christian man. They sailed from Truk on a Japanese ship (the Island at that time being under Japanese administration).

From Koror, the capital of Belau, the missionaries went to Babelthuap, where they finally settled. The village of Ngiual, where they built their first congregation, still has a strong church today, with its members involved in regular island-to-island and village-to-village witnessing and evangelism meetings on a bi-monthly basis.

Another "boat ministry" was initiated in 1968, this time to Yap in the Caroline Islands, now a part of the Federated States of Micronesia. This has encouraged the indigenization of the Church in this area, as outreach efforts are being made by the Belauan people themselves.

Today, 21 indigenous pastors, evangelists, four long-term missionaries, and Bible women are working with the Liebenzell Mission on Belau.

Mission work is also being conducted by the Assemblies of God on Belau, with two missionaries ministering there in 1985.

The Seventh-day Adventists also have a fairly strong presence.

CHRISTIAN ACTIVITIES

Bible Translation

A Liebenzell missionary, Hildegard Thiena, did a New Testament translation into Belauan in the 1950's. The Old Testament translation was completed by the United Bible Society in 1985.

Education

The Emmaus High School for Boys and Bethania High School for Girls -- both founded by the Liebenzell Mission -- are boarding schools in Belau whose students come from all over Micronesia.

Social Concerns

Campus Crusade for Christ had AGAPE teachers on Belau in 1981.

Other Religions

Jehovah's Witness had one congregation on Belau with 186 attendees in 1984.

Chapter Five: *New Zealand*

NEW ZEALAND

Profile

NATURAL FEATURES: Land area: 268,676 sq. km.; **Location:** 1,800 km. east of Australia. **Main islands:** North, South, and Stewart. **Others:** Chatham, Raoul, the Kermadec Group and Campbell. Only the Chathams are permanently inhabited. **Terrain:** Highly varied from snowcapped mountains to lowland plains.

CAPITAL: Wellington (pop. 342,500). **Other cities:** Auckland, Christchurch, Hamilton and Dunodin.

POPULATION (1985): 3.3 million. **Annual growth rate:** 0.8 percent. **Ethnic groups** (1982): European (85.7 percent), Maori (8.9 percent), Pacific Islanders (2.8 percent), Chinese and Indian (1 percent), Others (1.5 percent). **Urban:** (84 percent).

RELIGION (1981 census) **Christians:** Anglican and Protestant (59.7 percent), Catholic (14.4 percent), Eastern Orthodox (0.1 percent), Christian Cults (1.7 percent). **Non-Christians:** 0.6 percent. **Non-religious:** 23.5 percent.

LANGUAGE AND LITERACY: English, Maori, other Pacific Island languages. **Literacy rate:** 99 percent.

GOVERNMENT: Parliamentary. Constituent of the British Commonwealth. **Executive:** Monarch represented by the Governor-

General; Prime Minister. **Legislative:** Unicameral House of Representatives. **Judiciary:** three-level system Magistrates Court, Supreme Court, Court of Appeals.

ECONOMY: Annual GNP: (1984) US $21.43 billion. **Per capita income:** (1982) US $7,916. **Average inflation rate:** (1983) 3.6 percent. **Natural resources:** natural gas, iron, sand, coal, timber. **Agricultural products:** wool, meat, timber.

Historical Background

THE MAORIS

New Zealand was "discovered" by Europeans in 1642, but from at least 1300 A.D. has been inhabited by a race of Polynesians known as Maoris. They came from eastern Polynesia, moving from island to island to New Zealand. In New Zealand, they adapted themselves to a new physical environment and produced significant forms of social and economic organization and material culture.

EUROPEAN SETTLEMENTS

The first instance of Europeans forming any permanent settlements occurred in 1792. Whaling and trading stations sprang up around the New Zealand coast. The first immigrants arrived in Wellington in January 1840 from England. They arrived a week before an English-appointed governor for New Zealand landed in the north at the Bay of Islands to proclaim British sovereignty. This was formalized on February 6, 1840 when 46 Maori chiefs signed the Treaty of Waitangi in the Bay of Islands. All rights and powers of sovereignty were ceded to the Queen, all territorial rights were secured to the chiefs and their tribes, and the Maoris became British subjects. The Crown received sole rights of land purchase. This anniversary continues to be remembered as Waitangi Day.

First European contacts with the Maoris produced a series of tribal wars much greater and more devastating (due to the supply of new weapons) than had ever occurred prior to the coming of the Europeans. There followed battles and skirmishes between Maoris and representatives of the government and settlers concerning European purchases and seizures of Maori in particular. Later in the nineteenth century the Maori population was severely depleted by disease.

Initially, New Zealand was governed as a dependency of the colony of New South Wales, Australia. In 1841 it was constituted a separate colony, and in 1907 it received more autonomy as a Dominion. Complete autonomy followed in 1947 with the adoption of the Statute of Westminster.

People Groups

New Zealand's population in 1985 was 3.3 million. Urban concentration was 84 percent. Besides the pronounced rural-to-urban drift, New Zealand's population has been steadily moving north. In 1981, about 73 percent of the people lived in the North Island.

People of European origin predominate in the New Zealand population, although in recent years, declining birth rates and immigration has caused the proportion of Europeans to fall slightly. There are now several thousand Pacific Islanders in the New Zealand population. Ethnic Chinese and Indians have also increased marginally in importance, and together made up 1 percent of the population--18,500 and 11,200, respectively, in the mid-1980's.

Socio-Political Conditions

New Zealand is a monarchical state and a constituent member of the British Commonwealth. The elements of rule are the titular head, the monarch is represented by the Governor-General, (the English monarch being the monarch of the Dominion of New Zealand), the legislative authority, the executive and administrative structure, and the judiciary.

The supreme law-making authority is the House of Representatives or Parliament, whose members are elected triennially. The leader of the majority party in Parliament becomes the Prime Minister. Although there are three distinct political parties, two have alternately held control of the House of Representatives since 1935.

A further feature of New Zealand life is the high level of Government involvement in the economy. This dates from 1870 and has resulted in a high level of Government investment in transport, steel, petrochemical, forest, and other industries.

English is universally taught in schools and almost universally spoken. Until recently, Maori has not been taught at lower school level, but is still spoken by many of this group. Pacific Island and other immigrants tend to maintain their original language for a generation or so in the family, but the teaching of English in all schools tends to lead the younger generation to adopt this as the sole medium of speech.

Education is compulsory from ages 6 to 15, although most children commence primary school at age five. Almost one-half of the children, in the age-range three to four, are enrolled in free kindergartens or play centers. Rural programs and correspondence school programs make education available to every individual within the country. Tertiary education is increasingly taken. For instance, in 1976 less than 20 percent of those aged between 50 and 60 years had received a tertiary education. This proportion has risen to one-third among 30 to 40 year olds.

Economic Conditions

New Zealand is predominately a primary producer, especially of wool, meat, and timber. It enjoys a relatively stable economy and a fairly high degree of prosperity and standard of living, but, because it is heavily reliant on income from the export of primary products, it is unavoidably affected by general world conditions. Real income has declined in recent years.

Status Of Christianity

New Zealand is a Christian country with a high degree of nominalism in the major denominations and an increasing number of people who "object to state" or fail to specify, or claim to have "no religion" (23.5 percent in the 1981 census).

TABLE 7
COMPARATIVE IMPORTANCE OF 15 LARGEST
RELIGIOUS PROFESSIONS IN NEW ZEALAND[1]

	1971	1981	1971,%	1981,%
Anglican	895,839	807,132	31.3	25.7
Presbyterian	583,701	521,040	20.4	16.6
Roman Catholic	449,874	452,871	15.7	14.4
Methodist	182,727	147,195	6.4	4.7
Christian n.o.d.[2]	33,187	100,812	1.2	3.2
Baptist	47,350	49,536	1.7	1.6
The Church of Jesus Christ of Latter-Day Saints (Mormons)	29,785	37,431	1.0	1.2

Ratana	30,156	35,763	1.1	1.1
Brethren	25,768	24,216	0.9	0.8
Salvation Army	19,371	20,409	0.7	0.6
Protestant n.o.d.[2]	37,475	15,846	1.3	0.5
Jehovah's Witness	10,318	13,686	0.4	0.4
Assemblies of God	3,599	12,456	0.1	0.4
Pentecostal (Indigenous and unspecified)	1,859	11,652	0.1	0.4
Seventh-day Adventist	10,477	11,427	0.4	0.4
Religious Subtotal:	2,361,586	2,261,472	82.7	72.0
No Religion, Object to State and Not Specified	408,037	738,894	14.3	23.5
Total Population:	2,862,631	3,143,307	100.0	100.0

[1] Some of the groups have achieved this status only in recent years.

[2] Christian n.o.d. and Protestant n.o.d. are "not otherwise defined."

Source: NZ Census of Population and Dwellings 1971 and 1981 (provisional).

PLURALIST TENDENCY

Sociologists have noted the marked increase in the number of people who claim no religious or denominational affiliation, and the consequent decline in allegiance to the larger and long established churches. The religious character of New Zealand, they note, is becoming less and less homogeneous, more secular and more diverse with a rapid expansion in the number of small religious groups. Sociologists have termed this phenomenon "the pluralist tendency." Professor Lloyd Geering, writing on this trend in "Religions in New Zealand Society," concludes the analysis with this comment:

"The cultural bonding of New Zealand as a nation will not be of a religious character but will consist of a secular or religiously neutral base, in which each person will be responsible for choosing and adding his own religious component."

As a secular state, there is no commitment to nor affiliation with any religious tradition or ideology. When state functions require a religious dimension, the Anglican Church has given the lead as the single largest denomination or religious group. However, in the past decade, as the numerical strength and influence of the Anglican Church has declined, certain state or notable public occasions have been more ecumenical in character. Usually, Roman Catholics have been included.

The other striking feature of the pluralist tendency has been the impact of Pentecostalism and the charismatic renewal. Some data will be presented in a later section.

CHURCH UNION

One of the major issues of the 1970's was church union. The negotiating parties were the Anglican, Presbyterian and Methodist Churches, the Associated Churches of Christ and the Congregational Union. In 1978, a Covenant Agreement involved a statement of shared faith and a commitment to work toward more visible unity.

By 1981, the Methodists had indicated their willingness to proceed to full union with any or all of the negotiating churches as soon as it was constitutionally possible. The Presbyterians voted in mid-1981 on a simple "yes/no" option of uniting with one or more of the negotiating churches on the basis of the Plan for Union 1971. Of the three-quarters of the communicant members who voted, 52.7 percent were in favor, which was interpreted to indicate only moderate enthusiasm for proceeding with the 1971 plan.

The General Synod 1982 of the Anglican Church formally laid the Plan for Union 1971 to rest, in so far as the unification of ministries was concerned.

NATIONAL CHURCHES

This section discusses Anglican and Protestant, Catholic and Eastern Orthodox Churches and other religious groups. Background statistical data are contained in Tables 8 and 9 following the "Interpretations" section.

Anglican Church

BRIEF HISTORY

The **Anglican Church** has been present in New Zealand from the early days of European settlement. To Samuel Marsden of the

Church of England belonged the honor of preaching the first Christian sermon in the Bay of Islands on Christmas Day, 1814. Strong missionary activity followed among the Maori people, almost all of whom adopted the Christian religion. (Methodist and Catholic missionaries participated in this to a lesser extent, followed much later by Presbyterian and other missions.)

The Church of the Province of New Zealand was subsequently formed in 1857. Nine dioceses are part of the Province, including the Dioceses of Polynesia (South Pacific) and Aotearoa (Maori people throughout New Zealand). Although still the largest single religious profession, with 25.7 percent of the population in 1981, there has been a steady erosion of its relative importance throughout this century.

CHURCH DEVELOPMENT

There is considerable diversity within the Anglican Church -- Anglo-Catholic or High Church, liberal, evangelical, charismatic -- and these different streams have been accommodated with greater ease than in some other denominations. Among recent developments in the life of the Church have been the ordination of women to the priesthood and the ordaining of non-stipendiary priests, who remain in their secular jobs and develop a priesthood appropriate to their situation.

Missionary interest and activity are channeled through the Anglican Board of Missions and the semi-autonomous, evangelical Church Missionary Society. A single theological college, St. John's College, trains most Anglican priests and many Methodist ministers; about 50 of the 70 students are training for the Anglican ministry.

CHURCH MINISTRIES

The Latimer Fellowship and its magazine, *Latimer*, serve to unite the evangelical stream of the Anglican Church with Christian Advance Ministries, the latter group comprising the charismatics of the denomination. Christian Advance Ministries has a much broader constituency than the Anglican Church, but the Anglicans have provided much of the organization's leadership.

Day-school education is provided by 25 primary schools and 18 secondary schools; most began in the early years of European settlement and before a state system of education developed. In the past 20 years, Government assistance has involved grants and subsidies.

Since the passage of the Private Schools Conditional Integration Act in 1975, the voluntary integration of private schools into the State system has been possible. By 1981, seven Anglican secondary schools had taken this option.

Roman Catholic Church

After an initial wave of missionary endeavor among the Maori people, Roman Catholic activity after 1850 was directed more to European immigrants and their descendants. One hundred and thirty years later, however, there is a higher proportion (9.7 in 1976) of Maoris among professing Catholics than for any other major denomination, with the exception of the Methodist. In 1981, more than 450,000 New Zealanders professed to be Catholics, a growth of 24.4 percent since 1961, and 14.4 percent of the total population were Catholics, a drop from 15.7 percent in 1971. Certain parts of the country have a much higher proportion of Catholics, notably Westland, Taranaki, and Wellington.

In general, the historical root of New Zealand Catholics is Irish, the clergy having followed the laity as immigrants from Ireland.

RECENT DEVELOPMENTS

Since the Second Vatican Council (Vatican II) in 1965, there has been a renewed spirit of openness, both by and toward the Roman Catholic Church. The move toward a New Zealand Council of Churches has undoubtedly been aided by this openness. At the parish level, there is often even more extensive dialogue and cooperation especially where the charismatic renewal has influenced local congregations, including the Catholics. Christian Advance Ministries (the charismatic arm of the Anglican Church in New Zealand) has aided this fellowship, and for several years now, at least one full-time staff member has been a Catholic with particular interest in Catholic renewal.

Day schooling has been a strong feature of Catholic life since the passage of the 1877 Education Act, which ushered in a State system of education that was free, secular and compulsory. An extensive network of primary and, to a lesser extent, secondary schools emerged. Because of growing financial difficulties, much of the pressure for the Private Schools Conditional Integration Act came from the Catholics. Many of their schools are now integrated into the State system.

Social needs within New Zealand are addressed through the Catholic Social Services, with offices in each diocese. A broad range of activities is provided, with many of the religious orders being especially active; the Society of St. Vincent de Paul has a particular role in both New Zealand and overseas.

In respect to the overseas situation, the Commission for Evangelization, Justice and Development is the major avenue for mission, social and development activity. The Catholic Church produces two weekly newspapers, *The Tablet*, and *Zealandia*.

Eastern Orthodox Church

Because New Zealand has received comparatively few immigrants from Eastern Europe, Orthodox adherents comprise a very small part of the population. In 1981, 3,756 (0.1 percent of the total population) professed to be Orthodox; almost 75 percent of these were in the Wellington area. Both the Greek Orthodox Church and, since 1982, the Antiochan Orthodox Church are members of the National Council of Churches.

Presbyterian Church

A United Presbyterian Church has existed in New Zealand since 1901. Currently, it is the second-largest religious group in the country, a position that could shortly be lost to Roman Catholics. Relative strength has been declining during the twentieth century, and in 1981, 16.6 percent of the population claimed adherence to the denomination. Communicant members totaled 68,000 in 1982, a decline of 10 percent from 1977; and 38 percent were over 60 years of age, compared with 14 percent for the total population. In Otago and Southland, however, where Scottish migrants were in the majority during the second half of the nineteenth century, the proportion of Presbyterians in 1981 was 36.9 percent and 40.4 percent, respectively.

There is considerable theological diversity in the Presbyterian Church and no other denomination has publicly debated its theological differences so vigorously. The official magazine of the Presbyterian Church is *The Outlook*. Missionary activity is undertaken by the Joint Board for Mission Overseas, which includes the Methodists. This Board has been restructured recently and is now called the Council for Missions and Ecumenical Cooperation. Day school education has been provided by nine primary schools and twelve secondary schools. The evangelicals in the denomination are linked through the Westminster Fellowship and its magazine *Evangelical Presbyterian.*

Methodist Church

The third largest Protestant denomination is the Methodist Church, with 4.7 percent of the population in 1981. Between 1961 and 1981, Methodist Church adherents fell by more than 15 percent at a time when the total population increased by 30 percent. Other major denominations also suffered losses, though of lesser magnitude -- Brethren, 6 percent; and Anglicans and Presbyterians, each 3.5 percent.

Methodists have made the most unequivocal commitment to church union among the churches; moreover, the pursuit of union at the local level -- leading to "union" and "cooperating" parishes -- has meant that Methodist churches have been involved to a greater extent than Anglican, Congregational, Presbyterian or Associated Churches of Christ churches. The liberal and social activist tendencies of the Methodist Church have also been an obvious feature in recent years.

Baptist Union

The Baptist Union celebrated its centenary in 1982 and experienced its largest numerical growth in membership of any previous year. In 1981, there were almost 50,000 adherents or 1.6 percent of the total population; growth since 1961 totaled 21 percent. The denomination is more uniformly evangelical, which helps to distinguish it from the three larger Protestant denominations.

The *New Zealand Baptist* is the denominational newspaper. The Baptist Missionary Society oversees missionary activities in the Solomons, Papua New Guinea, Indonesia and Bangladesh.

Brethren

In 1961 the Brethren reached the peak of their numerical strength -- almost 25,800 adherents and 1.1 percent of the total population. By 1981, these figures had declined to 24,200 and 0.8 percent. Within Brethren Churches, resistance to charismatic renewal has been stronger than in other major denominations. Many adherents of previous years have moved into other churches. The theological position of the Brethren is conservative evangelical. The monthly newspaper is *The Treasury*, and their considerable missionary activity throughout the world is largely conducted by Christian Missions to Many Lands.

Salvation Army

Like the Baptists, the Salvation Army has been able to offset the declining numbers of the other major Protestant denominations. Over the 20-year period of 1961 to 1981, growth totaled 32 percent, slightly ahead of the national population growth. Adherents now total more than 20,000, or 0.6 percent of the population. This is the only major Protestant denomination having a higher-than-average representation in the service, production worker and laborer occupational groups -- a reflection of its strong social ministry. Additionally, the Salvation Army has the highest proportion of European adherents -- 94.1 percent in 1976 compared with 86.1 percent Europeans in the total population.

Pentecostal Churches

One of the most significant events in the changing religious profile of New Zealand has been the emergence of the various Pentecostal denominations and independent congregations. These include the Assemblies of God, the Apostolic Church, Elim Church and numerous independent fellowships, some of which are part of the indigenous Pentecostal Churches. In 1961, these various churches and fellowships, had 3,118 professed adherents; by 1971, this had increased to 10,149 and to 30,498 by 1981. Those professing to belong to the Assemblies of God comprised 41 percent of this total; the unspecified Pentecostal or indigenous Pentecostal group, 40 percent; Apostolic, 15 percent; and Elim, 4 percent. These figures need to be interpreted with caution since it is claimed that some who worship regularly in a Pentecostal church enter "Christian" on the census return.

The various Pentecostal churches are informally linked through the Associated Pentecostal Churches of New Zealand. On a proportional basis, the Assemblies of God are especially strong in Northland and Auckland; the Apostolic, in Hawkes Bay; and indigenous Pentecostals, in Canterbury and Westland. In Marlborough, the Elim Church has the support of 1.5 percent of the region's population, placing it well ahead of the Salvation Army, Baptist and Brethren denominations.

The Apostolic and indigenous Pentecostal churches have also been especially successful in attracting New Zealand Maoris. In 1976, Maoris comprised 8.6 percent of the total population, but 3.8 percent of the Apostolic and 21 percent of the indigenous Pentecostal adherents were Maoris. The Assemblies of God have been active among the Samoan and Fijian communities resident in New Zealand.

Indigenous Maori Churches

It could be questioned whether the indigenous Maori churches -- Ratana and Ringatu -- should be included under the heading of "Protestant" or under "Other Religions." Both retain many elements of Protestant belief but clearly avoid identification with any of the denominational groups of the *Pakeha* (European). Te Kooti Rikirangi, who played a prominent role in the Maori opposition to European settlement during the latter half of the nineteenth century, was behind the development of the Ringatu Church.

The Ratana church was begun in 1925. A Taranaki farmer, Tehupotiki Wiremu Ratana, was the initiator. Both churches draw heavily from Old Testament imagery and Maori culture and tradition; both have elements of what would now be termed "liberation theology."

In 1981, the Ratana church had almost 36,000 adherents and had grown at almost twice the rate of the New Zealand population during the previous 20 years. Growth in the Ringatu church was less strong. Obviously, a high proportion of adherents were Maoris-- 91 percent and 95 percent, respectively, in 1976. For many years now, the four Maori seats in Parliament, almost without exception, have been occupied by members of the Ratana Church.

Seventh-day Adventists

Some also question whether the Seventh-day Adventist Church should be termed Protestant, as its character is also very distinctive. In line with recent trends in the United States, Seventh-day Adventists in New Zealand are now becoming more closely identified with orthodox Christian belief and are starting to see themselves as part of the wider community of Christian churches.

TABLE 8

COMPARISON OF ADHERENCE AND AVERAGE CHURCH ATTENDANCE IN 1981 FOR SELECTED PROTESTANT DENOMINATIONS IN NEW ZEALAND

	Average Weekly Attendance of Adults	Percentage of Adult Adherents
Anglican	55,000	9.4
Apostolic	3,500	107.6
Assemblies of God	10,000	111.0
Baptist	30,000	83.8
Brethren	11,000	62.8
Churches of Christ (Assoc)	2,000	43.9
Elim Church of NZ	1,200	131.9
Evangelical Lutheran Church of NZ	1,000	26.1
Methodist	15,000	14.1
Pentecostal (Incl Indigenous Pentecostal)	10,000	118.7
Presbyterian	51,000	13.5
Reformed Church of NZ	1,000	59.2
Salvation Army	10,000	67.8
Society of Friends	400	52.1

Note: In concluding this section comment is necessary on the distinction between "adherents" as revealed by census data, and actual church involvement and commitment. The denominations with the largest numbers of adherents generally have the lowest level of involvement. Between 9 percent and 14 percent of adults attend church on the average Sunday in the case of Anglicans, Presbyterians, and Methodists. This proportion rises to 60-85 percent for the Salvation Army, Brethren and Baptists, and, according to Table 8, exceeds 100 percent for the Assemblies of God and other Pentecostal churches; in other words, the growing churches also enjoy the highest level of commitment. Indeed, in the case of the Pentecostal Churches, adults are attending their services who are not yet prepared to profess adherence; this is a sign for future growth.

For comparison, Darroch estimates that the 110,000 adults who are Roman Catholic attending church on the average Sunday, represent 33.6 percent of adult adherents.

Source: Average Weekly Attendance of Adults from Murray Darroch's "An Introduction to NZ Protestants" published serially in the *NZ Tablet*, June/July 1981. Estimates were provided by various denominations, as most do not collect attendance statistics.

TABLE 9

PERCENTAGE OF VARIOUS ETHNIC GROUPS IN NEW ZEALAND IN SELECTED RELIGIOUS PROFESSIONS, 1976

	European %	NZ Maori %	Pacific Island Polynesian %	Chinese %	Indian %	Other %
New Zealand, Total Pop.	86.1	8.6	2.0	0.5	0.3	2.6
Anglican	90.1	7.4	0.2	0.1	--*	2.1
Presbyterian	93.5	1.5	2.7	0.2	--*	2.0
Roman Catholic	84.9	9.7	2.3	0.2	0.1	2.7
Methodist	84.6	10.0	2.7	0.1	0.1	2.5
Baptist	93.3	2.4	0.8	1.2	--*	2.3
Ratana	8.2	91.0	0.1	--*	--*	0.7
Church of Jesus Christ of Latter-Day Saints (Mormons)	29.1	57.2	11.1	0.1	0.1	2.4
Brethren	88.2	8.6	0.6	0.1	0.1	2.3
Salvation Army	94.1	2.4	0.7	0.1	0.1	2.7
Seventh-day Adventist	64.1	7.5	23.5	0.1	0.1	4.6
Jehovah's Witness	78.0	16.1	3.1	0.3	0.2	2.3

Note: "Other" includes ethnic groups not listed and those who list their religious profession but not their ethnic origin.

*Less than 0.05 percent.

Source: NZ Census of Population and Dwellings, 1976,

ECUMENICAL AGENCIES

National Council of Churches

The major ecumenical agency, the National Council of Churches (NCC), was formed in 1941; member churches are Anglican, Presbyterian, Methodist, Baptist, Associated Churches of Christ, Congregational Union, Society of Friends (or Quakers), Salvation Army, Greek Orthodox, Cook Islands Christian Church, Liberal Catholic Church, and Antiochan Orthodox. Other churches have observers at General Meetings -- Roman Catholics since 1965, Lutherans since 1968, and other denominations on an irregular basis. This Council has a clearly-defined structure, with a paid secretariat, and is funded by the twelve member denominations.

In the report to the 39th Annual Meeting of the NCC (1982), the *modus operandi* of the NCC was expressed in the following way: "...the member churches have maintained their commitment to work together for the Gospel's sake." However, the diversity of the membership gives rise to several tensions. Probably the most important is between those who feel that the first priority of the Church is to preach the gospel of personal salvation and those who believe that the preaching of the gospel is inseparable from a deep involvement in political and social affairs.

The National Council of Churches is not a voting member of the World Council of Churches, although some of the member churches are WCC members. There is a close cooperation between the two bodies in the case of several commissions and programs, although this cooperation always remains under the authority of the New Zealand member churches. The NCC is a member of the Christian Conference of Asia and an observer to the Pacific Conference of Churches.

A Joint Working Committee of the National Council of Churches and the Catholic Church was formed 13 years ago. From this committee has come a series of proposals for a New Zealand Council of

Churches. The NCC has supported these proposals and given general approval to the draft constitution and rules. The Catholic Bishop's Conference has also approved the constitution and rules, and the proposals were discussed by the individual churches in 1983.

Pentecostal Churches

Although more loosely structured, the Associated Pentecostal Churches of New Zealand provides a forum for discussion and cooperation among the member groups of churches. The subject of "union" has also been raised, although not with any great enthusiasm.

PARACHURCH AGENCIES

New Zealand Evangelical Missionary Alliance

A large array of parachurch or interdenominational agencies fulfill a wide variety of both home and foreign (or national and overseas) activities. Most overseas mission agencies are associated with the New Zealand Evangelical Missionary Alliance (N.Z.E.M.A.) as full members. (There is no Evangelical Alliance or its equivalent in New Zealand). Agencies primarily involved with the various Pentecostal denominations are the main exceptions. A few denominational agencies are associate members, e.g., Baptist Missionary Society and Church Missionary Society; but in general, the denominational or ecumenical agencies are not part of N.Z.E.M.A.

Full members of N.Z.E.M.A. include foreign missionary societies such as Overseas Missionary Fellowship (OMF), Sudan Interior Mission (SIM), Bible Medical Missionary Fellowship (BMMF), and Worldwide Evangelization Crusade (WEC). Specialized evangelistic agencies include Open Air Campaigners (OAC), United Maori Mission (U.M.M.), Youth with a Mission (YWAM), and Far East Broadcasting Company (FEBC). Special purpose missionary societies are Wycliffe Bible Translators, Missionary Aviation Fellowship (M.A.F.), and Christian Leaders' Training College of PNG. There are training institutions like Bible College of New Zealand (B.C.N.Z.), and Capernwray Missionary Fellowship. Special interest organizations are also members, like Tertiary Students Christian Fellowship (TSCF), and Scripture Union, as well as relief and development agencies such as World Vision (WV) and The Evangelical Alliance Relief (TEAR) Fund.

N.Z.E.M.A. is a low-profile organization whose main service is to provide superannuation and resettlement facilities for members, to act as a clearing house for funds and inquiries and, most recently, to give a simple form of financial accreditation. The promotion of missionary interest is left to the individual members or ad hoc groups such as MOVE OUT, and to certain regional missionary associations. The first MOVE OUT Conference in 1981 attracted 500 participants and the largest missions display ever assembled in New Zealand. A second conference for 700 to 800 participants was held in 1983.

Evangelistic Agencies

Parachurch agencies whose main activities are within New Zealand are often evangelistic in orientation, e.g., Youth For Christ (YFC), Lay Institute for Evangelism (LIFE), Full Gospel Businessmen's Fellowship, Women's Aglow, Christian Businessmen's Association, Inter-schools Christian Fellowship (ISCF, a ministry of Scripture Union), and New Zealand Prison Fellowship.

Others provide an identity for Christians in a particular situation, e.g., Tertiary Students' Christian Fellowship (TSCF). Some seek to present a Christian perspective or dimension in a particular area, e.g., Christian Broadcasting Association New Zealand (C.B.A.N.Z. with its preparation of radio programs for secular radio), Energy Source T.V. and Seven Seas Television (the television equivalent of C.B.A.), Radio Rhema (in the establishment and operation of radio stations), the Association for Promotion of Christian Schools (in the encouragement of Christian day schools) and Sunflower Communications (publisher of a free paper, *Grapevine*, distributed in the Auckland area and available by subscription in other parts of the country).

Others promote prayer (Intercessors for New Zealand), Bible reading (Scripture Union and the Bible Society of N.Z.), audio-cassette teaching (Inspirational Tapes and many others), audiovisuals (Christian Audiovisual Society), ethical and moral standards (Integrity Centre), and Christian musicians (Christian Ministries International).

Other Groups

Various subsidiary committees and agencies exist for particular purposes. The oldest and best known is the relief and development agency, Christian World Service. In 1981/82, its annual income was $440,000. Other groups include the Youth Council, Churches Education Commission, Church and Society Commission, Women's Committee, and Mission and Evangelism Committee. Since 1975, the Inter-Church Commission on Immigration and Refugee Resettlement (ICCI), which includes Catholic and Jewish Welfare Agency representation, has made an important contribution to the settlement of refugees in New Zealand. Also established in 1975, was Ecumenical Secretariat on Development (ESOD) for development action and education.

Chaplaincies in prisons are coordinated by the NCC. A chaplaincy service for industry is run by a separate organization -- the Inter-Church Trade and Industry Mission -- which includes in its membership most of the NCC churches and the Lutheran and Catholic churches. The Churches' committees on broadcasting and on chaplaincies in hospitals and universities are now administered by ecumenical committees, following the NCC initiatives.

At the 1982 Annual Meeting of the NCC, the Maori section became the Maori Council of Churches (Te Runanga Whakawhaunga). This is now an autonomous body working in partnership with NCC, with membership open to the Maori section of any Church or Christian body.

All parachurch agencies seek financial support from the Christian community, and consequently need to develop good relationships with churches and congregations.

MAJOR CHRISTIAN ACTIVITIES

Evangelism

Various references have already been made to evangelistic agencies and activities in the preceding sections on the "National Churches," "Ecumenical" and "Parachurch Agencies." This section will enlarge upon those comments.

Mass Evangelization

Mass Evangelization is commonly associated with the major Billy Graham Crusades in 1959 and 1968. Although the 1959 crusade was probably the more effective in terms of lasting impact, both drew support and commendation from a wide spectrum of the Christian Church.

In the 1970's, mass evangelism was more frequently associated with the Pentecostal churches and agencies such as Full Gospel Businessmen's Fellowship and Youth for Christ (YFC). The Jesus Crusades of the 1970's and the YFC rallies were held in sports stadiums.

Although not characterized by mass meetings, there have been other nationwide thrusts involving home visitation and literature distribution, where the objective has been to present the gospel to every New Zealander within a comparatively short period. The latest activity of this kind was "Operation Resurrection," a nationwide outreach initiated by Youth With a Mission in 1983. The ship *Anastasis* was an integral part of the program.

Local Evangelism

Local Evangelism centers on individual congregations or groups of congregations within a suburb or town. Some activities have been coordinated across several congregations of a particular denomination to make use of a single, overseas evangelist.

A few denominations have full-time evangelists, others an evangelism committee or commission to enhance this evangelistic activity. Certain parachurch agencies already listed have an important role in local evangelism, either directly or through cooperative programs with local churches.

Many churches have also found that the establishment of home groups has enhanced the evangelistic thrust of the church, as the network of one-to-one relationships also grows.

Literature Distribution and Other Support

Certain agencies provide literature for evangelistic activities, e.g., Bible Society in N.Z., Lay Institute for Evangelism (LIFE), and ACTS International. Others give particular emphasis to the media, e.g., Radio Rhema, with its existing broadcasts in the Christchurch and Wellington areas and plans for total coverage of the country. *Challenge Weekly*, *Grapevine*, and *Shaker*, are published Christian magazines.

Training in evangelism through workshops, seminars and schools is also undertaken by LIFE, Open Air Campaigners (OAC) and various "Schools of Evangelism" run by local fellowships or individuals.

Other agencies specialize in the production and supply of cassette tapes, often for clearly defined audiences; films, and other audiovisuals.

In recent years, the use of mime and drama (e.g., The Covenant Players and YWAM's "The Toymaker and Son") have also been useful in extending the scope of evangelism.

Education

There are two facets of education to be considered, viz., day schools and theological or Bible schools. References have already been made to certain aspects of education under the "National Churches" section.

DAY SCHOOLS

Certain older denominations, especially the Catholic, Anglican, and Presbyterian churches, developed a network of day schools during the last century, particularly after the passage of the 1877 Education Act. This Act ensured that State education would be secular in its orientation.

More recently, a few interdenominational Christian schools have been established, as well as schools firmly based in a single congregation or fellowship. All are concerned with a strong biblical basis for all education, and curriculum materials reflect this concern. The Christian basis or content is comprehensive, in place of religious instruction as a separate subject entity. These newer schools are generally members of the New Zealand Association for Christian Schools. About two-thirds of the 25 members use Accelerated Christian Education (ACE) materials, curriculum resources developed in the United States, and the remaining schools use an assortment of overseas and locally-produced materials.

In 1981, there were 345 registered independent or private primary and secondary schools in New Zealand. With a few exceptions, all were denominational, interdenominational, or congregation-based schools. About 8 percent of the country's primary school children and 12 percent of secondary school children attended these independent schools in 1981.

The Private Schools' Conditional Integration Act of 1975 opened the way for the integration of these independent schools into the State school system. Certain safeguards were made to retain the integrating schools' distinctiveness and character, but certain conditions also had to be met. By early 1982, about one-third of the independent schools had completed negotiations for integration; another one-third were in the process of negotiating integration agreements. Most of the remaining schools were expected to retain their existing independent status.

THEOLOGICAL AND BIBLE COLLEGES

Training for the major denomination ministries takes place at the Holy Cross Seminary at Mosgiel near Dunedin (Catholic), St. John's College in Auckland (Anglican and Methodist), Knox College in Dunedin (Presbyterian), and Baptist Theological College in Auckland (Baptist).

Other ministerial and pastoral training is given at the Apostolic Bible College near Wellington (Apostolic Church), Zion Bible Training Centre in Auckland (Assembly of God and Elim Churches) and Bible College of New Zealand in Auckland (for several of the small as well some major denominations).

For general Bible training and preparation for overseas missionary service, the Bible College of New Zealand is the oldest and best known institution. Including its branch colleges, it has some 350 students, which is comparable to the combined student enrollment at the other colleges and schools listed above.

A diverse selection of courses is available, leading to degrees and diplomas of the Australian College of Theology and the Melbourne College of Divinity. The college also awards certificates and diplomas. Branch colleges provide evening and Saturday courses in Dunedin, Christchurch, and Nelson; comprehensive external study courses are also offered. The College operates three bookstores and publishes a bimonthly magazine, *The Reaper.*

Comparable courses are offered at Zion Bible Training Centre, a two-year course for students drawn from Pentecostal and charismatic churches. The New Zealand Assembly Bible School in Auckland offers one- or two-year courses for Brethren students. The Orama Christian Training School on Great Barrier Island, off Auckland, conducts a one-year Christian Workers' Course and three year Ministry Training Centre in a close-knit, community setting.

Shorter courses of up to a year's duration are available at Faith Bible College in Tauranga, Emmanuel Bible College in Whangarei,

Hebron Bible College in Auckland, and GLO Training Centre near Te Awamutu. Except for GLO (which mainly caters for students from Brethren assemblies) these institutions are Pentecostal-charismatic in orientation.

Social Concern

The Christian Church has always been at the forefront in caring for society's disadvantaged, elderly, and sick. Some denominations have become especially well known for their activities, e.g., the Salvation Army among alcoholics and the "outcasts" of society. The Anglican, Presbyterian, Methodist, and Baptist denominations have integrated social activities for the aged, orphaned, unemployed, handicapped and needy. The Brethren have run homes for orphaned children for many years, and more recently have added several aged-people's homes.

With high levels of unemployment in recent years, the Government has helped many churches set up community work schemes where the unemployed undertake work for the aged, disabled or sick.

Other congregations have supplemented inner city missions by acquiring property for use as hostels or temporary accommodation for those in need. Extended families and church-based communities are providing support for those with drug-related problems, psychiatric problems, and recent marriage or family breakdowns.

Although the following specifically refers to Anglican activities, it can be seen as an indication of the scope and nature of Christian social work. Other denominational groups, e.g., Presbyterian Social Services Association and Baptist Social Services, are based on similar principles and provide related services.

Social services within the Anglican Church are primarily structured at the diocesan level. An Association of Anglican Social Services, formed in 1980 and reporting to the General Synod, provides a forum for diocesan social workers and for information and advice concerning key areas of social need and local and national response to these needs.

Within each diocese are agencies coordinating every aspect of social need with a Director of Social Services usually providing executive direction. In the main centers, the City Mission is the focal point of this activity. In some areas, Methodists are linked with Anglicans.

Throughout the country in 1981, there were 13 children's homes (with 203 children) and 20 old people's homes (with 335 beds).

Chaplains are found in hospitals, universities, prisons, and the armed forces. There has traditionally also been a strong Anglican presence in the various Missions to Seamen.

Other Religions

One of the features of the "pluralist tendency" in New Zealand has been the growth of other religions. Two groups are especially strong, the Church of Jesus Christ of Latter-Day Saints (Mormons) and Jehovah's Witnesses. Others with less than 1,000 adherents in 1981 are Church of Christ, Scientist (Christian Scientists); Swedenborgians; Unitarians; and the Worldwide Church of God ("Moonies"). Christadelphians have maintained their strength of 1,500 to 1,700 adherents during the past twenty years.

CHURCH OF JESUS CHRIST OF LATTER-DAY SAINTS (MORMONS)

The Latter-Day Saints have shown strong growth in recent years, more than doubling in size since 1961 to 37,431 adherents, which represents 1.2 percent of the population. In 1981, some 57 percent of their adherents were Maori and 11 percent, Pacific Island Polynesian; this was five to six times their proportion in the whole population. This means that some regions in New Zealand have a much higher than average proportion of Church of Jesus Christ of Latter-Day Saints (Mormons), viz: Northland, East Coast and Hawkes Bay. The emphasis on genealogies is particularly attractive to Polynesians.

JEHOVAH'S WITNESSES

Jehovah's Witnesses (JW) have shown an even stronger growth rate during the past twenty years, reaching 13,686 adherents (0.4 percent of the population) in 1981. Here, too, is a higher than average representation of New Zealand Maoris and Pacific Island Polynesians; 16. percent and 3.1 percent, respectively, which is twice the national average; this group is also comparatively well-represented in Northland and East Coast.

In the past year or so, there have been several notable defections from the Mormons and JW's, resulting in considerable publicity and the formation of an organization called Ex-Mormons for Jesus. It is too soon to note what impact this will have on the continued growth of the two groups.

Chapter Six: *Polynesia:*

American Samoa
Cook Islands
French Polynesia
Niue
Pitcairn Islands
Tokelau
Tonga
Tuvalu
Wallis and Futuna
Western Samoa

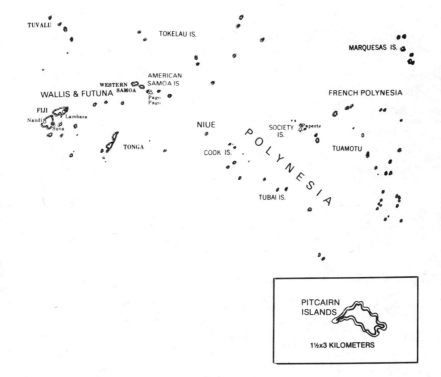

AMERICAN SAMOA

Profile

NATURAL FEATURES: Land area: 197 sq. km. (76 sq. mi.) consists of five islands and the tiny coral atolls, Rose and Swains. They are volcanic with mountains rising abruptly over the Pacific Ocean. Tutuila is the largest island.

CAPITAL: Pago Pago. **Population** 3,075. It has one of the finest harbors in the world.

POPULATION: 36,400, (1984 est.) **Annual growth rate:** 1.7 percent. About 65,000 American Samoans live in mainland U.S., and 20,000 in Hawaii.

LANGUAGES: Samoan, which relates to Hawaiian and other Polynesian languages. English is universally spoken.

RELIGION: Christians: 99 percent. **Largest denominations:** Congregational Christian Church in American Samoa, 60 percent; Roman Catholic, 20 percent; and Methodist, 5 percent. **Others:** Church of Jesus Christ of Latter-Day Saints (Mormons), 9 percent.

GOVERNMENT: An unincorporated Territory of the United States. **Branches of Government:** Executive -- Governor and Lt. Governor. **Legislative:** Bicameral-Senate with 18 Senators, House of

Representatives with 20 elected members. **Judicial:** High, District and Village Courts.

ECONOMY: Major funding comes from the United States. **Main industry:** fish canning, employing 15 percent of the work force. **Main crops:** coconuts, bananas, taro, pineapples, vegetables for local consumption. Tuna is the main export to the U.S.

American And European Contacts

The Samoas had considerable contact with Fiji and Tonga before the Dutch Admiral Jacob Roggeveen visited the islands in 1722. Subsequently, whalers, traders and castaway sailors arrived in increasing numbers. In addition, official British, German, and American expeditions in 1791, 1824, and 1838; respectively; expanded Western influence. Americans and Europeans came to dominate the economic life of the island as they made agreements with local chiefs.

While the foreign powers vied for trade, commercial, and strategic gains in Samoa, the chiefs in turn competed for political power. Through the ruling chief at that time, the United States obtained a treaty to use Pago Pago as a coaling station. Germany and Britain objected, nearly precipitating a confrontation. Eventually, the three powers established a system of joint rule in the Samoa Islands. In 1899, Britain withdrew; the United States took control of Eastern Samoa; Germany took Western Samoa. In 1900, Samoan chiefs formally ceded Tutuila to the United States, and the Manua Group in 1904. During World War II, the United States used the Islands as an advance training and staging area for its military forces. It also built roads, airstrips, docks, and medical facilities. Some Samoans volunteered for military service.

In the 1930's, a nationalist movement in Western Samoa started clamoring for independence. The *Mau a Pule* or *Mau* movement did not have a direct effect on American Samoa; however, the United States instituted some democratization and reforms. A bicameral legislature replaced an advisory board of local leaders. By 1978, American Samoa had its first native-born governor, Peter Tali Coleman. In 1976, the U.S. Secretary of the Interior approved American Samoa's Constitution.

American Samoans And Other People Groups

American Samoans are the descendants of Polynesians who are believed to have migrated to the islands 2,000 years ago. They are closely related to Tongans, Tahitians, the Maoris of New Zealand, and Hawaiians; they speak a related language.

Nearly 90 percent of the total population live in the island of Tutuila. While almost half of these live and work in the rural areas, a growing number reside and work in or near the Pago Pago area.

Five percent of the population are foreign-born, including Asians and Americans. There are approximately 1,500 Koreans and Japanese in American Samoa who work for the fishing fleets and the tuna canneries.

About 350 expatriate Americans, Australians, and Europeans are government officials, educators or businessmen. Tongans, Western Samoans and other Polynesians are also residents of the country.

THE *AIGA* AS A SOCIAL UNIT

As in Western Samoa, the basic social, political and economic unit in American Samoa is the *aiga*, or extended family, in which all kinspeople are related by birth or adoption. A *matai* or chief heads the group, directs the use of family land and other properties, and represents the *aiga* in traditional rites and ceremonies at births, deaths, weddings and other important occasions. In large communities, the *matai* appoints other members of the family to serve in some capacity in community affairs.

There are two types of *matais* at the present time: the *ali'i*, the high chief, who exercises ceremonial duties; and the *tutafale*, the orator, who is considered the new leader and the real source of authority in a community. Heredity is an important factor in the choice of the *matai*. However, the status of a *tutafale* can be achieved through election by the *aiga*, or the extended family, as a whole. A person's general competence, popularity, and ability to make a good speech are important factors.

American Samoans have emigrated in large numbers, particularly to California and Hawaii. Young men have enlisted in the U.S. Army; others have joined school football teams in the United States. Families have been reunited. This migration from the country compensates for its high population growth rate.

American Samoa: Its Political Status

"Unincorporated territory" refers to territory, such as American Samoa, which is not incorporated into the United States as are the other 50 states. "Unorganized" indicates that the United States Congress has not enacted organized legislation for American Samoa that will provide for congressionally-mandated powers of self-government. Instead, the Constitution of American Samoa forms the basic law of the Territory. This special arrangement ensures the inclusion of unique Samoan culture that otherwise can not be found in the United States Constitution and law. This pertains particularly to the customary pattern of land ownership and the holding of titles.

Thus, laws of the United States do not necessarily apply to American Samoa. Conversely, Samoans do not have automatic access to the court system of the United States. American Samoans are nationals, but not citizens of the United States. They could easily become citizens by establishing residence in the United States and complying with certain procedures.

The Territory is represented in the United States Congress by a non-voting Delegate.

Economic Conditions

American Samoa has a cash-based economy strengthened by American money and enterprise. More than 70 percent of the government budget comes from the Department of Interior and other Federal agencies. In the mid-1980's, the government employed about half of the work force. This has affected the traditional pursuits of farming, and most food is now imported. Social programs in the United States are also extended to the Territory.

Mission History

Before the arrival of the London Missionary Society (LMS) missionaries, some Wesleyans and indigenous movements with Christian ideas had begun in the islands. John Williams and Charles Barff came in 1830 and left some Tahitian teachers ashore. In 1836, Rev. Murray of the LMS settled on Tutuila where he stayed for many years. Within a few years, trained Samoan teachers began the spread of the gospel to Manua.

The missionaries and island teachers worked effectively through the conversion of the chiefs. Despite some political rivalries among the chiefs, they became key leaders in the Christian churches. At the same time, the status of the minister rose to the equivalent of a high chief.

Through the centuries, Christianity has interwoven the lives of the people. Nearly every village has an elaborate church, which remains the center of a way of life in the Islands. In most villages, the Sabbath Day is strictly observed. On this day, the people wear their best clothes and follow a regular prayer time. The majority of them observe these prayer hours at six in the morning and at six and seven in the evenings, praying and singing hymns.

The spread of Christianity in the Samoas is described in more detail in the section on Western Samoa.

Current Christianity

CONGREGATIONALISTS AND OTHER CHURCHES

Congregationalists are strong in American Samoa. However, while it remains the main denomination, it also loses many members to other groups. The Seventh-day Adventist Church has grown from 0.5 percent to 2.2 percent of the population since 1956. Newer denominations include the Assemblies of God, Church of Christ, Southern Baptist Convention, United Pentecostal Church, and Church of the Nazarene. The Assemblies of God recorded the fastest-growing group with 3.5 percent of the population as members. Other North American missionary groups have expanded their activities in the region.

Adherence and membership figures for the denomination include the following:

Congregational	16,500
Roman Catholic	6,000
Methodist	2,000
Seventh-day Adventist	600
Assemblies of God, Pago Pago	2,600
(1985, Baptized members)	
Church of Nazarene, Pago Pago (1970)	78
United Pentecostal Church (1972)	200
includes Tonga, Fiji, Tokelau	

| Church of Jesus Christ of Latter-Day Saints (Mormons) | 3,000 |

ROMAN CATHOLIC CHURCH

Catholic missionaries first arrived in 1845. In 1982, the Samoa-Pago Pago diocese was established. There are five parishes, with seven priests -- four diocesan and three religious -- three seminarians, seven brothers, 13 sisters, 28 catechists. There are 6,000 Catholics among the population of 30,000.

Catechists serve in rural villages after receiving an extensive four-year training course. Samoan seminarians study for the priesthood at the Pacific Regional Seminary in Suva, Fiji. The Samoans have the highest number of indigenous priests among those in the Pacific.

ASSEMBLIES OF GOD

In 1985, the Assemblies of God had 13 churches and 2 outstations, with 2,600 members and 1,100 other believers. Thirty-five credentialed ministers and three missionaries worked for the church. In 1985, the church had one Bible school with an enrollment of 30. This denomination is recently one of the fastest growing in the country.

INTERDENOMINATIONAL AGENCIES

The American Samoa Council of Christian Churches was organized on March 25, 1985. Its members include the Congregational, Roman Catholic, Christian Church in American Samoa, Methodist, Baptist, Congregational Church of Jesus Christ, and Church of the Nazarene.

Among its aims are to promote ways in which denominations can work together in common concerns, and to serve as the legal go-between in inter-ecclesiastical relations with other organizations. It also aims to identify new ways to strengthen the proclamation of the gospel in Samoa. The Council broadcasts a one hour Sunday service on government-sponsored radio and television.

CHRISTIAN ACTIVITIES

Educational Services

The first printed matter in Samoa -- several chapters of the Bible, source hymns, and a spelling book -- was introduced by the London Missionary Society, which came from Tahiti. By 1900, education was in the hands of various religious groups. The first government-run public school was established in 1903. Religious organizations still work with the governments to provide educational services.

Church and State are separate in American Samoa. While private church-related schools are allowed, they receive no subsidies from the government. After World War II, the government established a free school system from first grade to high school. Some students go abroad for university education, mainly to the United States.

The major churches established some secondary schools, including those of the Congregational Christian Church of Samoa and the Church of Jesus Christ of Latter-Day Saints (Mormons). In 1970, the Seventh-day Adventists and the Southern Baptists began elementary schools.

The Catholic Church has a primary school in Pago Pago and two secondary schools on Tutuila Island. In 1980, the Marist elementary school at Atu'u had an enrollment of 461; St. Francis Girls' School at Lepua had 412.

Broadcasting

Television is used for educational purposes. Local denominations participate in this function.

Literature

Bible translations into the Samoan language were completed in 1855. The Bible Society of the South Pacific distributes New Testaments, Bibles, portions and selection.

Service Agencies

There are about five service agencies in American Samoa which include Children's Evangelical Fellowship and the Interdenominational Committee of American Samoa, and Youth With A Mission.

Other Religions

CHURCH OF JESUS CHRIST OF LATTER-DAY SAINTS (MORMONS)

The Church of Latter-Day Saints grew rapidly in the 1960's, from 5.6 percent of the population in 1956 to 8.4 percent a decade later.

BAHA'IS AND OTHERS

Two small Baha'i congregation exist on Tutuila Island, as well as a small community of Jehovah's Witnesses.

INDIGENOUS CHURCHES

The Congregational Church of Jesus Christ, which split from the Congregational Christian Church in Samoa as early as 1846, has followers in both American and Western Samoa.

COOK ISLANDS

Profile

NATURAL FEATURES: Land area: 240 sq. km. Fifteen inhabited islands and over 100 small uninhabited ones comprise two clusters: the Northern Group of Pukapuka, Rakahanga, and Manihiki; and the Southern Group, of Aitutaki, Mangaia, and Rarotonga.

CAPITAL: Avarua on Rarotonga.

POPULATION: 17,754 (1981). The Cook Islands Maoris are Polynesians. About 24,500 Cook Islanders live in New Zealand. **Urban:** 27 percent.

RELIGION: Christians: 99 percent. **Major denominations:** Cook Island Christian Church (formerly London Missionary Society), 69 percent; Roman Catholic, 15 percent. **Others:** 16 percent -- includes Seventh-day Adventists; Church of Jesus Christ of Latter-Day Saints (Mormons).

LANGUAGE: Polynesian dialect similar to that of the Society Islands and the New Zealand Maoris. English is widely spoken.

GOVERNMENT: Self-governing state in free association with New Zealand. **Head of State:** British Monarch through a Representative. **Executive:** Prime Minister and Cabinet. **Legislative:** National Assembly with 24 members; a consultative Upper House, the House of Ariki, with 15 members representing all islands. **Local governments:** Island councils and village committees. **Judiciary:** Privy Council, the Court of Appeal, and the High Court. New Zealand is responsible for foreign affairs and defense.

ECONOMY: Per capita GDP: US $2,000 (1985 est.). **Main industries:** agriculture (coconuts, citrus, vegetables and fresh fruits); some tourism. **Main imports:** meat, dairy products, manufacturing. **Trading partners:** New Zealand, Australia, Japan, Hong Kong, and United Kingdom. New Zealand and Cook Island currencies are both legal tender.

Inhabitants And The Westerners

The Cook Islands people trace their origins to the Society Islands and the Marquesas Islands of French Polynesia. The inhabitants of the Islands settled into small states defined by the steep walls of mountain valleys. The social structure was hierarchical, with the chief or *ariki* occupying the highest position. Wars between the states led by the *arikis* were frequent before the Europeans' arrival.

The Spanish navigator Alvaro Mendana de Neira reached the Cook Islands in 1595. Portuguese navigator Pedro de Quiros arrived in 1606. In 1770, British Captain James Cook discovered five of the main islands in the Southern Group and the entire Island chain was eventually named after Captain Cook. Some of these islands were visited by the mutineers on the H.M.S. Bounty in 1789.

THE MISSIONARIES

During the 1820's, the missionaries of the London Missionary Society and their Polynesian teachers converted the people to Christianity, working effectively with the *arikis*. The *arikis* soon became high church officials. Thus evolved the so-called theocratic political system. During this time the culture was equally transformed as Western modes of dressing, housing and legal codes were adopted. The missionaries enacted blue laws which prohibited dancing, drinking of *kava* -- the traditional drink -- and wearing flowers.

The presence of Protestant missionaries and their proximity to New Zealand drew the Cook Islands into the sphere of British influence. In 1888, Rarotonga and later the southern group of Islands became a British protectorate. In 1901, the Southern and Northern Cook Islands became a part of New Zealand. After World War II through 1965, after a series of negotiations, New Zealand granted self-government to the Cook Islands. The country now has full self-government in domestic matters and remains in free association with New Zealand for defense and foreign affairs.

People Groups

The Cook Islands' Maori are Polynesian with ancestry from Samoa and French Polynesia. The Islanders are ethnically homogeneous. About 87 percent of the population lives in the southern group of Islands, especially Rarotonga. The population in the Cook Islands is declining in absolute terms, while that of Cook Islanders in New Zealand is increasing. In 1982, about 24,500 Islanders lived in New Zealand. Also, there is an increasing percentage of persons living in the urban area of Avarua. Less than half the population of this capital was born in Rarotonga. Since 1945, this pattern of migration has occurred from the outer islands to Rarotonga and from there to New Zealand. The population declined by 2.4 percent between 1976 and 1981.

The Cook Islands are predominantly Christian. There have been no reports of segments of the population which are socially or culturally distanced from meaningful Christian witness.

Socio-Political Conditions

MIGRATION

Since World War II, there has been an ever-increasing out-migration to New Zealand. Many Cook Islanders work in hospitals, large industries such as timber-milling, and transport. Further loss of the population occurred with the introduction of Air New Zealand services. The government has been very concerned about the effects on the economy and social life of this migration from the Islands.

POLITICAL STATUS

In their status as a self-governing territory in free association with New Zealand, the people are British subjects and New Zealand citizens. There have been several elections of the Premier and members of the Legislative Assembly. In 1981, the Constitution was amended to increase the number of seats in the Assembly from 22 to 24, one of the new seats being for a citizen resident in New Zealand. In 1984, Prime Minister Thomas Davis formed a coalition government composed of three members of the Cook Islands Party and four from his own Democratic party.

Post-World War II politics and the migration of people from Cook Islands have eroded the traditional power and influence of the *arikis*. This is particularly so in the Southern Group of islands; however, village politics still play a crucial role in the electoral process. A Constitutional Amendment in 1965 created an Upper House known as the House of Ariki, composed of up to 15 *arikis* from the Islands. This is a consultative body on issues related to customs and land tenure.

Health services are provided free by the government. The population is considered generally healthy; tropical diseases such as malaria are not endemic.

Economic Conditions

Economic and agricultural development in the country has always suffered from the Islands' isolation and smallness. Fruit and vegetable exports have been hindered by infrequent shipping and inadequate marketing in New Zealand metropolitan centers.

The country has a subsistence agricultural economy. Its primary crops include fruits and vegetables such as citrus, bananas, pineapples, pawpaw, beans, courgettes, avocados, sweet potatoes, yams, taro, and tomatoes. Livestock is also raised; fish is an important source of protein. Mother-of-pearl is collected. The country's main imports include food, textiles, fuel, vehicles and cement.

Most of the working population are engaged in agriculture, services and commerce. The government is a major employer. There are two clothing factories, a fruit canning factory, and four handicraft factories. Tourism is a developing industry; about 22,000 tourists a year visit the Islands. Remittances from migrants are an important source of revenue.

History Of Missions

LONDON MISSIONARY SOCIETY

The missionaries of the London Missionary Society (LMS) came to the Cook Islands from Tahiti. They eventually exercised a dominant influence over the chiefs and arranged for legislation which kept out other missions and preserved the land for the indigenous people. Islanders could not marry Europeans, which enabled the Islanders to keep their lands; leases were restricted. The missionaries also legislated moral codes, enforced by the Deacons.

When the Cook Islands became a Protectorate of Great Britain, the Church gradually lost its major influence on the government and in the field of education. The New Zealand government provided secular education in the country, mostly in the Southern Group. Because of isolation, the Northern Group Islands retained the pastors to provide schooling. They received remuneration from the government for their educational work.

Interest in religion seems to have declined as the country has developed economically. However, in Rarotonga, the center of modern developments, the Theological Training College of the Cook Island Christian Church continues to graduate well-qualified men and women for the ministry. Formerly, the Cook Islands had been the largest foreign mission-sending country, relative to its size and population.

OTHER MISSION GROUPS

After Great Britain abolished the laws prohibiting the entry of new missions, other churches tried to establish themselves in the Cook Islands. By the 1950's, one LMS missionary, 13 Roman Catholic, four Seventh-day Adventist, and six Mormon missionaries were present. The Catholics came from Tahiti and established schools which they did not relinquish to the government in later years. The secondary schools, run by the sisters of St. Joseph of Cluny, played a significant part in training the national leadership of the country.

The Church of Jesus Christ of Latter-Day Saints (Mormons) came after World War II. To attract people, they erected impressive church buildings in a uniform pattern from village to village. American and New Zealand Mormon builders and the local Mormon youth built these facilities. The latter learned valuable skills in the process. They also provided assembly halls for village functions and recreation areas for the village youth, mainly basketball courts.

Status Of Christianity

Cook Islanders are primarily Christians. The majority of them are affiliated with the Cook Islands Christian Church (CICC), formerly the London Missionary Society. For many years, the church and the pastors exercised strong power and influence in the society;

however, due to recent secular influence in the country, this power has somewhat declined.

NATIONAL CHURCHES

Cook Islands Christian Church (CICC)

This major Christian church in the Islands had its origin in the missionary work of the London Missionary Society in the 1820's. It played a significant role in the expansion of Christianity in the Pacific through its native missionaries. Between 1872 and 1896, the church sent about 70 missionaries to evangelize Papua New Guinea.

About 69 percent of the present population, about 14,000 people in 1985, adheres to the CICC. Church members who have migrated to New Zealand are affiliated with the Presbyterian Church of New Zealand.

Roman Catholic Church

The Catholic Church first came in 1894; in 1922 a Prefecture was established. The Diocese of Rarotonga is now a suffragan of the Archdiocese of Suva, Fiji. The bishop of Rarotonga is a member of the Episcopal Conference of the Pacific (CEPAC) in Suva, Fiji. The Holy See is represented in the Catholic hierarchy by the Apostolic Delegation to New Zealand and the Islands of the Pacific, based in Wellington, New Zealand.

In 1985, there was one diocese with 11 parishes. The religious included one bishop, 14 priests, four seminarians, four brothers, ten sisters, 33 catechists. Church membership was 3,000.

Anglican

An Anglican church serves the expatriate community. The church is administratively part of the diocese of Polynesia, in the Church of the Province of New Zealand.

Seventh-day Adventist (SDA)

The SDA first arrived in 1892 and have established a large community. Their membership was 2,500 in 1985. The SDA Cook Islands Mission is part of the Central Pacific Union Mission.

Assemblies of God

This church began its work from New Zealand in 1963. There were 100 affiliated members in mid-1970.

CHRISTIAN ACTIVITIES

Education

In 1971, there were 112 primary schools operated by Protestants, mainly by CICC. They also ran several secondary and technical schools. The Catholics operated two schools and a kindergarten.

There is no established church-state department to handle religious matters. The churches do not receive government subsidies, although they are exempt from certain taxes. Some charitable and educational institutions receive assistance from the government.

Broadcasting

The government radio station accepts religious programs with air time rotated among the four leading churches. Five-minute prayers are presented each night, and religious programs on both Sunday mornings and afternoons. Special religious services are occasionally aired live. The Catholic Church is affiliated with UNDA, an association of radio broadcasters in the Pacific.

Literature Distribution

Bibles, selections and portions are distributed by the Bible Society of the South Pacific. Translation of the scriptures to the Rarotongan language was completed in the 19th century: Portions in 1828; The New Testament in 1836; and the Bible in 1851.

Social Concerns

Four aspects of social change affect the lives of the Cook Islanders: the economic change that has brought independence to individuals; the end of the tribe and the beginning of urban life; educational advances that distance younger people from traditional ways of living; and the end of isolation and the ongoing exposure to the wider world arena.

Addressing the needs of the youth, the churches sponsor leadership training programs in the Islands, with youth rallies being very popular. There are about 24 women's groups which meet monthly, as well as a Women's Fellowship Council.

Other Religions

CHURCH OF JESUS CHRIST OF LATTER-DAY SAINTS (MORMONS)

This is the second largest church in the Islands, having expanded tremendously during the late 1960's. In their *Church Almanac 1985* the total membership figure was listed as 39,572. Many Maori missionaries from New Zealand came to work in the islands; many of the converts came from the CICC.

INDIGENOUS CHURCH

The Amuri Free Church came into being in Aitutaki Island through a schism within the CICC after World War II.

Cooperative Agencies

There is a Religious Advisory Council of the Cook Islands composed of four churches: The Cook Islands Christian Church, the Church of Jesus Christ of Latter-Day Saints, Roman Catholic Church, and the Seventh-day Adventist Church. A government statute named these churches as advisors on matters pertaining to life, mores, society, family, youth, etc. A sub-council on each of the islands works with the main council.

The Cook Island Christian Church is a member of the National Council of Churches in New Zealand. This council was formed in 1941.

FRENCH POLYNESIA

Profile

NATURAL FEATURES: Land area: 4,000 sq. km., scattered across four million sq. km. of the Pacific Ocean. Approximately 130 islands in major groups; the largest and most populated island is Tahiti. Most of the islands are of volcanic origin and have fertile soil with rich vegetation.

CAPITAL: Papeete. **Population:** 159,000 (1984) on Tahiti.

POPULATION: 200,000 (1986). Polynesians (75 percent), Asians, mainly Chinese (9 percent), Europeans (15 percent). **Annual growth rate:** 2.6 percent. **Urban:** 57 percent.

RELIGION: Christians: more than half of the population is Protestant, and one-third is Roman Catholic. **Others:** Jehovah's Witnesses and Buddhists. Church of Jesus Christ of Latter-Day Saints (Mormons), 6 percent.

LANGUAGE AND LITERACY: French is the official language, although Tahitian is used widely by the islanders and others. **Literacy:** 95 percent.

GOVERNMENT: French Polynesia is an overseas French territory with an internal self-government granted by France in 1968. It has a 30-member Territorial Assembly, seven members of which comprise the Government Council. The council works under the direction of a High Commissioner who is the chief executive appointed by the French government. Major legislative, judicial, and municipal systems follow structures and patterns established in France.

ECONOMY: Per capita GDP (1982): US $5,808. Subsistence agriculture (copra, tobacco, vanilla, tropical fruit), tourism, livestock, small boat building, fisheries. The nuclear industry and tourism have increased in importance since 1960.

Tales Of The South Seas And The Europeans

Remote islands of the French Polynesia Territory were inhabited when Magellan visited them in 1521. Roving explorers sighted them in subsequent years and in the mid-18th century, British and French navigators visited Tahiti. Historic tales of mutiny among sailors and public exhibition of "Noble Savages" aroused interest in Europe for the region. British missionaries were among the first expatriates to settle on the Islands. British and French forces subsequently fought over the region. In the mid-19th century, France annexed the Islands as its territory.

French colonists actively pursued their interests in the area. Their commercial interests became prominent. They established cotton plantations to which Chinese laborers were transported from Hong Kong. These plantations went bankrupt in 1873 and many of the Chinese were never repatriated. Their descendants account for the large number of Chinese in the population today.

SOCIAL STRUCTURE

French Polynesia originally had a hierarchical society. In the Society Islands the population was divided into three strata: the *arii* (ruling chief), the lesser chiefs, and the majority of commoners. The *arii* had extended power over the territory while the lesser chiefs had well-defined subdivisions. The chiefs ruled over areas with abundant resources. Wealth was distributed under established customs.

In the Marquesa Islands, only two ranks existed: the chiefs and the commoners. Not as powerful as those of the Society Islands, these chieftains were at war constantly. Droughts, lack of arable lands, and limited economic opportunities caused some of these conflicts. The old system of local chiefs had disappeared by the late 19th century.

THE FRENCH POLYNESIANS

The major ethnicities present in French Polynesia are Polynesians, Europeans (primarily French), Chinese and a scattering of peoples from other lands. The Polynesian population is further partitioned by geographic, social and cultural forces. Distinct cultural groups can be recognized, among them: Tahitians, Marqueseans, Tuamotuans and Austral Islanders.

These groups are all found to some extent on the island of Tahiti, which has over 70 percent of the population. Approximately 50,000 French Polynesians on Tahiti live outside the greater urban area of Papeete. These persons lead the traditional life of French Polynesia -- centered upon extended families, based upon subsistence agriculture and fishing, and focused on the village church.

In Papeete, the people generally live in smaller, nuclear families, work for wage labor, and are effectively unchurched. With more study, this people group could possibly be further subdivided into finer groups. It is essential to note that a new way of life is emerging for Polynesians in Tahiti, one that casts them into the role of workers in a wage-based system.

Socio-Political Conditions

Today, few traces remain of the traditional Polynesian social structures. The patterns derived from mission organizations can be found in some communities where the London Missionary Society was active. The *pupu*, a subdivision of the parish for purposes of Bible reading and other church activities, has become a meaningful unit for community organizations including secular ones.

POST-WORLD WAR II

Events of World War II significantly changed the lives of thousands of residents. Many young men fought alongside Allied servicemen in major Pacific confrontations. Residents of the islands were exposed to varying philosophies of politics and nationalism. Independence movements sprang forth during the 1950's. Political parties with opposing views became an important forum for expression of public opinion. In 1957, the region was defined as French Polynesia and residents expressed their desires for self-government. These proposals failed initially, but France granted internal self-government in 1968. Pouvanna a Oopa, a nationalist leader once forcibly removed from public office, became a representative to the French Senate.

SOCIAL SERVICES

As an overseas territory of France, French Polynesia receives social services including support of the secondary schools, grants for capital investment, and direct subsidies to the territorial budget.

THE PACIFIC TEST CENTER

In 1966, France established the Pacific Test Center (Centre d' Experimentation du Pacifique) on the atolls of Mururoa and Fangataufa in the Tuamotu group. France exploded 41 nuclear bombs at the site until 1974 when atmospheric testing was stopped. Countries in the Pacific, particularly Australia, Fiji, and New Zealand, protested strongly against these tests. Since 1974, testing is being done underground.

Economic Conditions

SERVICE-ORIENTED SECTOR

For most Polynesians, the establishment of the testing center stimulated the expansion of the service-sector largely at the expense of agriculture. In 1962, agriculture and fishing employed 46 percent of the labor force; services, including public administration, employed 35 percent. In 1977, the proportion was 18 percent and 64 percent, respectively, with industrial activities employing 19 percent. In 1976, agriculture and fishing contributed only 4 percent to the total GDP. By the early 1980's about 85 percent of all food consumed in the territory was imported.

In addition, the establishment of the testing center promoted the expansion of the service sector which has led to increased salaries and changed standards of living. However, in the 1980's the general state of the nuclear industry and the drop in tourism affected the economy of French Polynesia. Shifts in the political events in France also had an economic effect on the Islands.

Tourism, with its concomitant social effects, is an important part of the local economy. An international airport and international hotels and resorts attracted more than 90,000 tourists to Tahiti and the outer islands in the late 1970's. This influx of tourists provided employment for the service sector of the economy.

Mission History

EARLY CONVERSIONS

The missionaries of London Missionary Society first came to French Polynesia on board the ship "Duff" in 1797. They did not have converts to Christianity until 1813. They converted monarchs, particularly Pomare, and the principal chiefs. The support of the local leaders strengthened the missions. Many chiefs became pastors and deacons.

The Church became a focus for kinship groups, social life, and social status. Among the changes to the traditional patterns introduced by the missionaries were respect for the Sabbath, church-going twice on Sundays, "decent" clothing, attendance at semi-weekly hymn-singing and Bible classes. Monogamous marriages were promoted; the use of tobacco and alcoholic beverages was forbidden. The people accepted and/or adapted to the regulations well.

INDIGENOUS MISSIONARIES

The missionaries founded mission schools where they trained native pastors and encouraged the use of the local Tahitian language. During this time, Tahitian missionaries went all over the Pacific to spread the gospel.

THE PARIS EVANGELICAL SOCIETY

Political changes in the rule of French Polynesia in the 1860's meant the change from the London Missionary Society to the Paris Evangelical Society missionaries in the area. Among the outstanding workers of the time was Frederic Vernier, who revived and reorganized the Protestant church in the islands. He framed a concordat with the French government in the islands to accept internal autonomy of the church. The government paid for the pastors' salary in return for the right to veto decisions made by the church authorities.

The ecclesiastical organization formed under the concordat was modeled after that of the Reformed Church of France. Parish Councils were composed of the pastor and deacons, elected representatives of the six arrondissement councils. These members in turn chose 26 delegates to the Conseil Superieur, the highest local authority of the Polynesian Protestant Church. There were about 70 parish councils in the islands in the 1960's.

CATHOLIC MISSIONARIES

Two Picpus Fathers started the work of the Catholic missionaries in 1831; however, evangelization in the Marquesas islands only began in 1838 resulting in 216 baptisms in ten years. Although a vicariate was organized in 1848, real progress was not made until after the baptism of indigenous rulers in 1853. Persecutions caused missionaries to leave the islands several times. By 1908, despite the hindrances of Protestant opposition, disease, and other factors, the church had firm roots in the island.

Other Catholic missionaries came to French Polynesia. Among them were the Marist Fathers, the brothers from the Institute of Brothers of Christian Instruction of Ploermel, and the sisters of St. Joseph de Cluny. They took root in the Marquesas and the eastern and central Tuamotus. They made some progress in the Leeward and Austral Islands but they succeeded mainly, through their school system, in the Windward Group, particularly in Raiatea and Tahiti. During this time, antagonism existed among the followers of the Protestant and Catholic faiths, a reflection of the political rivalries between France and Britain.

About this same time, the civil administration granted permission to other sects to work in French Polynesia. The Seventh-day Adventists, the Jehovah's Witnesses, and Christian Scientists came into the colony.

Status Of Christianity

NATIONAL CHURCHES

The two largest religious communities in the territory are the Evangelical Church of French Polynesia with about 80,000 members and the Roman Catholic Church with 57,800 members in 1985, respectively. The Evangelical Church (L'Eglise Evangelique) originated from the London Missionary Society and the French Protestant missionaries. The dominance of Protestantism and Catholicism can be identified geographically. Catholicism continues to be the dominant religion in the Marquesas, Gambiers, and eastern and central Tuamotus. Protestantism prevails in the Leeward and Austral Islands. Rivalry persists in Moorea and Papeete. Up until the 1950's, there was minimal contact between the two hierarchies.

Smaller groups include Pentecostals, Seventh-day Adventists, and Assemblies of God. Non-Christian groups include some Jehovah's Witnesses and Mormons. Inroads of these groups have taken place among Catholics and Protestants.

Roman Catholic Church

After beginning its work in French Polynesia in 1838, the Roman Catholic Church had 57,800 baptized members in 1986. These individuals were in 78 parishes served by 35 priests, 31 brothers, and 63 sisters. The religious communities represented include the Oblates of Mary Immaculate, Missionaries of Our Lady of the Angels, Sisters of Charity of the Sacred Heart of Jesus, Brothers of the Sacred Heart, and the Clarisses (Lennoxville). The Diocese of Papeete covers this area.

The Vatican raised the territory's three Apostolic Vicariates to the rank of bishoprics in the 1960's. In 1985, a national archbishop headed the diocese of French Polynesia. Some chaplains of the French Armed Forces minister to the troops and naval units stationed on the territory. Papeete and its suburbs have three parishes: the Cathedral, St. Therese, and Pirae.

MINISTRIES AND CELEBRATIONS

Festivals

In the Roman Catholic Church the former missions have been transformed into parishes. The social life of church members is organized around religious feasts and traditional celebrations. The Feast of the Assumption on August 15th is a festive occasion for processions.

The *matutura* is a catechist's meeting that lasts from dusk to dawn, where speakers discuss religious matters. A little before midnight, the theological discussions are punctuated with songs by servers bearing food and beverages. The doctrinal discussions carry on until Mass at dawn.

The Feast of the Dead is the most picturesque of the local religious observances. Processions, vigils in the cemeteries, blessings by priests, preaching, prayers, and hymn singing characterize the occasion. People embellish the graveyards of dead members of the family.

Education

Education is one of the major ministries of the church. For many years, priests and sisters administered and taught in the schools. The College of the Brothers in the center of Papeete, together with its annexes, provide courses for baccalaureate degrees. The Sisters of Cluny and the Sisters of Our Lady of the Angels teach girls' schools. A junior seminary is located in Miti Rapa, where the local clergy is trained.

Languages

The Roman Catholic church uses the Tahitian language in its schools. It once had 30 language classes and was considered the authority in teaching the Tahitian language. Today, Tahitian is being used not only in schools, but also in government offices and in the media. Masses in the churches are in French and in Tahitian according to the make up of the attendants. However, most of the priests are French and many do not know Tahitian.

Publications and Media

The diocese publishes two periodicals: *Vea Katorika*, a monthly publication in Tahitian; and *Le Semeur Tahitien*, a bimonthly in French. Religious broadcasts in French and Tahitian are aired every Sunday.

Social Services

In its parish-based ministry, the church is involved in counseling, visiting of families, working with delinquent young people and other types of social ministries. The church has a residential facility for 30 delinquent young women. These women stay at the facility to the age of 17 or 18 and are provided training for trades during this time.

Together with the Protestant churches, the Catholic church has opposed the legalization of prostitution and gambling in Tahiti.

L'Eglise Evangelique

The Eglise Evangelique became independent in 1963. It has a re-formed Presbyterian organizational structure. The church ruling body is a synod of 48 persons -- half of which are lay members, the other half are pastors. Pastor Rapoto became the first Polynesian president of the Conseil Superieur in 1963. This coincided with the granting of full autonomy to the Polynesian Protestant church by the Paris Evangelical Society on the centenary of its installation in the Islands. The foreign missionaries act as advisors to the local pastors as needed.

There are 80 parishes within the Eglise Evangelique throughout French Polynesia. Forty-eight ordained pastors serve these parishes. Six hundred nonpaid deacons assist the pastors and provide leadership in the absence of the pastors.

The Protestant church has been intricately linked with the Tahitian traditions. Pastors are educated at seminaries in Papeete, in Suva at the Pacific Theological College or in France. Today, the great majority of the pastors are outer islanders. They use Tahitian as the language of the church. Some services are in French.

THE CHURCH IN THE URBAN AREAS

The place of the Church in the urban centers has been altered since the role of the Church in the lives of people is not as central as it used to be. Outside influences are said to be undermining the Church's ability to witness to a Christian way of living not only for the Islands but also for those outside the region. Nominalism has arisen as church participation has dropped. Although many claim membership in the Church, they are not generally participants. Some have actively disavowed church membership and their Christianity. This trend is found mostly in urban areas of Papeete and Faaa, not so much in the districts.

Church leaders lament the many outside influences coming to the area -- money, material goods, values, and new ways of doing things. Emphasis on material wealth and personal gain at the expense of community and other values has altered Christian practices. People in the tourist-related economy work all days of the week, not observing Sundays as days of rest.

Church membership by migrants to the city tends to be inactive despite letters from the pastors of the original village church. Language barriers have been cited as one reason. For example, persons from the Marquesas understand Tahitian as spoken in Papeete but they are not as clearly understood in turn. A greater barrier, however, seems to be the transfer of allegiance from the Eglise Evangelique in the church villages to the church in urban areas. Urban churches are large composite groups where the communal feel of a village church is lost. This tendency is common throughout the Pacific in urban areas.

CHURCH IN THE RURAL AREAS: TRADITIONAL CHRISTIAN EXPRESSIONS

Community-oriented rituals and ceremonies of the church continue to this day. They are stronger in areas outside Papeete and other rural areas. Among these festivities are the *pererina*, the *po matahiti*, the "blue cross," the *tuaroi*, and the *me*.

The *pererina* is colloquial for the term pilgrimage. It is essentially a way of keeping contact and strengthening or restrengthening the bonds between the church leaders and the people. The leaders visit homes, where the hosts display generosity, a sense of community, and festivity. Homes are gaily decorated. The other form of the *pererina* is the collective marriages of couples already living together to legalize an existent situation and to provide a firm structure for the family. The whole parish or district celebrates this collective event.

The *po matahiti*, the celebration of New Year's Eve, is important in Tahitian religious life. Parish worshipers, dressed in their best clothes, attend chapel for several hours while deacons and ministers exhort them to make a good preparation for the New Year. Young and old people alike celebrate through the early morning hours.

The *Tuaroi* is a Tahitian religious ceremony. Usually held on the eve of the first Sunday, this activity involves a crowd of about 100 to 120 children, young people, adults, deacons, ministers and missionary when there is one. For three to four hours, the crowd speaks in turns to expound and dissect a Bible verse chosen by the minister. The youngest of the group speaks first, then on to the highest ranking Church leader. It is a form of elocution where each one adds something new to the discourse.

The *Me* celebration has always been a part of Tahitian life. This is the Church collection that has existed for more than 150 years. Gifts in kind were given in the past during harvest time in May. These offerings concern young and old people alike. Children give their coins or *taras* while the adults give cash offerings. The ceremony is interspersed with singing and Bible verses in a festive atmosphere.

In all these festivals, the people are the center of the Church. Community togetherness and cooperation are central themes. Communal joy and giving are evident in the life of the Church.

CHURCH MINISTRIES

Evangelistic Outreach

One form of ministry is the evangelistic outreach by trained lay evangelists to inactive members of the church. They encourage participation in the Church life among those who have left the church.

Social Ministries

There are various social ministries also carried out by the Church. It has a residential re-education center, located in Mt. Moriah for young men who have difficulties. It treats about 50 young men who have problems such as family breakups, economic hardships, alcohol and drug problems, or criminal activities. This is a cooperative effort with the Roman Catholic church, which has set up a similar treatment center for young women.

A related ministry is a Girls' Hostel and Students' Hostel for low-salaried women workers and poor students who live in Papeete.

Another need for ministry is the recent problem of prostitution. With increasing numbers of tourists and military personnel, prostitution has become a means of livelihood for women who are without skills and resources to survive in Papeete. Attitudes towards this type of ministry to women are still mixed.

Leadership Training

Leadership training is given to youth leaders and is conducted at camps, seminars, and conference centers. Theological training includes training of those who like to preach. There are sessions for people to practice preaching in all the local churches. Seminars and opportunities are being encouraged for training women in leadership positions.

Religious Broadcasting

A religious broadcast is made on Sundays for half an hour on one of the local radio stations. The broadcast is in Tahitian and French. A 15-minute spot on television is also produced to spread God's word.

Literature Distribution

There is a wealth of religious literature in Tahitian. It includes the Bible, children's stories, Sunday school material, serious theological works, tracts, and a host of other types of literature.

MEMBERSHIP IN CHRISTIAN BODIES

The Eglise Evangelique has been a member of the Pacific Conference of Churches since 1961. It helps fund the Pacific Theological College in Suva, Fiji, both through scholarships to students from French Polynesia and through direct contribution. The Eglise Evangelique is an affiliate member of the World Council of Churches through the Pacific Conference of Churches. It is also a member of the Communique Evangelique Action Apostolic. This group includes 25 church bodies formerly with the Paris Mission Society. The group exists primarily to share ideas, materials produced in French, and personnel.

Two pastors from French Polynesia now serve in France and Switzerland.

The major churches of French Polynesia are concerned with the presence of many new sects and denominations in the Islands. Relationships among the old and the new groups is poor and virtually nonexistent. More interaction and cooperation in working out common problems are needed.

The Catholic Church is a member of CEPAC, composed of Catholic churches in the Pacific. It has joined the churches in the region in the condemnation of continued nuclear testing in the atolls of French Polynesia.

OTHER CHRISTIAN CHURCHES

Seventh-day Adventists first came to Tahiti in 1892. The French Polynesia Mission, organized in 1916, is part of the Central Pacific Union Mission based in New Zealand.

The Assemblies of God had 120 baptized members in 1985. It had three churches and three outstations in Tahiti. Four missionaries and one credentialed minister worked in the region.

There are some workers of the Baptists and the Youth With A Mission in the area.

CHURCH CONCERNS: UNREACHED PEOPLES

The Chinese People Group

Approximately 12,000 **Chinese** live in French Polynesia. Most live in Papeete, where they virtually control the economy. The few living outside Papeete tend to own and run small stores. Among the Chinese population there is a strong sense of identity, partly based upon ethnicity and reinforced by some social distance between them and the Polynesian and French populations. Increasingly, the vernacular language among the Chinese is Tahitian, with French continuing as the language of trade. Chinese, in its various dialects, is becoming less and less used, particularly by younger Chinese.

About 8 percent of the Chinese population has affiliated with a Christian church -- this is equally divided between the Protestant and Roman Catholic Churches. Another several hundred profess to follow traditional Chinese religious practices, with an emphasis on ancestor worship. The remaining Chinese profess no religious beliefs and are classified as secularists. Neither the Protestant nor the Roman Catholic Church has been able to attract significant portions of this population. However, there is one Protestant Chinese church in Papeete and about 500 Chinese persons who profess Christianity. As yet, this population is overwhelmingly unreached.

The French

Over 20,000 **French** live in French Polynesia, occupying the highest rungs of society. Many are connected with the French military or the nuclear testing facility. The French live a life apart from the rest of the population in French Polynesia. They live in the best housing areas, associate primarily with one another, and orient most strongly toward France and cultural life in France. Although most profess to be Roman Catholic, there is little participation in the life of the church. Churchmen in Tahiti describe them as secular and materialistic in their religious life. There is no evangelistic outreach directed toward the French in French Polynesia. The Eglise Evangelique has not seen this as a need, and other Protestant churches, such the Assemblies of God, Baptists, and Seventh-day Adventists, have focused their ministry on Polynesians.

Urban Polynesians

Another possible unreached people group are **urban Polynesians** in Papeete. These persons have been described as, "...Polynesians who have been marginalized and impoverished by the march of modernization." Increasingly, urban Polynesians are unchurched -- they have an allegiance to village churches which are inappropriate to their changed life in the city. Urban life is different from village life -- the extended family support networks and the range of mutual support and sharing are limited. Churchmen in Papeete report that the Protestant church is not meeting the needs of Polynesians living in Papeete, while the Roman Catholic church ministers primarily to immigrants from areas of French Polynesia which are heavily Roman Catholic. Neither church has found a way to evangelize those persons in Papeete who come from other areas outside of French Polynesia.

Other Religious Bodies

INDIGENOUS CHURCHES

Three groups have split from the Evangelical Church since World War II: The Keretitiano in 1950, the Autonomous Church in 1954, and the Polynesian Pentecostal Churches in 1968. A Chinese congregation attends the latter.

CHURCH OF JESUS CHRIST OF LATTER-DAY SAINTS (MORMONS)

The inroads of newer religions in French Polynesia are attributed to several factors. The success of the Mormons is attributed to not only the greater financial resources placed at the disposal by churches in the United States but also to the tenacity and dedication of its workers. Reportedly, the Protestant and Catholic missions have lost their fervor with the passage of time and have been replaced by a more tepid and tolerant form of Christianity.

OTHERS

The Reorganized Church of Jesus Christ of Latter-Day Saints, known as *Kanito* or *Sanito*, separated from the Mormons in the 1884. This began in the Tuamotu archipelago, where nativistic tendencies gave prominence to the magical powers of the priests. The *Mamaia* sect also flourished from 1823 to 1835, headed by a former LMS deacon who announced he was Jesus Christ or his immediate representative who came to evict all white people from the Islands.

The Jehovah's Witnesses started in Tahiti in 1958 with eight baptized witnesses. In 1985, they had six congregations with 617 full ministers in Tahiti. Two of these are in Papeete and four in rural areas of Tahiti. There are Jehovah's Witness halls on Moorea, Bora Bora, Huahine, and Raitea. Kingdom hall meetings and evangelism are the primary ministries of this group. Thirteen translators are working on the translation of materials into Tahitian.

NIUE

Profile

NATURAL FEATURES: Land area: 259 sq. km. **Sea area:** 390 sq. km. **Terrain:** an uplifted coral island; rugged and rocky with coral, limestone, and marble.

CAPITAL: Alofi. **Population:** 960.

POPULATION: 3,298 (1981). Niueans (Polynesians closely affiliated with Tongans and Samoans), 97.4 percent; Europeans and Chinese, 2.6 percent. Declining growth rate at -3.2 percent in 1975 to 1980 due to migration and lowered natural growth rate. About 5,600 Niueans reside in New Zealand.

RELIGION: Christians: 87.8 percent. **Major denominations:** Congregationalists belonging to Ekalesia Niue, 81.1 percent; Roman Catholics, 5.7 percent; Anglicans, 1 percent. **Others:** 12.2 percent. Church of Jesus Christ of Latter-Day Saints (Mormons), 10.4 percent; Jehovah's Witnesses, 1.7 percent; and Baha'is, 0.1 percent.

LANGUAGE AND LITERACY: Niuean, English. **Literacy rate:** 100 percent.

GOVERNMENT: Self-governing in free association with New Zealand. British Monarch is represented by the Governor-General of New Zealand. **Executive:** Prime Minister and three-member cabinet. **Legislative:** Island Assembly with 14 elected members from villages, and six from a common roll. **Judicial:** High Court under jurisdiction of New Zealand Chief Justice.

ECONOMY: New Zealand provides economic aid annually. **GDP** 1979: US $2,787. **Per capita income:** US $774. **Inflation** (1980): 14.9 percent. **Principal exports:** passion fruit, copra, lime, handicrafts.

Historical Background

Niue was originally populated by people of Samoan and Tongan descent. The first European to come to Niue was Captain James Cook in 1774. He named it the "Savage Land" because of the hostile reception given him. Niue became a British Protectorate, administered by missionaries of the London Missionary Society from 1846 to 1900. It became Christian during this period. In September 1901, Niue was annexed to New Zealand as part of the Cook Islands. In 1974, it became self-governing in free association with New Zealand, and Niueans were granted dual citizenship.

NIUEANS

The people of Niue have long been a homogeneous, ethnic community relatively isolated from other peoples. This continues to the present among the approximately 3,300 Niue people living on Niue. There are no recognizable social divisions; with such a low population and no real urbanization, it is hard to identify forces which would lead to social divisions.

In addition to Niue peoples, there are around 350 Samoans, Tongans and Europeans in Niue, many of whom are well integrated into the Niue community. The Church in Niue claims around 90 percent of the population as members.

Socio-Political Conditions

At present, there are about twice the number of Niueans in New Zealand (5,600) as in Niue. The high migration rate has been fostered by a search for wider economic opportunities, the attractions of city life, and the desire to join other family members. This migration has caused a decline in the Niuean work force and in the natural growth rate. The 1980-85 Development Plan of the government included stabilization of the population and the promotion of a "return home" scheme.

Another labor problem is the large size of the civil service in Niue. Over 80 percent of the work force is employed by the government; however, some leading government positions are headed by expatriates.

Economic Conditions

Subsistence agriculture is still predominant, although the low economic yield tends to dissuade people from making it a full-time economic activity. There are no known mineral deposits in the country. Small-scale industries include factory operations for the pulping of passion fruit, processing of lime oil and marketing of honey; coconut cream canning; handicrafts; and limited tourism.

The wide gap between domestic production and the demand for goods and services creates huge trade deficits, making Niue heavily dependent on foreign aid. New Zealand, Australia, the Netherlands and the U.N. Development Programme are sources of assistance.

Missions History

As in the Cook Islands and Samoa, the London Missionary Society (LMS) founded the Church in Niue. As early as 1830, LMS missionaries John Williams, Charles Barff, W. Gill, and H. Nisbet tried to land Polynesian teachers in Niue. They were unsuccessful until 1846, when Pentamina, a Niuean who trained at Malua, was accepted by the people. He paved the way for a Samoan missionary, Paulo, to work effectively in Niue. By 1852, through the work of Paulo, between 200 and 300 Niueans had become Christians.

The credit for the harvest falls to George Lawes, a gifted pastor, translator, and teacher who was the first western resident missionary in Niue. He translated the New Testament into Niuean and trained local pastors and teachers from among the people. His trainees became missionaries in the later years to other Pacific islands in the New Hebrides (now Vanuatu), Melanesia, Micronesia, and Papua New Guinea. These teachers, under the direction of the LMS, continued the conversion and training of their fellow Polynesians. They used the resources of their own languages and cultures to teach from the Bible and introduce their people to the power of Christ.

Status Of Christianity

After missionaries with the London Missionary Society introduced Christianity to Niue in 1830 the island was completely evangelized by 1900. Today, the Ekalesia Niue, which is an outgrowth of the LMS Church, continues to play an important role in the lives of the people.

About 88 percent of the population is Christian. Converts to other religions have occurred in recent years.

EKALESIA NIUE

To this day, Ekalesia Niue exerts great influence on the lives of the Niuean people. Its elders, pastors, deacons, and expatriate missionaries lead the people along traditional and religious ways, keeping a strict hand on the life of the island. Social status is still strongly associated with status in church activities.

The work of the Church is done primarily through individual members and collectively through local churches. In turn, the local churches form the Island Church Council.

Structure

Ekalesia Niue follows Congregationalist lines. There are 12 congregations in the island. The church minister heads up the local church. The members of the church supports the minister and family. One Elder, appointed by the local church and usually a Life Deacon, serves as the minister's special helper and pastoral supporter. This Elder must have been a church member for 20 years and had training as a Lay Pastor.

Deacons and officers of the church are elected by the local church meeting. Lay Preachers and Lay Pastors are appointed by the Island Church Council after they are nominated, trained, and examined by the local churches. Their work is at the request of the minister and deacons of the local church.

THE ISLAND CHURCH COUNCIL

The council is organized to guide, encourage and sustain the life and work of the local churches. It represents the membership to the wider council of churches in the world and to the government and people of Niue. It is a member of the Congregational Council for

World Mission (CCWM); the International Council for World Mission, the Pacific Conference of Churches, and the World Council of Churches.

The minister and three representatives from each local church comprise the Council. Each island-wide church organization is also represented. An Executive Committee administers, advises, plans and relates to different member churches and outside bodies.

The Island Church Council supports the training of ministerial students at colleges approved by the Council and CCWM. Trainees usually attend the Malua Theological College, the Pacific Theological College, or the New Zealand Congregational Theological College.

ROMAN CATHOLIC CHURCH

The Roman Catholic Church is served by a Marist priest at Alofi. In May 1972, it affiliated with the diocese of Rarotonga in the Cook Islands, separating itself from the Tonga diocese. The Catholic mission started in 1955. About 8 percent of the Niuean population belongs to the Roman Catholic Church.

OTHER CHRISTIAN CHURCHES

Small Christian congregations belong to the Anglicans, the Church of Jesus Christ, and the New Apostolic Church. The Seventh-day Adventists also have a following.

CHRISTIAN ACTIVITIES

The New Testament was translated into Niuean in 1866; the full Bible in 1904. The Bible Society of South Pacific distributes Bibles, New Testaments, and portions and selections of scripture. A new translation of the Bible is being organized by the Bible Society in the South Pacific.

Station ZK2ZN in Niue transmits educational programs, devotional services and local information services in Niuean. Overseas broadcasts are relayed in English and translated where possible.

Other Churches

The Church of Jesus Christ of Latter-Day Saints claims about 350 members on the island. It was established in 1953.

The Baha'is have a small group of adherents, about 0.1 percent of the total island population. A selection of Baha'i prayer was published in the Niuean language in 1970.

PITCAIRN ISLANDS

Profile

NATURAL FEATURES: Land area: 36.5 sq. km., comprised of two islands and two atolls: Pitcairn, Henderson, Ducie, and Oeno. Only Pitcairn is inhabited. The Islands are volcanic formations with steep elevations, rocky and cliff-formed coastlines.

CAPITAL: Adamstown.

POPULATION: (1983) 45 people of Polynesian and European admixture descent.

RELIGION: All inhabitants are Seventh-day Adventists.

LANGUAGE AND LITERACY: Pitcairn dialect and English.

GOVERNMENT: British colony, only one in the South Pacific. **Head of State:** British monarch represented by the British High Commissioner in New Zealand. The Island Council consists of a magistrate and nine members.

ECONOMY: People engage in subsistence agriculture and fishing. **Crops:** taro, coconuts, beans, sugarcane, bananas, yams, citrus fruits. **Export:** some sales of postage stamps.

Historical Background: Early Settlers

Although traces of pre-European habitation existed, the Pitcairn Islands were uninhabited when the British discovered them in 1767. In 1789, William Bligh sailed to Tahiti to gather breadfruit trees as a staple for the African slaves in the British West Indies. His first mate, Fletcher Christian, and 17 crew members mutinied and put Bligh adrift. Bligh landed in Timor, now Indonesia. Christian and the others took some Polynesian men and women from Tahiti and chose to settle in Pitcairn for its remoteness and isolation.

Demoralization, jealousy and violence characterized the early years of the settlement. The men killed each other until only one man remained, with nine women and 19 children. From this group descended the present inhabitants of Pitcairn. By 1856, the British government moved the entire population to Norfolk Island, northwest of New Zealand. In 1864, 43 persons returned to Pitcairn, due to homesickness. In 1883, the entire population became Seventh-day Adventists.

People Groups

Pitcairn people are descendants of the crew members of the H.M.S. *BOUNTY* who mutinied and Polynesian men and women from Tahiti.

In 1983, there were 45 local people and seven non-Pitcairners, most of whom were in the 16 to 55 age group. The population is declining, due to migration to New Zealand; there were 65 persons in Pitcairn in 1976 and 45 in 1983. Many people still carry the surnames of the original mutineers, such as Christian, Warren, Young, or Brown.

British Colonial Life

The Pitcairn Islands are administered by the British High Commissioner in New Zealand, who acts as the colony's Governor. An Island Council consists of the Island Secretary, four elected and five nominated members; it is responsible for the internal affairs of the Islands.

Social life revolves around families and the Seventh-day Adventist Church. Ringing of the church bells announces various events of community life, such as times of worship, public entertainment, public work, or the arrival of a ship.

Pitcairn Miscellany is a monthly four-page mimeographed news sheet produced by the Education Officer (a New Zealand teacher appointed for two years) and sponsored by the school. First published in 1959, it now has a circulation of 825, including distribution outside the Islands.

Education is compulsory for children 6 to 15 years old; students may attend post-primary school in New Zealand.

Barter System Economy

Barter, rather than cash exchange, is practiced; people barter their produce with passing ships.

The Island has a highly fertile volcanic soil and adequate rainfall. Its agricultural products include taro, coconut, beans, sugarcane, bananas, yams and citrus fruits.

The Island's only cash income is from the sale of postage stamps and a few curios. It receives some grants from the United Kingdom. Its currency is the New Zealand dollar.

Pitcairn has limited harbor facilities accommodating only small boats, while large ships must anchor off the islands. It has very few vehicles and no surfaced roads. Thus, supplies are often moved by wheelbarrow. Communication is maintained by radio and an AT&T service.

Missions History

At the beginning of European contacts there were very few inhabitants in the island. Missionary visits from America in 1886 and 1890 led the people to accept the Seventh-day Adventist Church. They have remained faithful to this denomination ever since. Occasional missionaries and later, more regular workers on two-year terms from Australia kept them in contact with that church and the outside church body.

Status Of Christianity

The entire population belongs to the Seventh-day Adventist Church, and a pastor is permanently assigned to the Island. People celebrate Saturday as their Sabbath, and alcohol and eating of pork are still forbidden today.

TOKELAU

Profile

NATURAL FEATURES: Land area: 10 sq. km. The group consists of three atolls: Fakaofo, Nukunonu and Atafu. These atolls have reef-bound islets encircling a lagoon.

CAPITAL: There is no capital in the island; it is administered from the Office of Tokelau Affairs based in Apia, Western Samoa.

POPULATION (1981): 1,572. The people are Polynesians, having family, linguistic, and cultural links with Western Samoa.

RELIGION: Christians: 98 percent. Most of the islanders (70 percent) belong to the Congregational Church of Samoa, while 28 percent of the population practices Roman Catholicism.

LANGUAGES: The Tokelauan language is similar to the Samoan and Tuvaluan languages; English is sometimes spoken.

Government: Tokelau is a non-self-governing Territory under the administration of New Zealand.

ECONOMY: Major funding is received from New Zealand. Sea products, coconut and pandanus palms are sources of revenue. Currency used is New Zealand dollar, Western Samoan tala and some tokelauan souvenir coins.

Historical Background

Not much is known of the origins of indigenous Polynesian people, although local traditions assume migration from the Samoas, Rarotonga, Cook Islands, and Nanumanga, Tuvalu. The three atolls were first sighted by European navigators in 1765. Horatio Hale, an ethnologist, described these atolls in 1841 during the U.S. Naval Exploration of the Pacific.

At that time, about 700 inhabitants lived in the atolls. Disease and raids by Peruvian slave traders reduced this number to about 200 in the late 1860's. Soon afterwards, European beachcombers and Polynesians from other islands arrived.

Tokelau became a British protectorate in 1889 and was incorporated in 1916 into the Gilberts and Ellice Island Colony. In 1925 New Zealand assumed administrative responsibility and in 1948 took full sovereignty. New Zealand's Ministry of Foreign Affairs assumed control over Tokelau's administration in 1974.

People

Tokelau's small population is ethnically homogeneous, with few immigrants. A substantial number of people from Tokelau have migrated to New Zealand; some visiting and interchange occur with people in Western Samoa. Virtually everyone in Tokelau professes faith in Christianity, and there are no unreached people groups.

The population in 1981 was 1,572. Fakaofo had 650 persons; Atafu, 554; and Nukunonu, 368. About 2,000 Tokelauans lived in New Zealand in the early 1980's. The people of Tokelau are British subjects and New Zealand citizens.

Socio-Political Conditions

In the 1960's, overcrowding became a problem in Tokelau. Due to pressures on the meager economic resources of the islands, the New Zealand government devised a resettlement plan, with a large number of families being relocated in New Zealand. Resettlement ended after achieving stability in 1976.

The New Zealand government provides primary education in the Islands, as well as scholarships for secondary and higher education at institutions elsewhere. Health services are provided by local medical officers and visiting ones from Western Samoa.

Limited government in Tokelau is in the hands of headmen (*faipule*) and village mayors (*pulenuku*). These officials are elected for three years. In mid-1984, the High Court of Niue had jurisdiction over criminal and civil cases; the Territory did not have prisons and only about seven police officers on duty.

Life in Tokelau still centers on the family group. A traditional form of patriarchal authority has been preserved; village affairs are conducted by a Council of Elders consisting of representatives of the families.

Economic Conditions

The economy of Tokelau is primarily subsistence agriculture and fishing, with a small amount of copra being exported. The sale of postage stamps to world philatelists provides additional revenues. Tokelau is heavily dependent upon New Zealand government subsidies.

The currency used is the New Zealand dollar; Western Samoan *tala* is also legal tender. Tokelau minted its first coin in 1978.

The Office of Tokelau Affairs, under the New Zealand foreign monetary system since 1974, was based in Apia, Western Samoa in the early 1980's; this arrangement has strengthened economic and cultural ties between the two island groups.

Mission History

Between 1845 and 1863, French Catholic missionaries of Wallis Island (Uvea) and missionaries of the London Missionary Society in Samoa utilized local teachers in their efforts to convert the Tokelaus to Christianity. By 1863, Protestant missionaries had succeeded in Atafu, and Catholic missionaries in Nukunonu. Catholic teachers later established themselves on Fakaofo. As a result, this atoll has both Protestant and Catholic adherents.

Status Of Christianity

About 70 percent of the people of Tokelau belong to the Congregational Christian Church in Samoa, having its origin in the London Missionary Society. About 28 percent are Roman Catholic. The people on Atafu are entirely Congregational; those of Nukunonu are Catholic. Both denominations are represented in Fakaofo with the work of both being directed from Western Samoa.

ROMAN CATHOLIC CHURCH

The church is part of the archdiocese of Western Samoa (Apia). In 1985, the church claimed 1,000 members. It has one parish with one priest, two sisters, and one catechist. The church also operates a school at Nukunonu.

TONGA

Profile

NATURAL FEATURES: Land area: 750 sq. km. Three main island groups with 162 islands: Tongatapu and Haapai in the south; Vava'u Group in the north.

CAPITAL: Nuku'alofa on Tongatapu. **Population** (1979): 18,400.

POPULATION: (1984 est.) 104,000. Tongans are mainly Polynesians. *Other groups:* some Europeans and other Pacific islanders. *Annual growth rate:* 2.1 percent. Large out-migration patterns; 65 percent live in Tongatapu.

RELIGION: Christians: over 70 percent. **Major denominations:** Free Wesleyan, Roman Catholic, Free Church of Tonga, Church of Tonga, Anglican. **Others:** Church of Jesus Christ of Latter-Day Saints (Mormons), Baha'is.

LANGUAGE AND LITERACY: Tongan, a Polynesian language; and English. **Literacy rate:** 95 percent.

GOVERNMENT: A constitutional monarchy consisting of a King, the Privy Council, Cabinet, the Legislative Assembly, and the judiciary.

ECONOMY: Per capita GDP: (1983) US $647. **Major exports:** food and livestock; crude materials. **Principal imports:** food, beverages and tobacco, minerals, fuel. **Aid sources:** New Zealand, Australia.

Population

Tonga's population is exceedingly homogeneous; over 98 percent of the population are Tongans. Two-thirds of the Tongan population lives on the main island of Tongatapu, and 26 percent of the population lives in urban areas. Social life, even in urban areas, is still regulated by traditional social forms and customs. There is little evidence of social or cultural divisions among the Tongan population. The non-Tongan population is made up of Europeans and other Pacific Islanders.

Church life in Tonga encompasses most of the population. There are no unreached people groups in Tonga.

Historical Background

TU'I TONGA AND THE SOCIAL STRUCTURE

Tonga is believed to have been settled in 1140 B.C. The Tongans' highly-developed social system existed long before the arrival of the Europeans. About 950 A.D., a dynasty began which has lasted into the present time. Its monarch, the *Tu'i Tonga*, was thought to have descended from a Polynesian god of the sun or sky, holding both spiritual and temporal powers. Eventually, the *Tu'i Tonga* exercised only spiritual authority, and a new ruler, called the *Tu'i Ha'atakalaua*, held temporal power. By the 17th century, a third dynasty arose, with the title *Tu'i Kanokupolu*. All three dynastic lines held power simultaneously but with very few disputes between them.

THE COMING OF THE EUROPEANS

The first Europeans to see the Tongan Island groups were Dutch navigators; however, it was Captain James Cook's visit to the islands in 1773 that initiated regular contacts with Europeans. During this period, Tongan social structures began to decline with civil war continuing from 1799 to 1852.

In 1845, Taufa'ahau, a soldier and leader christened George Topou, consolidated his rule over all the parties to become the undisputed head of the Kingdom of Tonga. Tupou, who became a Christian, introduced a new code of laws based on equality and set up a representative system of government, thus emancipating the people from semi-serfdom. The Tongan constitution, which he originated in 1875, is still in effect today.

Tonga became a British protectorate in 1900. Its foreign affairs were carried out by the British.

TONGAN MONARCHY

After obtaining independence from Britain in 1970, Tonga joined the British Commonwealth and appointed a high commissioner to London. In turn, Britain sent a high commissioner and deputy high commissioner to Tonga.

Tonga's traditional monarchy still exists today. Queen Salote Tupou III inherited the throne in 1918, reigning until 1965. Upon her death, King Taufa'ahau Tupou IV became the ruling monarch.

A strong sense of Tongan nationality, tradition and culture is preserved in its Church and society. Despite changes in Tongan political structures, noble families still wield great influence.

Socio-Political Conditions

SOCIAL ORGANIZATION

Traditionally, Tonga has a highly stratified society, with the Royal Family and nobility at the top, the *matapule* (or what used to be titled servants to the nobility) at the middle, and the commoners at the bottom. Thirty-three families trace their ancestry to the first *Tu'i Tonga* or to ancient Fiji chiefs. The highest-ranking male in the nobility usually holds the title and management of inherited land. Six titled *matapule* also inherit estates. Under the Constitution, the commoners are entitled to land allotment and are free from servitude to the nobles.

The extended family remains the basis of social organization, although the nuclear family is the main unit of a household. The men dominate the political and economic spheres of activity; however, males defer to their sisters on most important social occasions. Social ranking is based on complex bilateral kinship relationships, with social descent coming through the women. Sisters outrank brothers, exercise social control over them and name their brothers' children. This relationship, called *fahu*, is passed on to the children of the next generation.

As the economy modernizes, the traditional role of women as homemakers has changed, with more and more women becoming involved in marketing activities and formal employment.

Tonga's population growth has resulted in more migration to urban areas of Tongatapu, where people seek employment; others have migrated overseas as guest workers. The traditional family-oriented system is said to be breaking down, with youth becoming restless, and alcoholism on the rise. There is growing resentment over the rights of the monarchy and the nobility to retain ownership of much of the land.

Economic Conditions

The 1975-80 economic plans included investment in the productive sector of the economy. Every adult male was allotted 3.3 hectares of land for a garden and a building site in his village. However, all land remains the property of the monarchs and the nobility.

Unemployment is high: only a third of the labor force can be classed as income earners. Subsistence agriculture is the main occupation of the majority; coconuts, bananas, and vanilla are the principal crops for export.

Overseas remittances and aid from foreign countries have helped Tonga's economy, which improved slightly in 1983-84. Tonga's major trade partners include Australia, New Zealand, Japan, the European Economic Community (EEC), and Federal Republic of Germany. The government has encouraged the growth of tourism and industry.

Large numbers of Tongan men migrate to New Zealand as guest workers, where unemployment and illegal entry have become a problem. In Tonga, an imbalanced population and lack of skilled labor have resulted from this migratory trend.

History Of Missions And Churches

Ten missionaries of the London Missionary Society introduced Christianity to Tongatapu in 1797. Most encountered suffering, and some death. In 1822, the Methodist minister, Rev. Walter Lawry of New South Wales introduced Methodism to Tonga. He suffered from bad health but succeeded in persuading his mission to send out the Rev. John Thomas from England. Two Tahitian missionaries, Haepe and Tafeta, arrived in 1826.

The Methodist mission officially started with the arrival of the Revs. Thomas and Hutchison in 1826. Thomas stayed for 25 years. When he left in 1851, almost all the Tongans had become Christians. Thomas was regarded as "the father of Methodism" in Tonga. Missionaries who came later also worked successfully through the chiefs, foremost of whom was Taufa'ahau, later known as King George Tupou I.

SCHISMS, REUNIONS AND SCHISMS

Tongan church history has been characterized by schism, reunion, and further schism within the original Wesleyan Methodist Church. The churches formed through these splits and reunions include: the Free Wesleyan Church of Tonga, the Free Church, and the Church of Tonga.

In 1885, King George Tupou I set up the Free Church of Tonga, independent of the Australian and British Methodist missionaries. This he did at the prodding of his Prime Minister, the former Methodist missionary Shirley Baker. Some Wesleyans remained with the Australian missionaries.

After years of conflict, the Wesleyan Methodists and the Free Church of Tonga tried to reconcile in 1924. Tongan Queen Salote supported this reconciliation, but the union was not complete. Some chose to remain with the Free Church of Tonga, headed by the Methodist missionary Jabez Watkin, who had served as the president since 1885.

However, the Free Wesleyan Church of Tonga was formed and became the major religious church body in the country, with the Royal Family as its patron. Eventually, its ministers were highly-educated indigenous church leaders of the Pacific. In recent years, these leaders have also been high officials of pan-Pacific Christian organizations, theologian organizations, and theological colleges.

In 1929, Finau 'Ulukalala and about one-third of the members of the Free Church of Tonga broke away from the leadership of Jabez Watkin and formed the Church of Tonga.

During this period, other small churches and religions were established in Tonga. The Roman Catholics initiated their first mission in 1837; the Seventh-day Adventists, in 1893; the Church of England and the Mormons, in 1902. Today, the Assemblies of God, the Brethren, the Church of Christ, the Salvation Army and the Tokaikolo (a split from the Free Wesleyan Church) all hold services regularly. The Baha'i World Faith and the Jehovah's Witnesses are also present on the island.

Status Of Christianity

CHURCH AFFILIATIONS

Tongans are devout Christians, whose national anthem is "E'otua Masimati" ("Oh, Almighty God Above"). Their Constitution declares it unlawful to work, play, or trade on Sunday. This is a day of rest, prayer, feasting, and visiting friends and neighbors.

In 1983, 30 percent of the population belonged to the Free Wesleyan Church. There was a steady decline in membership in the last early 1980's. Part of the loss of members has gone to the fast-growing Seventh-day Adventist, Assemblies of God, and Mormon churches.

According to the 1966 census, latest figures available, denominational affiliation, membership, or adherence were as follows:

	Number
Free Wesleyan	42,680
Roman Catholic	14,510
Free Church of Tonga	12,324
Church of Tonga	8,031
Seventh-day Adventists	1,919
Anglican Church	874
Assemblies of God	338
Others	813
Not Stated	233
Church of Jesus Christ of Latter-Day Saints (Mormons)	8,350

CHURCH LIFE

The Tongan people respect their churches and fear their ministers. "The King may ruin a subject's riches or rank, but a *faifekau* (minister) may ruin the chance to dwell in heaven." Fear of hell and excommunication are powerful behavior control mechanisms.

Rank differentiations and promotions within various offices in the church vary from one church to another. Generally, a man is allowed to be called a catechumen (*lotu fehu'i*) if he attends church services regularly and demonstrates good conduct. For continuing in this manner for several years, he may become a lay preacher (*malanga*). A few excellent men among the lay preachers may be promoted to church minister (*faifekau*) by the church president. Great honor and respect are accorded them.

Although the majority of the villages have more than one church, there is still cooperation among the people. The socially-accepted value of cooperation has persisted in some aspects of social and economic life. However, the *misinale*, or annual fund raising for a church, is confined to the members of the same congregation. Recently, people who have had exposure to life outside Tonga have questioned the function of *misinale*. They feel that poor people may suffer hardship in order to donate large sums of money to win the approval of the minister and other members of the church or to enhance their status in the church.

Although the church continues to influence people in the community, this influence is said to be diminishing. Within the churches, too, there has been conflict between the opinions of conservative and progressive members. Some promote the status quo of Tongan society, with its class, authority, and power structures. Others want changes. The progressives are classed with the *fakaongo*, whose worldview is toward a modernized society. They also espouse strong nationalistic sentiments.

THE CHURCHES

Free Wesleyan Church

The Free Wesleyan Church of Tonga embodies much of the institutional and cultural patterns of the society. The King is the titular head of the church, where his influence remains strong. He confirms the election of the church president (who is also the Royal

Chaplain), and has the right to appoint a president when the incumbent cannot fulfill his duties.

The position of the ordained minister, the *faifekau*, is prestigious. Education and skill are requisites for holding this office, and once ordained, the minister assumes status equivalent to a minor chief. The power and authority of the president of the church is more extensive and encompassing, reflecting the traditional values and behavioral patterns in Tonga.

From 1925 to 1971, the presidents of the church were expatriates, receiving stipends and allowances at a level set by the Board of Overseas Missions of the Methodist Church in Australia. Since the early 1970's, Tongan ministers have occupied this position. The Rev. Sione 'Amanaki Havea is the president of the church today. He was formerly the Principal of the Pacific Theological College in Suva, Fiji.

Despite the occurrence of leadership crises from 1977 to 1982, the Free Wesleyan Church tries to maintain basic harmony and to nurture its institutional and spiritual life.

Two patterns are emerging in the church: on the one hand, there is traditional adherence to hierarchical structure with dependence on advice and orders from the top. On the other hand, the church also supports development movements, such as the Program of the Tonga National Council of Churches. This association aims at discovery and development of the intrinsic worth of the individual.

Free Church Of Tonga

The original Free Church of Tonga was founded by King Tupou I or King George I, at the inducement of Shirley Baker. Tupou's followers became the first members of this church. However, when it became the Free Wesleyan Church of Tonga, some members decided to remain with the Free Church.

Today, the Free Church is still Methodist by tradition. Its history has been characterized by a continual power struggle. As previously noted, one of its members, Chief 'Ukulala, severed ties with the group in 1929 and formed the Church of Tonga. Subsequently, European and Tongan ministers have occupied the post of the President at different times. Until 1984, the family of Fonoa was associated with a leadership of the church described as strong and autocratic.

Roman Catholic Church

Marists started missionary work in 1842, many years after the Protestants. By 1880, the Catholic population numbered 1,700. Tonga and Wallis and Futuna comprised a single diocese until 1935, with a single bishop overseeing it. The situation in Tonga, where Catholics were a struggling minority, was entirely different from that of the other two islands. The church was established in the capital in 1901; the Missionary Sisters of the Society of Mary began their educational work in 1924.

The Catholic hierarchy was established in Tonga in 1966. As of 1985, the church had one diocese, with 11 parishes. The bishop heading the diocese is also a member of the Episcopal Conference of the Pacific (CEPAC) based in Suva, Fiji. Church membership in 1985 was estimated to be 14,000 with 27 priests, five seminarians, 13 brothers, 53 sisters, and 54 catechists. There is also a Senate of priests on the Island.

The Holy See is represented in the Catholic hierarchy by the Apostolic Delegation to New Zealand and the Islands of the Pacific, based in Wellington, New Zealand.

Assemblies Of God

In 1985 the Assemblies of God had 281 baptized members and 500 other believers. There were also four missionaries, 26 credentialed ministers, 16 churches, 15 outstations, and one Bible school with an enrollment of 20.

Other Churches

The Anglican Church and the Seventh-day Adventist Churches 874 and 1,919 members, respectively.

CHRISTIAN COOPERATIVE AGENCIES

The Tongan National Council of Churches was formed in 1973. It started with three churches and now has six full members and three fraternal members. In 1975, it organized a seminar on Land and Migration. It also has a Rural Development Program aimed at setting up village development projects, and human development emphasizing the abilities of the individual.

CHRISTIAN ACTIVITIES

Education

The history of institutionalized education in Tonga is related to the history of the early missionaries, who started the first schools at a time when the Holy Bible was the only book available. Later, government schools opened, but many of them were run by Tongan pastors, men of devotion and some formal theological training. They taught the children to read the scriptures and hymns in the vernacular and to write a few letters.

Out of the 110 primary schools in Tonga today, 97 are government-run and 13 run by the church. There are three government secondary schools and one private school. The Free Wesleyan Church operates four schools: Queen Salote College for women, Tupou College for men, Mailefihi/Siu'ilikutapu, and Nuku'alofa College.

The Roman Catholic Church runs St. John's, Takuilau and St. Mary's High Schools. The Anglicans operate St. Andrew's School. The Mormons operate Liahona High School. The Seventh-day Adventists operate Beulah College. Free Church of Tonga operates Tailulu College.

Social Concerns

The churches conduct various training programs for young people and adults. The Free Wesleyan Church of Tonga trains young men as farmers at Hango Agricultural College on 'Eua Island, Toafa on Vava'u Island and Mahinae'a on Tongatapu. It also supports the training of men and women at the Sia'atoutai Theological College.

The Roman Catholic Church supports the training of farmers at Fuaalu Rural Training Center, as well as an adult education program and training in the administration of credit unions.

Missions Outreach

Tongan missionaries work with churches in Fiji, American Samoa, Papua New Guinea, the Solomon Islands, Australia, New Zealand, Trinidad, and the U.S. states of Hawaii and California. They work with the aboriginal people in the north of Australia; and in the Uniting Church parishes in West Australia, South Australia, Victoria, New South Wales, and Queensland.

There are about 24 foreign missionaries in Tonga working with six agencies or church groups, including two members of Campus Crusade for Christ.

Literature Distribution

The Scripture Union and the Bible Society of the South Pacific widely distribute religious materials to the churches, groups, and villages in the country. Church newspapers are issued regularly by the different denominations. *Koe Tohi Fanongonongo* is the Free Wesleyan's Church's monthly newspaper.

The Tonga Chronicle/Kalonikali-Nuku'alofa is the weekly newspaper sponsored by the government. It has a circulation of 6,000 in Tongan and 1,200 in English.

Broadcasting

The government Tonga Broadcasting Commission provides air time for the different denominations in proportion to their size. Protestant churches buy an extra one and one-half hours weekly; the Catholics, an extra one-half hour weekly. The *Haafe Houa Uesiliana* is the official voice of the Free Wesleyan Church. The Catholic Church is a member of UNDA.

Other Religions

The Church of Jesus Christ of Latter-Day Saints (Mormons) members comprised 7 percent of the total population of Tonga in 1966. A recent estimate by the LDS claimed 30 percent of the population as adherents.

The Baha'i World Faith represented 0.3 percent of the population. They have a national Faith Center in Tongatapu.

Membership in the Jehovah's Witnesses group constituted 0.2 percent of the population.

TUVALU

Profile

NATURAL FEATURES: Land area: 26 sq. km., consisting of nine island atolls -- eight are inhabited. Sea area covers 900,000 sq. km. Elevation is no more than five meters. **Climate:** tropical, average temperature 27°C (80°F).

CAPITAL: On Funafuti atoll. **Population:** 2,120.

POPULATION: 1981 - 7,500. Tuvaluans (97 percent), Kiribati (1 percent), Euronesian (1 percent), European, Chinese (1 percent). Non-resident Tuvaluans living or working overseas -- about 2,500. **Population density:** 288/sq. km.

RELIGION: Christians: 97 percent. **Major denominations:** Church of Tuvalu, mostly Congregationals, 95 percent; Catholics, 2 percent; Seventh-day Adventists, 2.5 percent. **Others:** Baha'is and Jehovah's Witnesses, 2.5 percent.

LANGUAGE AND LITERACY: Tuvaluan -- closely related to Samoan; English; Gilbertese (Kiribati), mainly on Nui. **Literacy rate:** 95 percent.

GOVERNMENT: Independent with special membership in the British Commonwealth. **Executive:** Governor General and Cabinet.

Legislative: 12-member Parliament. **Judicial:** High, Magistrates and Island Courts.

ECONOMY: Per Capita GDP (1981): US $667. Subsistence agriculture, small-scale fishing. Foreign exchange earned from remittance abroad and from sales of postage stamps and coins.

Historical Background

The islands, originally known as the Ellice Islands, came under the influence of the United Kingdom between 1850 and 1875 through the activities of slave-traders, known as "blackbirders."

In recent times, these Islands were linked administratively to the Gilbert Islands, now known as Kiribati, which became a British colony in 1916. In 1974, the colony began to move toward independence, but the Polynesian Ellice Islanders pressed for sovereignty for themselves. The people chose to separate from Kiribati in a referendum. The Islands became a separate British dependency in 1975. They were named Tuvalu (a Tuvaluan word meaning "eight standing together") and achieved complete independence in October, 1978.

People Groups

Approximately 97 percent of the 7,500 people in Tuvalu are native Polynesians. In addition, approximately 2,500 people from Tuvalu live in Nauru, Kiribati, or Banaba. There is neither urbanization nor social division among the Tuvalu people. There are no unreached people groups in Tuvalu.

Socio-Political Conditions

The Tuvaluans share similar social customs with other Polynesians, such as the Samoans and Tongans. The family, the village, and the church are the center of their daily activities. The villages are closely knit and self-contained. Tuvaluans place a high value on working within accepted traditional channels.

Tuvalu is a special member of the British Commonwealth, which is represented in the Island by the Governor-General. The leader of the majority in the 12-member parliament is the Prime Minister. Each of the eight inhabited islands has its own local island council, and there is a town council in Funafuti.

A Maritime School in Funafuti, the most heavily populated island, trains Tuvaluans as seamen. Following graduation, the government arranges their employment. About 2,000 of them are now working all over the world.

Economy

There is very little economic activity in the Islands. Most foreign exchange comes from the earnings of Tuvaluans working abroad and through the sale of postage stamps and coins. The soil is of poor quality, limiting agriculture to native plants such as coconut. Some copra is exported. Fishing and tourism have not been exploited as major industries.

Introduction Of Christianity

Christianity was brought to Tuvalu in 1861 by a group of ship-wrecked Cook Islanders, of the London Missionary Society (LMS). Four years later, the Rev. A. W. Murray of LMS, based in Samoa, visited the group and soon placed Samoan pastors on the different islands. Tuvalu was evangelized fully by the early 1900's. The link between the established church in Samoa and in Tuvalu continued for more than a century. In 1977 Tuvaluans received a translation of the New Testament in their own language, replacing the Samoan translation they had previously used. A local translation of the Old Testament was published in 1986.

Status Of Christianity

More than a century after the first missionaries came to the islands, Tuvaluans today are predominantly Christian. Religion plays an important part in their everyday life. With an estimated population of 8,000 in the mid-1980's, church and religious memberships were as follows:

Tuvalu Church (Protestant/Congregationalists)	7,700
Seventh-day Adventists (mainly in Funafuti)	200
Roman Catholics (in Nanumea and Nui)	50
Other Christians	30
Baha'is	30
Jehovah's Witnesses	20

THE TUVALU CHURCH

The Tuvalu Church includes 95 percent of the Christians in the country. Established in all eight inhabited islands, it is led by a local pastor, although the President of the country is considered the titular head of the church.

The church developed along Congregational lines. Parish ministries focus on nurturing the spiritual growth of the people. Emphasis is placed on church attendance, and participation in the church is now part of the cultural tradition.

Since there is only one main church in Tuvalu, a Church Assembly serves as the national church council. It is a contributing member of the Pacific Conference of Churches and also a member of the Congregational Council for World Mission and the World Association for Christian Communication.

Among the social concerns confronting the church is a tendency toward alcohol abuse among young men. While not a major issue at this point, church leaders are trying to address it.

In 1964, freedom of religion was decreed, and now some church leaders are concerned that expatriates are returning to the Islands, bringing non-Christian religions with them.

The church established the first primary school system in the country and continued to administer it until the government took over the role in the early 1980's. There is still joint administration of the only secondary school in Tuvalu. A chaplain works with the students in the high school, while pastors also work with primary school students.

Women are active and highly effective in church activities. They raise funds and maintain health programs in the villages. Youth are involved too, both in church administration and in church youth programs.

Available printed Christian resources include the Bible, worship materials and a hymnal in Tuvaluan, and a monthly church magazine, *Lama (The Torch)*. A Christian bookshop, *Maina* in Funafuti, sells Christian materials. The government-owned radio station broadcasts morning devotions and Sunday services.

SEVENTH-DAY ADVENTISTS

The Seventh-day Adventists have had a small presence in the country since 1975. They are part of the Gilbert and Ellice Mission, now the Central Pacific Union Mission, which began in Abemana, Gilbert (now Kiribati).

ROMAN CATHOLIC CHURCH

Two Roman Catholic congregations, numbering about 50, exist in Tuvalu -- one in Nanumea, the other in Nui. Until 1964, Catholics could not openly work in the country nor could priests or catechists enter because of the "Closed Island" Ordinance, a government proclamation prohibiting outsiders from entering Tamana, Arorae, and Tuvalu. In 1972, only one lay-brother worked in Nanumea.

The Roman Catholic church belongs to the Archdiocese of Tarawa, Nauru, and Funafuti.

Other Religions

The Baha'is have gained some converts from among Congregationals. In 1969, a small section of land in Funafuti was leased to them to build a meeting place.

Jehovah's Witnesses number about 20 adherents.

WALLIS AND FUTUNA

Profile

NATURAL FEATURES: Consists of the islands of Wallis (Uvea), Futuna, and Alofi. Alofi is uninhabited. Wallis is surrounded by a barrier reef.

CAPITAL: Mata Utu on Wallis Island. **Population:** 600.

POPULATION: (1983) 12,000. Two-thirds live in Wallis; one-third on Futuna. People are mainly Polynesians; few Europeans -- mostly French government officials. Large population in New Caledonia and Santo, Vanuatu. **Annual growth rate:** (1978-80) 3.8 percent.

RELIGION: Christians: 100 percent, Roman Catholics.

LANGUAGE AND LITERACY: Wallisian and Futunan. French is official language. **Literacy rate:** 95 percent.

GOVERNMENT: Overseas territory of France. **Executive:** a French administrator assisted by a Territorial Council. **Legislative:** a Territorial Assembly. An elected deputy or senator represents the country in the National Parliament in Paris.

ECONOMY: Major funding is received from France. Subsistence agriculture. *Main crops:* coconuts, taro, cassava, bananas, yams, breadfruit. Income derived from remittances and grants from France.

Historical Background

WALLIS ISLAND

Wallis and Futuna had separate histories before they became French protectorates. Tradition points to the Tongan influence in Wallis Island. Contact was frequent during the 100 year period from 1450 to 1550. Power struggles among the chiefs existed during the early part of the 19th century.

Wallis was named after the European captain who came to the Island in 1767. Other Europeans came in 1825 and had violent encounters with the local people. In 1837, a French Catholic missionary of the Society of Mary, Father Pierre Bataillon, arrived. At first, he competed with the Protestant missionaries from Tonga. Later, he succeeded in converting the most powerful of the native chiefs to Catholicism. He arranged for the Island to become a French protectorate in 1842.

FUTUNA

The early settlers of Futuna and Alofi came from Samoa and from the Marshall Islands. In 1616, Dutch navigators landed in the Island and called it the Hoorn Island, after a town in Holland. From that time on, whalers put into the Islands for provisions and refreshments. Some seamen became beachcombers.

The chiefs asked for French protection in 1842. Thereafter, the political history of Futuna and Alofi ran parallel with that of Wallis. They became an overseas territory of France on July 29, 1961.

People Groups

The people in Wallis and Futuna are Polynesians. They trace their ancestry from the Tongans and Samoans who settled in the area in the 1500's. About 2 percent of the population is comprised of Europeans, mainly French government officials. There has been no differentiation of the population into people groups mainly because of homogeneity and the lack of urbanization. In addition, with all of the native population professing faith in Christianity, there are no unreached people groups in the Islands.

Socio-Political Conditions

The territory is divided into three administrative districts. These correspond to the three ancient kingdoms of Wallis, Alo (Futuna), and Sigave (Futuna). A French administrator is the head of the territory, assisted by the Territorial Council. The latter is composed of the French administrator as the ex-officio president, the *Lavelua* (King of Wallis), *Tuiagaifo* (King of Alo), *Sau* (King of Sigave), and three members appointed by the administrator. The Council decides on matters of general policy.

The Islands do not have significant urban settlement. Mata Utu, the capital town, has about 600 people. Through the years the inhabitants have migrated to New Caledonia and elsewhere. Some have returned with new ideas and experiences.

The people became French citizens in 1984. Adults vote a deputy or senator to the French National Assembly.

There are no local newspapers but the *Fetu'u Aho* published in New Caledonia is available in Wallisian. The government gazette, the *Journal Officiel* is published monthly. Radio Wallis broadcasts six hours a day.

Economic Conditions

The people practice subsistence farming. There is negligible export. About 4,000 hectares of coconut trees provide produce for use as food, forage, for animals, soap and oil. Fish is the principal source of protein. Some livestock are raised for local consumption.

In the late 1940's, an infestation of beetles ruined the coconut production. The economic hardship that followed led to the first migration of people. They were drawn by employment opportunities elsewhere.

About 11,000 Wallisians live in New Caledonia now. For a long time, remittances to the country sustained the local economy. These remittances, however, diminished in the early 1980's due to the poor economic condition in New Caledonia and the "attenuation of ties between islanders developing new roots abroad and those still in the territory."

Tourism is underdeveloped in the country. However, air flights serve Wallis from Nauru, New Caledonia and Apia, Western Samoa.

Limited port facilities are located at Mata Utu, Halalo on Wallis, and on Sigave at Futuna.

National income also comes from import taxes, fishing right licenses to Japan and Korea, and from French government subsidies.

Mission History

ROMAN CATHOLIC MISSIONARIES

The French Marist missionaries first evangelized the islands in 1836 and 1837. The entire population of the two islands were baptized by the end of 1842 (Wallis) and 1843 (Futuna). Father (later Bishop) Pierre Bataillon was one of the first missionaries in Wallis. He remained despite great difficulties. He succeeded in converting the native king and all of the Islanders.

Father Pierre Chanel, a Marist missionary, was the first to settle in Futuna and Alofi. He was murdered in 1841 at the instigation of the native king. He was the first martyr of the Pacific. His successors converted the Islanders to Christianity later. Recently, the Vatican canonized Chanel as saint and his relics were flown back from France to Poi, Futuna to be enshrined.

CHURCH LIFE

Wallis and Futuna developed a vigorous church life. The ancient social structures were preserved and incorporated into Christianity. Warfare was abolished and family life strengthened. Special houses for men and boys were established. There were strong religious fraternities among the lay people and many vocations to religious life. The indigenous priesthood appeared here sooner than anywhere else in the Pacific. The church operated the schools with financial assistance from the government.

THE CLERGY

During the colonial period, the clergy exercised vast influence and power, sometimes exceeding the civil authorities. Until 1970, the bishop carried the title of "co-prince" just like the traditional rulers. The first indigenous priests were ordained in 1886. Such indigenous clergy has grown since as the European clergy in the Islands diminished. In 1974 there were eight national priests, 76 percent of the total clergy. Some priests serve as missionaries to other parts of Oceania.

Until 1935, Wallis and Futuna were part of the Vicariate Apostolic of Central Oceania, based in Tonga. Later, a separate vicariate apostolic was established for Wallis and Futuna, mainly because of transport and communication difficulties. Now it is a diocese administered by a native bishop.

Status Of Christianity

NATIONAL CHURCH: ROMAN CATHOLIC

As a small island nation isolated from outside influences, Wallis and Futuna developed as a unified society around a single church. In 1985 the Diocese was administered by Monsignor Lolesio Fuahea. The Diocese had five parishes. Religious workers included 19 priests, three seminarians, seven brothers and 47 sisters. Most of these workers were indigenous Polynesians.

The Holy See is represented to the hierarchy by the apostolic Delegation for New Zealand.

COOPERATIVE AGENCIES

The Diocese of Wallis and Futuna is a member of the Bishop Conference of the Pacific (Conference des Eveques du Pacifique, or CEPAC). The priests have formed the Presbyterial Council.

CHRISTIAN ACTIVITIES

Education

The Marist mission originally developed the educational system in the country. Father Bataillon first instituted a school in Wallis. The sisters of the Third Order of Mary and the Marist brothers ran the schools.

Today, all children of school age attend school. In 1971 the Roman Catholic Church was responsible for 11 schools. When the islands became a French territory, the government took over the responsibility for funding and coordinating educational policies. The Catholic Church retains its influence on matters of staffing and curricula.

The Vice-Rector of Mata Ulu of the Education Ministry supervises the secondary school system. There are two junior high schools: one in Salauniu in Futuna and the other in Alofivai in Wallis. The

Catholic Church provides boarding facilities at Lano. Some qualified students go to senior high school in Noumea, and some obtain scholarships for tertiary education in France.

Social Concerns

The Catholic Church has five charitable institutions. The religious sisters and brothers work in these institutions. These hospitals and dispensaries were established during the early part of the evangelization of the Islands.

The Catholic mission in Lano (Wallis) and the experimental station on Matalaa Peninsula run a small cattle industry. Lack of suitable pasture remains a problem.

WESTERN SAMOA

Profile

NATURAL FEATURES: Land area: 3,000 sq. km. Consists of two large islands, Savai'i and Upolu, and seven small islands. The islands are volcanic in origin with rugged interiors and narrow coastal plains. Upolu contains about 75 percent of the population.

CAPITAL: Apia on Upolu. **Population** (1981): 33,170.

POPULATION: (1983 est.) 159,000. Polynesian Samoans comprise 89 percent of the population. Euronesians (mixed Samoan and European, Chinese, Fijian and Tongan descent) comprise 10 percent. **Annual growth rate:** 3 percent. **Urban population:** 21 percent. Over 30,000 Western Samoans live in New Zealand, American Samoa, and the U.S. **Urban:** 35 percent.

RELIGION: Christians: 98 percent. **Major denominations:** Congregational Christian Church, Methodists, Seventh-day Adventists, Assemblies of God, Roman Catholic. **Others:** Baha'is and Church of Jesus Christ of Latter-Day Saints (Mormons), 2 percent.

LANGUAGE AND LITERACY: Samoan is the universal language, but English is used in commerce and government. **Literacy rate:** 95 percent.

GOVERNMENT: Parliamentarian democracy with syntheses of certain *fa'a* Samoan practices. **Executive:** Head of State and Cabinet. **Legislative:** Assembly with a single chamber; 47 members, 45 of which are chosen or elected *matais* and two universally elected members. **Judicial:** Supreme Court. Local government conforms to traditional system.

ECONOMY: Per capita GDP: US $1257 (1985).**Major exports:** copra, cocoa, banana, other fruits and vegetables, wood and wood by-products. **Major imports:** food, manufactured goods, machinery, equipment, chemicals, minerals and fuels. Overseas remittances are sources of revenue.

Historical Background

The Samoan Islands are believed to be among the first populated in Polynesia. The first European sighting of Samoa in 1721 was by Jacob Roggeveen. Subsequently, other explorers landed in the Islands. John Williams of the London Missionary Society arrived in 1830. Other missionaries followed and eventually converted the people to Christianity.

MAJOR POLITICAL POWERS IN SAMOA

The Samoan Islands were traditionally ruled by chiefs in tribal units until the 1860's, when they came under the Colonial rule. Between 1830 and 1900, Samoan factional fighting involved the people, the resident European population, and the three major powers in the area -- Great Britain, the United States, and Germany.

The quest for South Pacific Island bases led to a series of conventions whereby the eastern part of the Islands (now called American Samoa) was annexed by the United States and the western part (now Western Samoa) by Germany.

After World War I, the Treaty of Versailles gave New Zealand the mandate to govern Western Samoa. Sustained agitation centering around the Mau nationalist movement on the part of Euronesians and Samoans led to independence for Western Samoa in January 1962.

People Groups

Western Samoa has not seen the degree of social change and intrusion of Western economic systems that has occurred in other nearby Pacific nations, such as American Samoa. Accordingly, its population is much more homogeneous, in terms of both ethnicity and social division. Over 90 percent of the population is native Polynesian, with the remaining 10 percent being Euro-Polynesian. Although 30 percent of the population live in the urban center of Apia, alienation among urban youth does not appear to be as widespread as reported from America Samoa. There are no unreached people groups in Western Samoa.

Socio-Political Conditions

THE *Aiga* SYSTEM

Today, as in the past, the family or *aiga* remains the traditional political unit in Samoa. It consists of parents, children, and the extended family group of blood, marriage and adopted connections. The *matai*, or chief, heads this family group. He or she is chosen by the *aiga* to direct the use of family lands and other properties and to direct or to represent the group in political or social events. This is especially true on such occasions as births, deaths, marriages, the investiture of new chiefs, and the hosting of visitors.

THE *Matai* LEADERS

Matais are of two kinds: the *ali'i* or "chief" and the *tulafa le* or "talking chief." The former are the ceremonial, respected, powerful leaders of Samoa. The latter are the stewards and executives of the chiefs, serving as oral historians and orators, and custodians of group knowledge. There are four highest *matais* or the *tama aiga* (royal sons): the *Malietoa, Tupua Tamasese, Mata'afa,* and *Tuimalea liifano.* Altogether there are 12,600 *matais* in 360 villages in Western Samoa. About 100 women are titled *matais.*

The *matais* belong to the village *fono*, or council, which sets policy and adjudicates grievances. They once held the power of life and death. Each village also has a women's committee responsible for health matters, handicrafts, and some agricultural projects.

As contact with the Western world increases, the *matais* try to balance the traditional elements of the culture with the new influences impacting the family groups. While adhering to the *fa'a*

Samoa, or the old customs, they are open to new ideas that can be adopted or assimilated to meet specific needs. An example of their openness is the increasing acceptance of modern technology to raise the standard of living of the people.

PRESENT POPULATION

About 60 percent of the present population is under 20 years old. As the younger people learn more of the outside world, they tend to migrate to urban areas such as Apia. They also tend to turn away from the land as their means of livelihood. Out-migration continues to flow to such places as New Zealand, American Samoa, and the United States.

Economic Conditions

The United Nations lists Western Samoa as one of the least developed countries of the world. Its main physical resources are soil, forest, streams and the sea. There are no known deposits of valuable minerals.

About 75 percent of the people are subsistence farmers, using traditional methods to grow coconuts, cocoa, bananas, and taro for export and for their own needs. Of the land under cultivation for coconuts and cacao, the government controls extensive tracts. It also has jurisdiction over the prices paid to small farmers for their crops. Some livestock is raised in Western Samoa, but it is mainly for local consumption.

The economy is heavily dependent on foreign aid and remittances from abroad. To improve its balance of payments, the government is attempting to increase revenues from exports and tourism, particularly from New Zealand, the country's principal trading partner. For instance, the fishing industry, an area with good potential for growth, is being encouraged to use more modern facilities and equipment. Also, taro, which is in demand among Polynesian communities abroad, is being pushed as a potential major export crop. However, during the period from 1970 to 1981, exports stagnated and imports continued to rise, causing a worsening of the country's trade balance. Until there is a better market for Western Samoa's exports, the economy will continue to rely on external assistance.

Mission History

WESLEYAN MISSIONS AND LONDON MISSIONARY SOCIETY

Christianity came to Samoa in the form of the Wesleyan Mission in 1828, when a Samoan convert from Tonga established a mission on Savai'i. Within the next two years Methodist chapels were located in several Samoan villages. The London Missionary Society became interested in the Islands in 1830, following a visit by John Williams and a small group of Tahitian teachers. Williams returned two years later with more teachers and missionaries to open formally the LMS effort in the Samoas.

INDIGENOUS MOVEMENT

The early missionaries found an indigenous millenarian movement already in existence. Called the *Siovili,* or Joe Gimlet, cult it had introduced many Samoans to alien religious ideas. The cult was founded by Siovili, a Samoan leader thought to have been influenced by Wesleyans he encountered in Tonga, and by the Mamaia, or "visionary heresy," movement that swept the Society Islands in the late 1820's. The cult spread across Upolu, Savi'i, and Tituila in the early 1830's, but within five years membership had waned from a high of 6,000 adherents to almost none. Many of the cultists were converted by the Wesleyan and Roman Catholic missions.

RESPONSES TO MISSIONS

The response of the Samoans to the early missionaries was generally positive. There was no organized non-Christian priesthood in the Islands to oppose Christianity, and Christian rites fit well with the Samoan taste for ceremony. Also, the missionaries worked within the political structure of the villages to gain converts. Because the chiefs often found that their status was enhanced upon conversion, they generally favored the process and were allied with the mission effort.

On occasion, however, village and district politics worked against the progress of evangelism and contributed to denominational diversity within the Islands. In their dependence on the protection of the chiefs, missionaries and mission teachers sometimes became involved in local politics, inadvertently alienating the chiefs' political opponents. They in turn extended their protection of missionaries of another denomination, such as the Wesleyans or

Catholics, and encouraged a sense of rivalry among the adherents of the various denominations.

CONGREGATIONAL ORGANIZATION AND MINISTRIES

London Missionary Society (LMS) missions were organized administratively according to local districts and sub-districts. Samoan villages were autonomous, and the local congregations developed as autonomous bodies, also. In general, mission teachers, who depended on the chief's goodwill, were willing to modify formal mission policies to meet local political circumstances. This pattern of local congregational organization and autonomy still exists in Samoa today.

Mission stations operated in different parts of Samoa to instruct the people. The missions also published and distributed reading materials widely. The schools and the publishing program played an important role in spreading the gospel and increasing the literacy rate.

In 1844, the LMS established a seminary in Malua to train Samoan teachers for the work of evangelization. Over the next 25 years, 1,143 students and their wives were enrolled, many of whom were eventually assigned to villages for teaching and ministry. Others became members of a small, educated elite.

Today, every village has a church; many have several churches. The churches are always the largest buildings in the village, and the pastors nearly always live in the largest homes. The congregation provides for the pastor's food, house, and salary. The pastor is respected and considered a person of high rank.

STATUS OF CHRISTIANITY

The motto *Faavae i'le Atua* (Founded on God) appears on the national emblem of Western Samoa, reflecting the nation's long association with Christianity. The first contact with Christian missionaries was over 150 years ago and the area has been predominantly Christian through the years. The Congregational Christian Church of Samoa, an outgrowth of the London Missionary Society, the first organized mission in the Islands, is today the major denomination of Western Samoa.

By denomination, the church affiliation in 1984 was as follows:

	Adherents
Congregational Christian Church of Samoa (LMS)	75,679
Roman Catholic	33,500
Methodist	23,864
Assemblies of God	3,000
Seventh-day Adventist	2,840
Anglican	426
Congregational Church of Jesus Christ	N/A
Church of Jesus Christ of Latter-Day Saints (Mormons)	12,000
Jehovah's Witness	N/A
Baha'i	N/A

The diversity of denominations can be seen even in small villages, where with only 200 to 300 people there may be two or three denominations, each represented by a resident pastor and a church building. This situation is a reflection of a long-standing tendency among the people to change church affiliation not only for doctrinal reasons, but also in line with the shifting political affiliations of the *aigas* and *matais*.

National Churches

CONGREGATIONAL CHRISTIAN CHURCH OF SAMOA

The transition from LMS mission to church was officially recognized in May 1961, when the General Assembly of the LMS voted to change the name of the organization to the Congregational Christian Church of Samoa (CCS). This church comprises 52 percent of the population, however, recently, it has been losing members to Pentecostal denominations, the Assemblies of God, and the Mormons.

Indigenous Missionaries to the Pacific Islands

From the beginning of the LMS missions, this church has dedicated itself to spreading the gospel to other South Pacific islands. Its missionaries were instrumental in introducing Christianity to Tokelau, Niue, the Gilbert and Ellice Islands (now Kiribati and Tuvalu), and Vanuatu. By 1972, over 210 Samoan Congregationalists had served as missionaries in other parts of the Pacific.

Congregational Organization

The congregational organization in villages consists of the Samoan pastor, lay pastors, deacons, official members, and adherents. The congregation selects its Samoan *faife'au* pastor from the graduates of the Malua Seminary or from the pool of pastors who are not currently serving a congregation. It enters a *feagaiga*, or lifelong "kinship relationship" with the minister, who looks after the spiritual needs of the congregation in return for which the congregation attends to the pastor's material needs. Pastors are usually members of high-ranking descent groups and marry well-educated women of good families.

Church Leaders

The pastorate constitutes an educated elite in Samoan society, comparable in prestige and status to a high-ranking title. Pastors are highly respected and actively participate in village affairs affecting the church.

Lay pastors are chiefs who have not completed formal theological training but after private study have passed a special examination administered yearly by the CCCS. They are permitted to preach in village congregations. After ten years with a congregation, they may preach in any village in the Islands.

Deacons are invariably senior-ranking chiefs who are formally recognized church members. They are well-respected men who actively participate in church affairs and decision-making at all levels of church administration. Their most important responsibilities involve the financial affairs of the congregation. They work closely with the village pastor in raising and administering funds for the local church, the national church organization, and the pastor's personal upkeep.

Church Membership

The *ekklesia*, or "ecclesiastical membership," consists of those who are baptized, have taken communion, and are formally recognized as full-fledged members of the church. Adherents who wish to become members must attend Bible classes for about six months and then be examined by the pastor. If they pass and if their behavior has been satisfactory, the new members are accepted into the church and receive communion. To remain in good standing, members are expected to maintain an acceptable standard of moral behavior and meet obligations toward the church. Adherents who are not formal members may attend church services and participate in church activities. They usually contribute to the pastor's maintenance and various church projects.

Other Ministries

Women are active in fellowship groups, worship services, and choirs. Sunday School teachers conduct Bible-reading classes for older children. Special daily prayer services, except on Sunday, are conducted in one or two households assigned by the deacons. Each dusk when the church bell strikes, the villagers assemble in their homes for a short family service consisting of a hymn, the reading of a Bible passage, and a prayer conducted by the household head.

ROMAN CATHOLIC CHURCH

A relative late-comer to Samoa, the Roman Catholic church has grown rapidly in the 20th century. It was first brought to Samoa by French Marist missionaries from Wallis and Futuna, a Catholic territory at that time.

By 1966, 20 percent of the people adhered to Roman Catholicism. Included were many of the principal Island rulers, who were educated in Catholic educational institutions. Also included were those of part-European extraction, who were served by the Catholic schools and recreational facilities.

Church Structure and Leaders

The Bishoperic of Apia covering the three territories of Western Samoa, American Samoa and Tokelau was established in 1960 when the Pope set up a hierarchy the South Pacific Islands. A Cardinal oversees this diocese. In 1968 the first indigenous bishop, a Samoan, was consecrated Bishop of Apia.

Eighty percent of the priests in the diocese were assigned to Western Samoa in 1974, while the remainder of the large diocese lacked enough priests. This problem was partly solved by an extensive catechist system, which by 1974 had 135 catechists serving 23 parishes.

Among the religious congregations working in Samoa are the Marist Brothers, Missionary Sisters of the Society of Mary, Discalced Carmelite Nuns, Sisters of our Lady of Nazareth, and Sisters of Our Lady of Missions.

Other Ministries

In 1973 the Catechetical School of Moamoa was selected as the training center for permanent deacons in all of the Pacific dioceses. In addition, the Diocese of Apia supervised 18 primary and six secondary schools, seven of which had all-Samoan staff. There were ten homes for the aged supervised by the Diocese.

The church also works with the government and the United Nations Food and Agriculture Organization in several major socio-economic plans for land reform in Samoa.

WESLEYAN METHODISTS

Tongan and Samoan Link

The early ties between Samoan and Tongan Methodism brought both strength and problems to the Methodist Church in Samoa. The constant encouragement and support given by the Tongans to the first Wesleyan missions enabled them to make rapid progress in their evangelism program.

At the same time, the preferential treatment given Tongan ministers often extended to their being given positions of leadership above Samoans and led to resentment among the Samoan Christians. The Tongans tended to be favored within the church even as recently as the early years of the present century.

This situation gradually disappeared as the Samoan church developed a special relationship with the Methodist Church in Australia. Even the ties with Australia were loosened in 1964 when the Methodist Church of Samoa became a separate conference within the Methodist Church.

The early years of Methodist missionary work were marked by uncertainty and conflict with other missions, the effects of which can still be seen today.

Educational Ministries

The Methodist Church supports four schools ranging from primary to sixth-form levels. In addition, the Avoka Girls' School is maintained by the church as a vocational training center for young women. The Joint Board of Mission Overseas supports one staff member working with the Samoan church and provides scholarships and grants for Samoans.

Church Ministers

The church's ministers are trained at Piula Theological College, which enrolls about 50 to 60 students in a four and a half year program. The staff is entirely indigenous. Many ministers support themselves outside the church as plantation workers, teachers, and in other capacities. Within the society, they generally occupy a prestigious position, deriving from their education in theology and their work as ministers.

Challenges

Church leaders see renewal of faith as an important task for the church, and efforts are being made to strengthen the spiritual life and commitment of the members. As have other churches in Polynesia, the Methodist Church has lost members to the Church of Jesus Christ of Latter-Day Saints (Mormons), and the spiritual renewal program is seen as a way of preventing further inroads of this nature.

OTHER CHRISTIAN GROUPS

Other Christian groups include the Assemblies of God, Brethren, Nazarenes, the United Pentecostal Church, and the Seventh-day Adventists.

In 1985 the Assemblies of God had 32 churches and five outstations in Western Samoa with a baptized membership of 1,700 and an additional 1,500 adherents. It had 185 credentialed ministers and four missionaries working in the country.

Among the indigenous churches of Western Samoa are Ponesi's Church, the Congregational Church of Jesus Christ, which split from the main Congregational Church; Makisua's Church, which split from the Assemblies of God and consists of two small Pentecostal groups; and the Samoan Full Gospel Church.

Interdenominational Organizations

The National Council of Churches, organized in 1963, includes as members the Congregationalists, Roman Catholics, Methodists, Anglicans, and Seventh-day Adventists. The Council, which meets annually, is a member of the Pacific Conference of Churches. Its funds come from contributions from the member churches.

Among its activities are the observance of a Week of Prayer for Christian Unity and an hour-long religious broadcast on Sunday evenings. The women in the council have an International Executive Committee, which organizes special retreats two times a year.

Christian Activities

EDUCATION

Education has long been an important part of the work of the missions in Western Samoa. They originally set up primary schools in each village, conducted by the local pastor, but these have been gradually replaced by government-run schools.

Today, many of the churches operate post-primary central schools, some of them founded in the early days of the missions, as for example, the Malua Theological School, the Leulumoega School for youth, and the Papauta School for girls, all established by LMS and all still affiliated with the Congregational Church. Western Samoa churches run five out of the six schools preparing students for the New Zealand school certificate level and three out of the four schools providing sixth-form instruction preparatory to entrance in New Zealand universities. They operate in close cooperation with the Department of Education, although no government subsidies are provided.

In 1979 the Congregational Church established the University of Samoa, which is now awaiting formal accreditation. Church-operated theological seminaries have produced a surplus of pastors in Western Samoa, and some of them now serve as missionaries in Papua New Guinea.

Youth With A Mission runs a Discipleship Training School in the country.

LITERATURE DISTRIBUTION

Christian literature is widely available in Western Samoa. The Bible was translated into Samoan in 1855, and the Bible Society of the South Pacific continues to distribute New Testaments, selections and portions of scripture, newsletters, and prayer guides. The Wesley Bookshop, Ia Malamalama Bookshop, and Malua Press, among other commercial outlets, distribute Samoan Pulpit Bibles. Three libraries carry religious materials, and the churches publish 14 separate periodicals for Western Samoans.

BROADCASTING

The government radio station broadcasts daily morning devotionals and Sunday evening programs for which six Protestant church groups share responsibility. The Roman Catholic Church in Western Samoa is a member of UNDA, an association of Catholic broadcasters in the Pacific.

Concerns

The Methodist Church of Samoa administers the Samoa Methodist Land Development, a rural development program. It involves the development of over 1,000 acres of church land for traditional export crops, horticulture, and grazing. The program also includes a master mechanic and carpentry training, sewing classes and nutritional education.

Recently, the Methodist Church of Samoa has been speaking out on various social concerns, particularly the issue of a nuclear-free Pacific.

UNREACHED PEOPLE

There are no unreached people in Western Samoa. However, there are thousands who need to be challenged to a personal commitment to Christ. In the communal context of the culture, there seems to be a need to develop individual responsibility.

Other Religions

THE CHURCH OF JESUS CHRIST OF LATTER-DAY SAINTS (MORMONS)

The Church of Jesus Christ of Latter-Day Saints (Mormons) are numerous in Western Samoa. They, too, are engaged in extensive educational programs. Many of the converts are from the Congregational Church.

BIBLIOGRAPHY

AFEAKI, Emiliana, CROCOMBE, Ron, and McCLAREN, John
    1983   *Religious Cooperation in the Pacific Islands*, Suva, Fiji: University of the South Pacific.

AGENCY FOR INTERNATIONAL DEVELOPMENT
    1980   *Fiji, A Country Profile*, Washington, DC: U.S. Government Printing Office, January.

    1980   *Tonga, A Country Profile*, Washington, DC: U.S. government Printing Office, March.

    1980   *Western Samoa, A Country Profile*, Washington, DC: U.S. Government Printing Office, March.

ANSOUL, Richard.
    1984   *Beautiful Feet: Australian Baptists Enter Papua New Guinea*, cited by Barton Magasim in "Status of Christianity Profile: Papua New Guinea, A Study," Port Moresby: Manuscript.

ARBUCKLE, Gerald, Fr.
    1978   *The Church in the South Pacific, Asia-Australia*, Dossier 8. Belgium: Pro Mundi Vita.

ARCHDIOCESE OF SUVA
    1985   *Contact*, Fiji's Catholic newspaper. 15 September.

    1985   *Official Directory of the Archdiocese of Suva*, Fiji 1985-1986.

ASOR, Mackenzie
    Anglican Pastor, Port Moresby, formerly member, Melanesian Council of Churches. Interview by Leonora Mosende, 18 September 1985, Port Moresby, Papua New Guinea.

BARRETT, David, editor
    1982   *World Christian Encyclopedia*, Nairobi: Oxford University Press.

BAYS, Glen, and FLANNERY, Wendy
1983   *Religious Movements in Melanesia Today*, Point Series 1-3.
        Goroka, Papua New Guinea: The Melanesian Institute
        for Pastoral and Socioeconomic Service.

BIBLE SOCIETY IN THE SOUTH PACIFIC, THE
1984-   "Minutes of the Meetings of the Advisory Board," Suva,
1985   Fiji: Bible Society in the South Pacific.

1985   "God's Word Open for All," a quarterly newsletter, Suva,
        Fiji: Bible Society in the South Pacific, February.

BIDDLECOMB, Cynthia
1981   *Pacific Tourism, Contrast in Values and Expectations*,
        Suva, Fiji: Lotu Pasifika Productions.

BOOTH, Robert
1985   "The Two Samoas, Still Coming of Age," *National
        Geographic*, October. pp. 452-472.

BOUTILIER, James, HUGES, Daniel, and TIFFANY, Sharon,
editors
1978   *Mission, Church, and Sect in Oceania*, Ann Arbor, Michi-
        gan: The University of Michigan Press.

BOVORO, Maika
1984   "Status of Christianity: Fiji," manuscript.

BRENNIS, Donald L.
1984   *Dangerous Words: Language and Politics in the Pacific*,
        New York: New York University Press.

BRETHREN CHURCH
1984   *Golden Jubilee Fiji Gospel Churches*, Brethren Conven-
        tion, Souvenir Programme, 10-12, November.

BRITISH INFORMATION SERVICE
1977   *Tuvalu*, London: British Information Service, April.

BUNGE, Frederica and COOKE, Melinda W., editors
1984   *Oceania: A Regional Study*, Washington, DC: U.S.
        Government Printing Office.

BUREAU OF STATISTICS
1979   "Statistics of Religious Organizations Year Ending June

1977," *Papua New Guinea Statistical Bulleti*n, Port Moresby: Papua New Guinea Printing.

BURTON, J. W.
1930   *Missionary Survey of the Pacific Islands*, London: World Dominion Press.

BUTTRESS, Rev. R. L.
1982   *Mission Issues for the Eighties*, Suva, Fiji: Lotu Pasifika Productions for Diocese of Polynesia.

CAMPUS CRUSADE FOR CHRIST
1984   *South Pacific Ministry Campus Crusade for Christ*, 1984 Statistical Report.

1985   "1984 Annual Report and 1985/86 Goals." Sydney, Australia: South Pacific   Campus Crusade for Christ.

CARR, Charles
1986   (Executive Director of General Baptist Foreign Mission Society and Missionary in Saipan 1967-1973.) Interview by Mary Janss Forrest, 13 March.

CARTER, John, ed.
1984   *Pacific Islands Yearbook*, 15th ed., Sydney: Pacific Publications.

CHANDRAN, Russell, FORMAN, Charles and TUWERE, I. S.
1984   "Theological Education in the South Pacific Islands," report of a study team in Suva, Fiji. June through September.

CHARLES, Hubert E.
1976   "Essays on   Palau," M.A. thesis, Fuller Theological Seminary.

CHOWNING, Ann.
1977   *Introduction to the Peoples and Cultures of Melanesia,* 2nd ed., Menlo Park, CA: Cummings Publishing Co.

CHURCH HOUSE, DEAN'S YARD
1985   *The Church of England Yearbook, 1985*, London: CIO Publishing.

CHURCH OF JESUS CHRIST OF THE LATTER-DAY SAINTS
1985   "Summary of Church Membership - South Pacific," *1985 Church Almanac*, pp. 252-257.

CHURCH OF THE NAZARENE
1984   "Church of the Nazarene, South Pacific Region, Annual Statistics for International Districts, 1984," *World Mission* (Nazarene).

CLIFFORD, James
1982   *Person and Myth,* Los Angeles: University of California Press.

COLLESS, Brian and DONOVAN, Peter, editors
1980   *Religion in New Zealand Society*, New Zealand: Dunmore Press.

COLLINS, Bernie
        "Not to Destroy But to Fulfill: Southern Highlands Culture and Christian Faith," Papua New Guinea: Evangelical Printers.

CONKEY, Calvin
1983   "A Trailblazing Report of the Tokelau Islands," Pasadena, California: Youth With a Mission, June.

CONNAN, John
1985   "A Study in Authority and Power in the Free Wesleyan Church of Tonga, 1977-82," Masters thesis, Fuller Theological Seminary, Pasadena, California.

1982   "Tonga, Land of Traditions," *Response*, May, pp. 12-13.

COOP, William, editor
1982   *Pacific People Sing Out Strong*, New York: Friendship Press, Inc.

COPPELL, W. G.
1983   *Bibliography of Pacific Island Theses and Dissertations,* Canberra: Australian National University.

COUNCIL ON WORLD MISSIONS
1979   *Pacific Report.*

CRAIG, Robert D.
1981   *Historical Dictionary of Oceania*, Westport, Connecticut: Greenwood Press.

CRAWFORD, David.
1967   *Missionary Adventures in the South Pacific*, Rutland, Vermont: Tuttle.

DARROCH, Murray
1981   "An Introduction of New Zealand Protestants," *New Zealand Tablet*, issues between 3 June and 8 July.

DAVID, Herb
1986   "Whirlwind of Change in Papua New Guinea," *Lutheran World Information*, February, pp. 11-13.

DECK, Northcote.
1963   *Romance of Rennell Island*, Westchester, Illinois: Good News Publishers.

DEPARTMENT OF STATISTICS
1982   *New Zealand Official Yearbook*, New Zealand Government.

DE VRIES, Janet M.
1982   *Learning the Pacific Way, a Guide for All Ages*, New York: Friendship Press.

DIVISION OF FOREIGN MINISTRIES
1985   *1985 Official Statistics: Assemblies of God*, Springfield, Missouri: Assemblies of God.

DOVEY, J. W.
1950   *Gospel in the South Pacific*, World Dominion Press.

DUVULOCO, Jovilusi
1986   (Methodist Overseas Missions Secretary, Suva, Fiji.) Interview by Leonora Mosende, 11 September, Suva, Fiji.

EKALESIA NIUE
n.d.   Proposed Constitution for the Church in Niue, Ekalesia, Niue, CCWM, manuscript.

EMMOTT, Bill
1985   "Fiji: Islands in the Wind," *The Economist,* July 27, pp. 33-40.

EUROPA PUBLICATIONS LTD.
1984   *Europa Yearbook, 1984,* London: Europa Publications Ltd.

EVALUATION CONFERENCE ON CHRISTIAN COMMUNICATION IN THE PACIFIC
1972   *Market Basket Media,* a report, Honiara, Solomon Islands: Provincial Press.

EVANGELICAL MISSIONARY ALLIANCE
1984   *Prayer Calendar.*

FIJI COUNCIL OF CHURCHES
1985   Sunday Broadcast of Church Services, 1984 roster, January-December.

FORMAN, Charles W.
1982   *The Island Churches of the South Pacific,* Maryknoll, NY: Orbis Books.

FOY, Felician, editor
1986   *1986 Catholic Almanac,* Huntington, IN: Our Sunday Visitor Publishing.

FRANCO, Angela, DUPON, Jean, HAMMETT, Michael et al.
1982   *Country Profiles* (South Pacific), Honolulu: Pacific Islands Development Program, East-West Center.

GARRETT, John, editor
1985   *The Methodist Church in Fiji, Foundation Years,* Suva, Fiji: Lotu Pasifika Productions.

GARRETT, John
1982   *To Live Among the Stars, Christian Origins in Oceania,* Geneva: World Council of Churches Publications.

GARRETT, John and MAVOR, John
1973   *Worship, the Pacific Way,* Suva, Fiji: Lotu Pasifika Productions.

GREEN, Richard, editor
1985   *Asia and Pacific Review 1985*, London: World of Information.

1986   *Pacific Business Guide*, London: World of Information.

GRIFFEN, Vanessa
1982   "Women in the Pacific Islands," *Response*, June.

GRIFFEN, Vanessa, WAQAVONOVONO, Makerta
1980   *Studies on Women in the Pacific*, Kuala Lumpur, Malaysia: APCWD.

HANCE, James
1985   (Director, Assemblies of God International Correspondence Institute for the Pacific.) Interview by Leonora Mosende, 16 September, Suva, Fiji.

HENDERSON, John W.
1985   *Area Handbook: Oceania*, Washington, DC: U.S. Government Printing Office.

HERB, Carol Marie, editor
1982   "People of the Pacific Islands," *Response*, May.

HERR, Richard
1986   "South Pacific Islanders Question U.S. Friendship," *Far Eastern Economic Review*, 16 January, pp. 26-27.

HEWETT, Robert B.
1981   *Political Change and the Economic Future of East Asia*, Honolulu: Pacific Forum.

HEZEL, Francis X.
1978   "Indigenization as a Missionary Goal in the Caroline and Marshall Islands." In *Mission, Church and Sect in Oceania* edited by James A. Boutilier, Daniel T. Hughes, and Sharon W. Tiffany, Ann Arbor, MI: University of Michigan Press.

HINTON, Harold C.
1985   *East Asia and the Western Pacific*, Washington, DC: Stryker Post Publication, Inc.

HODEE, Paul
1983   *Tahiti 1834-1984*, Tahiti: Archeveche de Papeete.

HODGES, Ronald
1974   "A First for the Indigenous Churches of Guam," *General Baptist Messenger*, 18 April, pp. 6 and 9.

HOWE, Christopher et al.
1984   *The Far East Australasia, 1984-85*, 16th ed. London: Europa Publications Ltd.

HOWE, K. R.
1984   *Where the Waves Fall*, Honolulu: University of Hawaii Press.

HYND, Douglas
1984   *Australian Christianity in Outline: A Statistical Analysis and Directory*, Australia: Lancer Books.

INDER, Stuart, editor
1980   *Papua New Guinea Handbook and Travel Guide*, 10th ed., New York: Pacific Publications.

JACOB, Alain
1985   "New Caledonia: The Strategic Implications," *Manchester Guardian Weekly*, 3 February, p. 12.

JACOBS, Charles
1972   *South Pacific Travel Digest*, Los Angeles: Paul Richmond and Co.

JOHNSTONE, Patrick
1985-   (Operation World), personal correspondence.
1986

1986   *Missions to Oceania.*

KELLEY, Allen E., editor
1985   *The Episcopal Church Annual*, Wilton, Connecticut: Morehouse-Barlow Co., Inc.

KING, D. and RANCK, S., editors
1982   *Papua New Guinea Atlas: A Nation in Transition.* Waigani: University of Papua New Guinea and Robert Brown and Associates.

KNIBB, David
1985   "Pacific Islands are Drifting Away from West," *The Wall Street Journal*, 30 December, p. 9.

KOHLER, Jean-Marie
1981   "Mission aux Iles Fidji," Samoa et Tonga, du 6 au 29 Octobre, typescript.

KUFE Lau Mua
1985   [Tuvalu pastor.] Interview with Leonora Mosende, 21 September, Port Moresby, Papua New Guinea.

LANGUAGE AND INTERCULTURAL RESEARCH CENTER
1977   *People of Samoa*, Provo, Utah: Brigham Young University.

LATOURETTE, Kenneth Scott
1982   *Twentieth Century Outside Europe, Vol. 5: The Americas, The Pacific, Asia, and Africa*, Grand Rapids: Zondervan.

LINDSTROM, Lamont
1984   "Manna for Man Tanna," *Columban Mission*, October, pp. 28-34.

LOELIGER, Carl
1982   "Christian Missions." In *Papua New Guinea Atlas: A Nation in Transition*, ed. by David King and Stephen Ranch. Australia: Robert Brown and Associates Ltd., pp. 24-25.

MAGASIM, Barton
1984   "Status of Christianity: Papua New Guinea, Solomon Islands," manuscript.

MANNING, Robert and QUIMBY, Frank
1983   "Micronesia: A Sort of Independence," *Far Eastern Economic Review*, 14 July, pp. 19 and 20.

MANTOVANI, Ennio, editor
1984   "An Introduction to Melanesian Religions," *Point*, series no. 6, Goroka, Papua New Guinea: Melanesian Institute.

MASTAPHA, Daniel
1984   Address at the Church Leaders Meeting at the Pacific Conference of Churches, 9 January, Suva, Fiji.

MAUER, Daniel
1970   *Protestant Church at Tahiti*, Dossier 6. Paris: Societe des
        Oceanistes.

MAY, R. J. and NELSON, Hank
1982   *Melanesia: Beyond Diversity*, Vols. I and II. Canberra:
        The Australian National University.

MCADAMS, D. G.
1984   *Wholistic Development in the South Sea Evangelical
        Church*, manuscript cited by Barton Magasim, World
        Vision International Port Moresby office.

MCARTHUR, Gil
1985   "A Strategy of Mission to the Year 2000," personal cor-
        respondence, August.

1985   (Consultant, World Vision International.) Interview,
        18 September, Australia.

1981-   "International Leadership Retreat," papers, South Pacific
        Leaders' Fellowship.

MCCONNELL, Doug
1985   "An Accurate Picture of the Evnagelical Church of
        Papua--Port Moresby," a paper on Church Growth, Fuller
        Theological Seminary, Pasadena, California, 2 January.

1986   Phone interview with Mary Janss Forrest, 18 September.

MCDONALD, Hamish
1985   "Brothers and Strangers," *Far Eastern Economic Review*,
        15 August, pp. 15-17.

1985   "Chiefs and Indians," *Far Eastern Economic Review*,
        31 October, pp. 44-45.

1985   "Letter from Noumea," *Far Eastern Economic Review*, 18
        April, p. 25.

1985   "Pacific Paradox," *Far Eastern Economic Review*, 31 Oc-
        tober, pp. 122-123.

MONTGOMERY, Helen B.
1909   *Island World of the Pacific*, New York: Macmillan
        Publishing Co., Inc.

MYERS, Ched
1986   "The Eye of a Geopolitical Storm, Nuclear Politics in the
        South Pacific," *Sojourners*, 8 March, pp. 8-9.

NATIONAL COUNCIL OF CHURCHES IN NEW ZEALAND
1984-   *Annual Reports.*
1986

1984-   *News Service.*
1986

NATIONAL STATISTICAL OFFICE
n.d.   *Citizen Population of Papua New Guinea: Provincial
        Projections, by Province, 1980-2000,* Papua New Guinea,
        Government of.

NICHOLS, Alan
1970   *Crusading Down Under,* Minneapolis: World   Wide
        Publications.

NICOLE, Jack
1985   [Lecturer, Pacific Theological College.]   Interview   by
        Leonora Mosende, 27 August in Suva, Fiji.

OLIVER, Douglas L.
1961   *The Pacific Islands,* rev. ed, New York: Doubleday &
        Company, Inc.

O'LOUGHLIN, PETER
1986   "Missionaries Compete to 'Save' Tongan Souls," *Los An-
        geles Times,* October 12.

O'REILLY, P.
1969   *Tahitian Catholic Church,* Dossier 5.   Paris: Societe des
        Oceanistes.

OSBORNE, Robin
1985   "The Island People Begin to Make Waves," *Manchester
        Guardian Weekly,* 10 February, p. 8.

OVEREND, Ray
"I Have Overcome the World," unpublished manuscript.

PACIFIC CHURCHES RESEARCH CENTER
1980   *Reo Pasifika, Voice of the Pacific*, Journal of Pacific
        Churches Research Center, No. 1, Port Vila, Vanuatu.

PACIFIC CONFERENCE OF CHURCHES
1985   *National Council of Churches Secretaries Meeting*, Suva,
        Fiji: Lotu Pasifika Productions.

1984-   *Pacific Conference of Churches Newsletter*, several issues,
1985   Suva Fiji: Lotu Pasifika Publications.

1985   *Partnership in Aid and Mission*, Suva, Fiji: Lotu Pasifika
        Productions.

1979   *Women in Development, the Role of Women in Church and
        Society*, Suva, Fiji: Lotu Pasifika Productions.

PACIFIC REGIONAL SEMINARY
1985   *Pacific Regional Seminary Handbook*, 1985. Suva, Fiji:
        Assembly Press.

PACIFIC THEOLOGICAL COLLEGE
1980-   *Pacific Theological College Newsletter*, several issues.
1985

1983   "Record of Pacific Islander Missionaries," Suva, Fiji:
        Pacific Theological College.

POPULATION REFERENCE BUREAU
1985   1985 *World Population Data Sheet*, Washington, DC:
        Population Reference Bureau, Inc., April.

QUASS, Susan
1985   "Micronesians: On the Edge of the Future," *Response*,
        September, pp. 4-7 and 39.

QUIMBY, Frank
1983   "The Strategic Trusteeship," *Far Eastern Economic Review*,
        14 July.

READ, Carlos
1986   Itinerant missionary, Assemblies of God, the Samoas.
        Interviews and tapes, January.

RICHARDS, Charles
1970   *Christian Communication in the Southwest Pacific*, Tanza-
        nia: Central Tanganyika Press.

RITI, Philemon
1985   [Secretary to the Solomon Islands Christian Association.]
        Interview by Leonora Mosende, 21 September 1985, Port
        Moresby, Papua New Guinea.

ROCHE, Paul, editor
1981   *Catalyst*, Social Pastoral Magazine for Melanesia, Vol. 11,
        No. 1, Port Moresby: Melanesian Institute for Pastoral
        and Socioeconomic Service.

SAMS, Rev. Ronald W., W. J.
1986   [Director of Development, Diocese of the Carolines and
        Marshalls.] Letter to Mary Janss Forrest, 2 January.

SCHWARZ, Brian, editor
1985   "An Introduction to Ministry in Melanesia," *Point*, series
        no. 7, Goroka, Papua New Guinea: Melanesian Institute.

SCRIPTURE UNION
1984-   *Scripture Union in Fiji Annual Report 1984*, Suva, Fiji,
1985   Monthly Reports.

SHIFFER, Jim Fr.
1984   "Tanna Report," *Columban Mission*, October, pp. 4-9.

1984   "Coming of Age," *Columban Mission*, October, pp. 13-14.

SINCLAIR, Tim
1986   "Wingti Demands His Brave New World," *Pacific Islands
        Monthly*, January, pp. 10 and 13.

SMITH, Elsabe
1979   *Yesterday and Today, With the Indian in the Church in
        Fiji*, Suva, Fiji: Lotu Pasifika Productions.

SOUTER, Gavin
1963   *New Guinea: The Last Unknown*, Sydney: Anges and Robinson.

SOUTHERN BAPTIST CONVENTION
1983   *Southern Baptist Statistics*, South Pacific Islands.

SOUTH PACIFIC BUREAU FOR ECONOMIC COOPERATION
1982   *SPEC (South Pacific Bureau for Economic Cooperation) Series on Trade and Investment in the South Pacific*, Fiji: SPEC and Asia Pacific Research Unit, Ltd.

SPERRY, Armstrong
1962   *Pacific Islands Speaking*, New York: Macmillan Publishing Co., Inc.

STEELI, Ian
1982   *Pacific*, New York: UN Fund for Population Activities.

STERBA, James
1986   "Vanuatuans Await the Second Coming of One John Frum," *Wall Street Journal*, 10 January, p. 1.

1986   "Evri Samting Yu Wantem Faenem Aot About Pacific Pidgin," *Wall Street Journal*, 23 January.

SUNDA, James
1963   *Church Growth in the Central High Andes of West New Guinea*, India: India Lucknow.

TAGOILELAGI, Faigame E., coordinator
1980   *The Dancing Convention, Youth of the 80's*, Suva, Fiji: Lotu Pasifika Productions.

THOMPSON, Virginia and ADLOFF, Richard
1971   *The French Pacific Islands*. Berkeley: University of California Press.

THORKELSON, Willmar
1977   "Papua Beset by Babel of Tongues," *National Catholic Reporter*, 15 August, 1977.

TIERNEY, Art, Fr.
1984   "Custom Village," *Columban Mission*, October, pp. 22-25.

TINDALE, Norman B.
1974   *Aboriginal Tribes of Australia*, Berkeley: University of California.

TIPPETT, Alan R.
1971   *People Movements in Southern Polynesia*, Chicago: Moody Press.

1967   *Solomon Islands Christianity, A Study in Growth and Obstruction*, New York: Friendship Press.

TONKINSON, Robert
1982   "Vanuatu Values: A Changing Symbiosis." In *Melanesia: Beyond Diversity*, edited by R. J. May and Hank Nelson, Canberra: The Australian National University, pp. 73-90.

TUAFA, Lopeti
1968   "Change and Continuity in Oceania," M.A. thesis, Fuller Theological Seminary.

TUPOUNIUA, Penisimani
1977   *A Polynesian Village, the Process of Change in the Village of Hoi, Tonga*, Suva, Fiji: South Pacific Social Sciences Association.

TUPOUNIUA, S., CROCOMBE, R., and SLATTER, C., editors
1983   *The Pacific Way, Social Issues in National Development*, Suva, Fiji: South Pacific Social Sciences Association.

U.S. CATHOLIC MISSION ASSOCIATION
1985   *Mission Handbook, 1985-86*, Washington, DC: U.S. Catholic Mission Association.

U.S. CENSUS BUREAU
1980   *Number of Inhabitants*, Trust Territory of the Pacific Islands, Washington, DC: U.S. Government Printing Office.

U.S. DEPARTMENT OF STATE
1981   *Papua New Guinea*, Washington: U.S. Government Printing Office.

UNDA
1983   *Mass Media Education for Youth in the South Pacific*, Training Manual. Suva, Fiji: UNDA Oceania.

UNITED BIBLE SOCIETY
1985   *Bulletin of the United Bible Societies: World Annual Report, 1984*, Number 138/139 (First/Second Quarters).

UNITED METHODIST CHURCH
1985   *Methodist Church in Fiji 1835-1935*, 150th Anniversary Celebration Souvenir Programme. Suva, Fiji: Lotu Pasifika Productions.

1985   *Methodist Church in Fiji 150th Anniversary*, a newspaper issue. 18 August.

1984   "The Methodist Church in Fiji," a workshop on Culture and Faith. Suva, Fiji: Lotu Pasifika Productions.

UNITED NATIONS FUND FOR POPULATION ACTIVITIES
1982   *The Pacific*, Population Profile 18, New York: United Nations.

UNITED PRESBYTERIAN CHURCH
1982   "Proceedings of the 34th Session of the General Assembly of the Presbyterian Church of Vanuatu, 1982," pp. 76-77.

VANOUSEN, Henry P.
1945   *They Found the Church There*, New York: Friendship Press.

VICEDOME, G.F.
1961   *Church and People in New Guinea*, London: Butter Worth Press.

VIDICH, Arthur J.
1980   *The Political Impact of Colonial Administration*, New York: Arno Press.

VON OEYEN, Robert
1985   "Church in the Pacific," manuscript.

1985   "Vanuatu," manuscript.

WALDO, Myra
1977   *Myra Waldo's Travel Guide to the Orient and the Pacific*, New York: Collier Books.

WARREN, Don
1984   *New and Ongoing Religious Movements in Melanesia*
(Revival movement among the Telefomin Baptist Churches), cited by Burton Magasim.

WATCH TOWER BIBLE AND TRACT SOCIETY OF
PENNSYLVANIA
1985   "1984 Service Year Report of Jehovah's Witnesses Worldwide." *The Watchtower.* 1 January, pp. 20-23.

WEICHERDING, Robert, editor
1985   *The Official Catholic Directory, 1985,* Wilmette, Illinois:
P. J. Kenedy & Sons.

WEIMIER, Bob
1986   "Church of the Nazarene, Statistics," correspondence.
February.

WESLEYAN CHURCH
1984   "Field Statistic Chart," *Wesleyan World,* July-August.

WHEELER, Daniel
1942   *Memoir of Daniel Wheeler,* Philadelphia: The Book
Association of Friends.

WHITEMAN, Darrell
1984   "An Introduction to Melanesian Cultures," *Point,* series no.
5, Goroka, Papua New Guinea: Melanesian Institute.

1983   *Melanesians and Missionaries,* Pasadena: William Carey
Library.

1982   "Melanesia, Islands of Diversity," *Response,* May, pp. 7-9.

WICKLER, Howard
1982   "Lay Leadership is Key in the Solomon Islands," *Response,*
May, pp. 22-23.

WILLIAMS, Sue
1986   "Tension, Violence Grow in New Caledonia," "New Caledonia's 'Third Force' Faces the Future," *Pacific Islands
Monthly,* January, pp. 15, 18, 23-24.

WILTGEN, Ralph M.
1979   *The Founding of the Roman Catholic Church in Oceania*

1825 to 1850, Canberra: Australian National University Press.

WORLD ASSOCIATION OF PRESBYTERIAN CHURCHES
1981   *WAPC Membership Statistics,* Australasia. p. 83.

WORLD COUNCIL OF CHURCHES
1985   *Directory of Christian Councils,* Geneva: World Council of Churches.

WORLD METHODIST COUNCIL
1982   "Statistics of World Methodism," Pacific Annual of 1982, World Methodist Council, p. 123.

WORLD VISION AUSTRALIA
1972   *Missions Reference File,* Canberra: World Vision Australia.

WORLD VISION INTERNATIONAL
1977   *World Vision International Report,* Pacific Survey Stage 1, July.

WORSLEY, Peter
1957   *The Trumpet Shall Sound: A Study of "Cargo" Cults in Melanesia,* London: Macgibbon & Kee.

WRIGHT, Cliff
1979   *Melanesian Culture and Christian Faith,* Vila, Vanuatu: Pacific Churches Research Centre.

1979   *New Hebridean Culture and Christian Faith,* Port Vila, Vanuatu: Pacific Churches Research Centre.

WURM, S. A.
1981   *Language Atlas on the Pacific Area,* Canberra: Australian Academy of Humanities.